The Quaker Economist

D1502566

Horizon Society Publications
4875 Sioux Drive #001
Boulder Colorado 80303
September 2002

NOTE: Horizon Society Publications has no bank account. Please make checks out to Jack Powelson and send to above address. $5 per copy, plus mailing cost, $2 for first copy, $1 per copy thereafter.

ISBN 0-9618242-3-9

Table of Contents

Preface

This Quakerback contains the first 48 letters of an online series on current economic and related events of special interest to Quakers. No knowledge of economics is required.

The first 48 Letters were originally named *The Classic Liberal Quaker* and may be found on the web at http:// tqe.quaker.org. This web site will also contain Letters subsequent to 48. Because of the original title, references may appear in this volume to "CLQ." These should be changed to "TQE."

Because readers would comment after seeing a Letter, in the web version the comments on each Letter appear after the following Letter. For example, comments on Letter 5 appear after Letter 6. In this book, they appear immediately following the Letter to which they apply.

Friends are invited to subscribe (free) to subsequent Letters, by sending an empty email (no message, no subject) to tqe-subscribe@quaker.org. You may unsubscribe at any time by sending an empty email to tqe-unsubscribe@quaker.org. If you subscribe, each Letter will be sent to your email address when it is published.

Comments may be sent to tqe-comment@quaker.org.

We are indebted to the Earhart Foundation for a grant to allow publication of this book. Gregg De Vito and Ann Dixon assisted in the publication. My daughter, Carolyn Powelson Campbell, drew the globe on the cover. Stephen Williams made many valuable contributions.

We are also indebted to the following persons, who either currently serve, or at one time have served, on the editorial board. The board receives Letters one week in advance and comments on them, but is in no way responsible for the final product.

Roger Conant, Mount Toby Meeting, Leverett (MA).
Caroline Conzelman, Boulder (CO).
Ann Dixon, Boulder (CO) Meeting of Friends.
Virginia Flagg, San Diego (CA) Friends Meeting
Herbert Fraser, Richmond (IN) Friends Meeting.
Merlyn Holmes, Unitarian, Boulder, Colorado.
Asa Janney, Herndon (VA) Friends Meeting.
Janet Minshall, Anneewakee Creek Friends Worship
       Group, Douglasvillle (GA).
J.D. von Pischke, a Friend from Reston (VA).
Bob Schutz (deceased), Santa Rosa (CA) Meeting.
Wilmer Tjossem, Des Moines Valley (IA) Friends
       Meeting
Faith Williams, Bethesda (MD) Friends Meeting
Geoffrey Williams, Attender at New York Fifteenth
       Street Meeting.

Jack Powelson, editor
Russ Nelson, publisher

THE QUAKER ECONOMIST

March 12, 2001

Letter No. 1

Dear Friends:

Classic Liberalism, or the economic philosophy adopted by seventeenth-century Quakers, carries the Inner Light into economics. It holds that there is that of God in every worker, trader, investor and CEO of a multinational corporation. It would tilt public policy toward seeking the good more than controlling the bad (though both are necessary).

There is that of God in every Chinese. Let us see if we can find it.

Shall we admit China to the world of economic powers? (Who are "we" to decide?)

Trade and Economic Prosperity

The Government of China wants desperately to have Permanent Normal Trading Relations (PNTR) with the rest of the world. Member nations of the World Trade Organization grant PNTR automatically to each other, but China is not yet a member. PNTR means no discrimination among members. If a member of the WTO grants a trade concession to another member, such as a lower tariff, it is required to grant the same concession to all members. If China joins the WTO, its exports would gain access to all member countries on the same basis as those of any other member.

The objectors argue that China has an atrocious human rights record - which we will describe later in this letter - and that by withholding membership we can pressure China to improve. Something similar is happening with Turkey, whose membership in the European Union is being postponed until it complies with European standards on human rights. (We will come to that in a subsequent letter.) In both cases, the nations say, "We don't want to admit to our club a country whose behavior is below the minimum standards of civilized peoples in the twenty-first century."

The proponents say that only as China joins the rest of the world will it gradually adopt the human rights found in other countries. Only as its government and businesspeople travel abroad and make close contact with others will the Chinese copy these traits. As a classic liberal I must join this camp, despite the risk that it may be wrong. My belief in that of God in every Chinese helps me also believe that trading with them will help build trust.

Still others say the United States wants China as a business partner: to buy our goods, as we buy theirs. We all trade the products of our specialties for those of others. I earn money by teaching my students; I spend it at the grocery store. All three of us benefit.

China has a long history of trading, from ancient times until the fifteenth century. With shipping that extended East to Africa and West across the Pacific, China came to possess the most advanced economy in the world by 1100 AD. It also pioneered in agriculture and industry, constructing canals, and building great cities.

In 1433, however, the Chinese Emperor canceled the voyages of one of the world's greatest sailors, Zheng He, and from that point on China languished economically, and its people sank into poverty. Historians have often taken the fifteenth century as the dividing line for China, in two ways: (1) It stopped trading with the rest of the world, and (2) It lost its ascendancy among the world of nations. Although far from conclusive, this correlation supports my belief - a classic liberal one - that trade may be a major force for conquering poverty all over the world. In subsequent letters, I hope to show that the correlation between trade and economic advancement is widespread. For now, we see only that it probably applies to the history of China.

Abuse of human rights

"Soon after his arrest on trumped-up charges. Li Kuisheng was beaten to a bloody mess. . . he was forced to jog naked in the snow, handcuffed and shackled. Then one arm was forced back to his shoulder, the other arm was forced up from behind and his thumbs were tied together, an agonizing position that he says left him wishing to die. He was deprived of sleep for days on end, had rifle butts repeatedly slammed into his back and served as a target dummy for flying kung fu kicks. Last month, after 26 months in custody, Mr. Li was cleared of all charges and released." (*New York Times,* 2/13/01).

Stories such as this one appear with alarming frequency. Nor is the torture confined to the central government. Police in villages throughout the country regularly kick and beat their charges. Also, "Human Rights Watch [has] charged that thousands of children have died in China's state-run orphanages from deliberate starvation, medical malpractice, and staff abuse. Pictures of starving children were smuggled out by a former doctor. . . Countless abandoned children, most of them girls [who are less valued than boys]. (*New York Times,* 1/06/96).

Ever since prehistoric days, China has been hierarchical, with laws designed to preserve state power, not to protect the rights of individuals. Inequality has been legalized, with different rules applying to persons of different ranks. For centuries the upper classes consisted of rich farmers whose tenants were virtual slaves, or the military, or the emperor and his bureaucracy. With the advent of the People's Republic in 1949, many Friends hoped that Chinese society would become more egalitarian. But it did not. Instead, classes of privileged persons emerged on both national and local levels, who believed they had rights to treat their "subjects" in unspeakable ways. This has happened in industry, agriculture, education, and urban and national politics.

Why would the Chinese do this? Here we can only speculate. My guess is that the idea of power has become so ingrained in Chinese society that even a revolution "in the name of the people" adopts it. Though the national economy has improved since the mid-seventies, much of the old power structure remains, with inefficient state enterprises sopping up the bulk of national resources while private effort to earn a living is repressed.

"On the tiny plots that are leased to each family [in the villages], farming is inefficient and costly, and the returns are not enough to pay local taxes. And yet, under China's controls over land and residency, these families cannot sell their land, or even give it away, nor can they move permanently to the cities to take up new jobs. Now the farms do not pay, and young people have no choice but to seek menial jobs in the cities, in part to help meet the farm taxes at home, where villages are dispirited and often populated by women, children and the aged. Under China's rigid system of residence controls, most cannot move permanently and must work illegally, at the bottom of the ladder." (*New York Times,* 12/24/00).

The repression of the Falun Gong has puzzled Westerners. Here is a spiritual/exercise group with no political pretensions, being jailed, tortured, and sometimes forced into suicide. Most recently, "the official press here has openly suggested that believers are mentally disturbed and need treatment. Hundreds of defiant followers have been forcibly hospitalized and medicated, . . ." (*New York Times,* 2/18/01.)

Why? Quakers can hark back to the seventeenth century, when our own spiritual ancestors were incarcerated. At that time, it was widely believed in both England and the Continent that unity in religious belief was essential to the integrity of the nation, and deviance could lead to common disaster. The Chinese government feels the same threat today. Many times in their history social rebellions (such as "Red Eyebrows," 9 to 23 CE, "White Lotus," 1775-1804, Taiping, 1850-64) did indeed threaten the power of the overlords, and they may well assume the same from the Falun Gong today.

Abuses of human rights were common in the Western World in centuries past. Some continue today, but they are enormously decreased. How did they diminish? No one knows for sure, but I would agree with the usual explanation of the Enlightenment of the seventeenth through eighteenth centuries (the time that Quakerism was born).

But why did the Enlightenment occur? Though we are on more speculative ground, I am intrigued by the correlation between increased trade and the rights of individuals. Traders learned that if they did not fulfill contracts and treat other traders with respect, they themselves would lose out. This movement led the English and the Europeans into classic liberal societies, in which power became increasingly diffuse. If that is right, then the same may be so for the Chinese, if they are admitted into the trading societies of the world.

Sincerely your Friend,
Jack Powelson

READERS' COMMENTS ON LETTER NO. 1

The parallel of early Quakers to Falun Gong is very interesting and seems germane to the current world situation. I feel your economic justification is not as intuitive of the current situation because it does not address the inherent ecological aspects of current societies. Curiously, it seems that early

Quakers and Falun Gong both address(ed) the spirit of God within as reflective of a fundamental state of the planet; and both attempt to allow that spirit to manifest by waiting for the light or spirit to declare itself.

Bernard Macdonald, Mendocino Monthly Meeting, Albion, CA

Long ago I adopted a personal notion that if a culture, group, or country has to choose between order and chaos [or words to that effect] it will [should?] choose order and pay the price. Without necessarily defending autocratic government, I reluctantly try to understand/accept that in a vast country of over a billion population the requirements of political and economic order must be enormous — and at times brutally arbitrary. And I have to think about alternative consequences such as I believe we're seeing in Russia. This of course is easy for me to say, being as I'm so comfortably insulated here in the middle of Iowa!

Wilmer Tjossem, Des Moines Valley (IA) Friends Meeting

If China should draw close to the western world, there is the fear that without a hostile power, the U.S. could no longer justify its huge military establishment, its military industries, its power bases everywhere in the world (Taiwan), its financial and economic domination of the world. Indeed, there are those who believe that no great power can long exist without an offsetting enemy, insuring thereby a unity among its people. The historical record is replete with illustrations.

Clarence Boonstra, Gainesville, FL

THE QUAKER ECONOMIST
March 19, 2001

Letter No. 2

Dear Friends:

What would Friends do about school shootings?

Here I've been on the job for only a week, and already I want to take a break. These Letters were designed to analyze the world economy, but a news item has gripped my attention, and I want to talk about it. Because it is about me.

School shootings have occurred throughout our country, some leading to deaths of high-school children. The first to gain national attention took place in Littleton, Colorado, only thirty miles from my home. Only this month a 14-year-old girl shot a classmate in a school in central Pennsylvania, and a 15-year-old, who killed two classmates in Santee, California, faces possible life imprisonment without parole. There have been others.

Why is this about me? Because, like the children who committed these shootings, I was bullied by my classmates. My mother, brought up on a farm in Scotland, had dropped out of school in the sixth grade. Later she studied nursing in a New York hospital and became an R.N. She had always felt ashamed of her lack of education, though I was proud of her for putting three children through college after my father died, bankrupt in the depression, at age 49. She had wanted her children to receive the best education there was. So she taught me to read before I entered kindergarten and then arranged for me to skip a grade. Always thereafter I was with older boys and girls, and I never adjusted.

As if that weren't enough, I was given a scholarship at the most chic school in town, called Pebble Hill. It was populated by the "rich crowd," to which my family didn't belong. One day a mother was driving several of us home from some sporting event. One of my classmates noticed our laundry hanging on the line, something he had never seen before. For the next several days the boys called out to me, "Nyah Nyah, laundry hanging on the line!" One time they pinned me to the floor and pounded my shoulders until they hurt because I wouldn't tell them my middle name. Once as I was going out the front door, the older boys were having a snowball fight. As soon as they saw me, both sides turned on me - it was fifty against one - and chased me into the silo (the school was on an old farm). There they pummeled me with snowballs until they tired of it and went away laughing. I ran crying into the headmaster's office, which was the worst thing I could have done.

As soon as I heard of the Littleton shooting, I thought, "Well, I wouldn't shoot anyone, but I know exactly how they felt!!"

All during high school and into college, I had few friends. I was always the "odd-one-out," playing in the bushleagues while my classmates were on the team. At prep school - yes, I was sent away to school to have the "best" education - I lived in a sophomore house while I was a senior, because no one would room with me on the senior campus. Only when I was in college did I begin to "come out of it."

One summer while in college I had a job in the Berkshires, where I learned square and contra dancing. Later, I started a square dance group with the Young Friends in New York. The American Friends Service Committee heard of this and asked me to call square dances and conduct discussions on economics at their high-school institutes. Then they invited me to do the same on a student ship going to Europe right after the war. As I stood on the top deck calling the dances for hundreds of joyous young people, I knew I was not the same guy who had run crying into the headmaster's office at Pebble Hill.

What had happened? The AFSC had given me positions of responsibility, where I could serve others, and where others would look up to me. Many Friends speak of the AFSC as their "introduction to Quakerism." For me, the AFSC provided the "introduction to life," for which I am eternally grateful.

In college, I had envied my professors but thought they knew so much more than I did, that I could never become one. Somehow, calling dances and lecturing in economics for the AFSC gave me more confidence. I went to grad school, got my PhD, and I am still teaching at age 80. (Well, it wasn't all that simple, but the AFSC did play a role that it never knew).

Still later, one of our daughters was "picked on" in school, as Robin (my wife) and I looked on helplessly. Later, majoring in physics in college, she decided there were not enough women physicists, so she offered to tutor ιan who wanted to go into physics. Her students looked up to r, and brought her gifts. She became a respected woman, and ι an important position in Silicon Valley.

From a... _ his, I have concluded that high schools should reach out to those who are picked on. These misfits should be put into positions of importance, where others will look up to them. This will be difficult, because such positions are usually gained by merit. Whatever is done for the "picked-on" must be done quietly and carefully, so that they do not appear to be "favored."

Unfortunately, when a murder has been committed, it is too late. The child must be punished, but the kind of punishment is widely debated. A 14-year-old in Florida has just been sentenced to life imprisonment without parole for killing a 6-year-old. Surely this is too severe, and it must be hoped that Governor Jeb Bush will re-set the balance.

Why did I not pull a gun at Pebble Hill? Times were different (so I was lucky). Today, child psychiatrists "point to the easy availability of guns, but they also wonder whether the violent student outbursts are a byproduct of communities like [Santee], where children come and go as they please, and where the ups and downs of student life and cliques are magnified by a school's position as the center of the local universe" (*New York Times*, 3/9/01).

Dorothy Rabinovitz of the *Wall Street Journal* (3/9/01) is less sympathetic. She blames more the premises of the world in which students live than she does bullying, which has occurred through the centuries. "It is a world that has elevated pains like harassment — bullying — to a crime second only to homicide. And it is a world whose premises the young . . . have entirely internalized. Given the assumptions of a society that stresses, as ours now does, the inviolable right to freedom from insult, and from all the slings and arrows that are and always will be a part of life's experience, it shouldn't be surprising that a teenager who perceives himself as bullied will absorb the message that he has been made victim of a monstrous crime, and that the entire world around him will understand it as such — as they will also understand why he had to wipe out his oppressors."

It is not necessary to decide whether it is one thing rather than another. I believe it is all of these. But I am persuaded by Dr. Daniel R. Weinberger, Director of the Clinical Brain Disorders Laboratory at the National Institutes of Health. Dr. Weinberger writes (*New York Times*, 3/10/01) that "the human brain has required many millennia and many evolutionary stages to reach its current complex status. It enables us to do all kinds of amazing and uniquely human things: to unravel the human genome, to imagine the future, to fall in love. As part of its capacity for achievement, it must also be able to exercise control that stops maladaptive behavior. Everyone gets angry; everybody has felt a desire for vengeance. The capacity to control impulses that arise from these feelings is a function of the prefrontal cortex." He goes on to say that the prefrontal cortex is not fully developed in the brain of a 15-year-old, and therefore he or she will not understand the realities of what he or she does. That is why teen-agers need supervision from parents and school. I believe, along with Ms. Rabinovitz, that not only has our society changed as she says but also that parental supervision has declined. I have witnessed the change, taking place gradually, slowly, ever since I left grad school in 1950.

You don't have to agree with me. Please write what you think. Try to keep it short, because I expect (hope?) that many Friends will have ideas, and I may have problems publishing them all.

In the meantime, I promise to get back to an economics focus for the next *Quaker Economist.*(How about population? The drug war? The International Monetary Fund? I haven't decided, so keep posted).

Sincerely your Friend,
Jack Powelson

READER COMMENTS ON LETTER NO. 2

Jack, it was a very moving letter, with much clarity earned from experience and thought.

Joe Franco, American Friends Service Committee

I think that all kids need to be given responsibilities and ways to make a positive contribution to their homes, schools, communities — not just those who are picked on. Not all of the kids who are shooting other kids are doing so because they themselves were picked on. Some of them are probably totally alienated from their peers and families, just don't care about anyone or anything much. Some do cause trouble to retaliate against general or specific others, but some do it because they don't know who else to be except the Bad Kid. If they had any other way to be someone, they might not have to act out. Anyway, I do know that the way to stop it is not just to put more armed police offers in schools. That sort of low level intervention will be all that people like Dubya can think of.

Rachel Janney, Blacksburg (VA) Friends Meeting

I would try to make the practice of bullying and insulting socially unacceptable. I have seen the miracles that occurred in the Alternatives to Violence Project workshops that many of us conducted in the California medium-security prison in San Diego County. At the beginning of the workshops, we listed the ground rules. The most important, in my view, was NO PUT DOWNS. We strictly enforced that rule, and I think that is what made it possible for the different races and groups to come together at the end as friends. We even found members of two different gangs becoming friends during the workshops! Of course this wouldn't eliminate the put downs that occurred outside our controlled environment, but if the rule were enforced where possible, the perpetrators at least might feel a twinge of guilt outside the classroom. There would still be plenty of opportunity for the victims to learn to adapt to the real world.

Virginia Flagg, San Diego (CA) Friends Meeting

Something only implied in the article was the effect of the example our national "leaders" set using guns and bombs to solve problems. Unfortunately the kids don't perceive how ineffective that strategy is or the multiplicity of alternative strategies that were not covered by the press. Do we get the children we deserve? God help us!

Bruce Hawkins, Northampton (MA) Friends Meeting

Hi Jack, Thanks you so very much for interrupting your planned schedule of topics to deal with your concern about school shootings. I am most impressed that you are willing to expose your very un-macho feelings and experiences in order to suggest a possible course of action to deal with this very painful issue.

Janet Minshall, Atlanta (GA) Friends Meeting and co-editor of *The Friendly Woman*

The tendency for people, including children, to take the law into their own hands exists when the world around them is sufficiently permissive (or the perceived abuse is great enough) is widespread….think of the Red Guards in China, and currently the Bakassi boys in Nigeria, and uprisings in Palestine and elsewhere all over the world. Why, when you and I were growing up, did we not take such action? Mainly, I think, because we were impregnated from an early age onwards with respect for authority (and the law) by our immediate surroundings, our parents, and other adults. Maybe self-esteem has something to do with it, but mainly it was just that such extreme violence was outside our frame of reference. Today, that is not the case. Whether it is the violent TV (remember that kids watch many hours a week) or the video-games, or lack of parental role-models, or the permissive school enviroment (even mild corporal punishment is not permitted), kids don't have the kind of restraints today that used to exist.

Tom Selldorff, Weston (MA)

One time I was at my job cleaning the coaches' office, and I found a starters blank gun, apparently without shells in it. Of course I had a little imaginary drama with it, and imagine my horror when the 5th pull of the trigger finally brought its one blank shell into the top position and it made a deafening blast in that small office. Fortunately no one heard it and I aired out the smoke and got away with it. Just illustrates that give a kid a gun, even a non-violent kid, and it can be bad news. So I do blame the availability of weapons.

Steve Willey, Sandpoint (ID) Friends Meeting

I, too, was bullied in public school. I think that's where I learned the lesson that violence doesn't solve anything. The bullies didn't materially affect my life, and when I fought back, I didn't stop them either.

Russ Nelson, St. Lawrence Valley (NY) Friends Meeting

Like Jack, I too was bullied. Like many kids now, I had fantasies about shooting up the school. I never acted on them, even though I had access to guns. Perhaps it was the times; perhaps it was my caring and loving parents who devoted hours every week to the family; and perhaps it was the Scouts where I could be a leader and achieve the success I didn't find in school.

Doug Stevenson, Boulder (CO) Friends Meeting

THE QUAKER ECONOMIST
March 26, 2001

Letter No. 3

Dear Friends:

How do we feel about the "drug war?"

The London *Economist* (9/9/00) says it all. Well, not quite. I have a bit more to add, for Quakers.

> If you want to see money thrown at a problem to no good effect, you need look no further than America's "war on drugs". The federal government will spend roughly $18.5 billion on drug-control policies this year, and over $19 billion in 2001; state and local governments annually pitch in another $22 billion or so. By comparison, the entire Justice Department will have a budget of about $21 billion this year.

> The war also carries social costs. Among the more than 2m people imprisoned in America, for example, over 450,000 are incarcerated for drug offences—more than are in jail in the European Union for crimes of every kind. Blacks and Latinos are jailed for drug offences in striking disproportion to their numbers: according to Human Rights Watch, black men are sent to prison on drug charges at 13 times the rate of white men. Mandatory minimum sentences sometimes keep drug offenders behind bars longer than violent criminals.

As if this were not enough, our "war on drugs" has spurred a real war in Colombia. For decades, guerrillas - who called themselves Marxist - had been fighting the government "on behalf of the poor." More recently, they have turned to drugs. To create civil unrest, they murdered mayors (over 30 in 1997) and killed and kidnapped civilians. At least 300,000 farmers and ranchers were driven from their homes in 1999 alone, and others were ordered to grow coca to process cocaine for the United States. In 1985, sixteen-year-old Carlos Castano gathered a small band of armed farmers to avenge his cattle-ranching father, killed by guerrillas. His movement spread,

13

until today the "paramilitaries" have become a formidable army of 5,000, some say stronger than the national army. Both the guerrillas and the paramilitaries butcher peasants, whom each accuses of favoring the other side. The paramilitaries have been known to take over a town, order all the men into the main plaza, judge them and execute them, and then finish off the afternoon with liquor and music. By 1999, one family in four had lost a member to violence, while violence caused 25% of the cases of mental illness (according to the government).

In 1998, President Andres Patrana withdrew the army from a "demilitarized zone" the size of Switzerland, in exchange for an agreement by the guerrillas to enter into talks. He then declared that the demilitarized zone would not be administered by the national government. Instead, the guerrillas set up a government, courts, and appointed police and civil officials. They finance themselves with "taxes" in the form of coca.

The United States ships military equipment to the Colombian army. It has offered assistance in spraying the coca plants and subsidizing the farmers to produce alternative crops. However, it did all of this earlier in Bolivia and Peru, but the coca merely shifted to Colombia. Now, wealthy Colombians are buying land in Ecuador, in case the cultivation should move there. Many places all over the world can grow coca. So long as it is demanded, it will be supplied, and if one spot is shut down, it moves to another.

Here is the story of a small town in Peru (*New York Times,* 3/17/01):

> This isolated town used to be as sedate and dirt poor as all
> the rest. Then came coca and its byproducts, discos and prost-
> itutes, pool halls and cantinas, cheap hotels and the businesses
> that cater to newcomers, . . .

> The change began more than a year ago . . . but accelerated
> with a huge American-backed campaign to destroy coca fields in
> adjacent Putumayo Province. The effort, the officials said, dis-
> placed coca growers and their crops, sending them to the jungles
> here in Nariño Province.

As alternative crops are grown in formerly coca areas, coca displaces similar crops in the new areas to which it moves. Net effect: probably zero. Viewing drugs from a Quaker standpoint, Eric Sterling recently wrote in the alumni magazine of Haverford College:

Taken altogether, I believe that Quakers must balance their concern about the serious problems of drug use and abuse with the egregious problems created by the efforts to control such use and abuse. Examining our anti-drug strategy in the light of Friends' traditional concerns - respecting the individual, abhorring violence, caring for the community, and protecting the environment - reveals a strategy dramatically inconsistent with these views; in short, the worthwhile social objectives of reducing drug use around the world are being pursued by means that are very hurtful to individuals, to society, and to the environment.

I agree with Elkin and go further. Early Quakers not only respected the individual; they placed responsibility upon him or her. Many have suggested that if all the money we spend on imprisonment and war were used instead for treatment, the results would be better. Treatment is good; it works. But I believe the problem should be attacked at its roots: why are drugs used in the first place? I recall my parents saying to me, with respect to smoking and drinking, "The Lord provided enough stimulants in the wind, the sun, and the trees, that we do not need artificial ones."

I believe the drug problem resides mainly in the family, the church, and schools. But schools and church have failed. My own students (in the University of Colorado) tell me the evils of drugs were drummed into them repeatedly in high school, but they paid no attention. Nor have churches generally assumed this is their problem. On the other hand, loving families, attention to children, and every once in a while telling them what my parents said to me (but don't overdo it) will go a long way (I think).

This would be the classic liberal approach. Classic liberalism is the liberalism that grew up in England in the seventeenth century, closely associated with Quakerism. It means freedom from the dictates of king, nobility, and feudalism, freedom to choose one's religion. It respects the individual and places responsibility upon him or her. Though it helps the poor and those who get into trouble (healing the sick, treating the addicted), nevertheless it teaches that the individual is ultimately responsible for his or her actions, including addiction.

May I leave you with a question? Do you feel that the drug problem is best handled by the classic liberal approach, which puts responsibility on families, churches, and schools? Or has it gone too far for that, and more drastic action is needed, by more stringent laws and government fighting a "drug war?"

Sincerely your Friend,
Jack Powelson

READER RESPONSES TO LETTER NO. 3

I agree with everything in the letter, but it didn't quite say out straight: The war on drugs does much more harm than drugs do. The harm is disproportionate to minorities and women and innocent people. The Manhattan (NY) Bar Association documented that several years ago. It is chilling to read at: http://www.druglibrary.org/schaffer/library/studies/nycla/nycla.htm.

Bruce Hawkins, Northampton (MA) Friends Meeting

God created us with free will. We should try to act in His image and do the same for those around us. At the same time we have to use all our powers of persuasion to help our young people to "just say no." We don't need more lawyers and policemen to control the supply side; we do need more sophisticated, skilled marketers/persuaders to work to reduce the demand side. So long as there is a market, someone somewhere will find a way to meet the demand. The greater the risks on the supply side, the greater the profit when they succeed. We have to take the profit out of the supply side, and that won't happen until there is diminished demand.

A well enforced tax and tariff plan on legalized drugs would provide funds for education and treatment, and, even more important, might bring production back inside this country where it would be more controllable and less damaging than it is now in the backwoods of the Andean countries.

Gordon Johnson, Episcopalian Church, Alexandria, VA

My first exposure to the arguments for decriminalizing drug abuse was in articles Milton Friedman wrote shortly after WWII. Other "conservatives", such as Bill Buckley, took up the cause. I argued this position at several annual gatherings of the FCNL, AFSC and FGC during the 1980s and was assured by many Friends, such as Alison Oldham, that Friends never would subscribe to that position. Recent discussions with Quakers, however, convince me that that this position is very widely shared by Friends now.

The drug war is simply an attempt at crop restriction with the only direct effect, if any, being to support cocaine prices—an activity enthusiastically supported by the Mafia. But the chief beneficiary appears to be the prison-industrial complex.

Herb Fraser, , Richmond (IN) Friends Meeting

We lost a nephew to a drug overdose. At Universal Woods we test for drugs whenever there is an accident. That is the only time. We had a person seriously hurt himself while on drugs. We felt we had no choice but to terminate him. Would these things happen more frequently or less frequently if drugs were legal? There is no use comparing to booze. You can smell when booze is used inappropriately, and everyone knows it.

Lee B. Thomas, Jr, Friends Meeting of Louisville (KY)

I am disturbed by allegations that elements with CIA connections were allied with the South East Asian opium producers. Then there were allegations that drugs were used to help finance the Nicaraguan Contras. Then we were a supporter of Manuel Noriega, who apparently had drug trade involvement, until he got too big for his britches and uncooperative. In more recent years, while the US Coast Guard was doing its best to interdict drugs coming across the Gulf of Mexico, substantial amounts of drug importation were discovered arriving via commercial aircraft in Miami right under the noses of the enforcement people. Most recently, and most disturbing to me, there have been allegations that a "quota" of drug importation has been permitted with the purported justification that such an approach would limit the over-all amount of drugs coming in, despite the fact that such action would represent government complicity with international criminals. I have no way of knowing which if any of these allegations may be true, and I hope none are true; but I fear that where there is smoke there's also some fire.

Spending money on education and treatment may be the best approach after all, though I hasten to add that "legalization" goes right back down the "pact with the Devil" path; and, so as long as a substantial drug problem persists, some form of drug-law enforcement will be necessary and require funding.

Frank Galloney, Episcopalian Church, Montrose (AL)

THE QUAKER ECONOMIST
April 2, 2001

Letter No. 4

Dear Friends:

Can Quakers Learn Anything from the Russians?

After World War I, Quakers were feeding Russians and Germans. I was too young to know about it at the time, but during the thirties my mother handed me a copy of *The New Russia Primer,* produced (I believe) by the Soviet Government. I was most impressed by how the Soviets would hand power to the people, through communist cells and collectivized agriculture. By the time I was in high school, I was a thorough socialist, posting notices on the bulletin board. I was thrilled when Norman Thomas, socialist candidate for President, came to our school to speak. Later on, I became acquainted with his brother, Evan, through New York Friends Meeting, which I had joined.

To me, common morality required collectivized land. God gave us the land, so why should anyone "own" it? But as I studied economics, politics, and history, I came to understand that for every piece of farmland, someone must manage it, someone must plant seeds, someone must cultivate, someone must harvest, someone must sell the crop, and someone must eat it. We can't all do all those things on any given piece of land. If farms are private, the farmer does most or all the above. If land is public, a governmental elite commands these operations, but the government does not (usually) know as much about farming as the farmer does. In the Soviet Union, the government gave orders to the farmer, and the collective farms failed vastly to supply the people with enough food. To overcome this partially, the Soviets allowed farmers to cultivate their own crops on small pieces of land, and by the end of the Soviet Union private farming - though on only a tiny percentage of land - was supplying about half the food crops of the country.

What is the condition of Russians today? Is it time for Quakers to offer help once again?

A few years ago I was invited to speak to officials in the land privatization program in four cities of Ukraine, whose collectives are similar to the Russian. I discovered that they were not acquainted with how real property was bought and sold in other countries; they knew nothing of mortgage markets, title searches or insurance, or registration of titles. If they were to privatize the land, they had much to learn.

When State enterprises were auctioned off at the end of the Soviet Union, certificates were handed out to the people, which could be exchanged for stock. But the elite friends of the Kremlin amassed most of them. Ministers in charge of state monopolies became the owners, converting them into private monopolies that continued to operate as wastefully as before. Whereas under the Soviet Union they had rewarded themselves with high emoluments and privileges, they now milked the enterprises for their private benefit. Much of this "milk" has been placed in secret deposits abroad in the names of the elite owners.

Government agencies still own vast amounts of property. "If it were a business, the presidential property office would be one of the largest in Russia. It owns, by its own account, sanatoria, farms, garages, hundreds of properties, an airline, and a publishing house. Many Russians believe there is much more" (*The Economist,* 1/30/99.) "The central bank commands an empire that stretches across Russia and beyond. It employs 100,000 people and owns a rich selection of properties, like holiday spas, apartment buildings and stables, as well as branch offices, valued in 1996 at $1 billion" (*New York Times,* 7/30/99.)

The vast majority of collective farms have not been privatized. They are complete communities, with administrative offices, businesses, and schools, all dominated by officials jealous of their powers. Though farmers have been given shares of collective ownership, the officials usually make it difficult or impossible to trade them in for land over which they have decision-making power. Those few farmers who have managed to obtain private land are hard put to buy seeds and fertilizer, or to sell their output. These purchase/sales channels have been monopolized by the collective, which usually denies them to the private farmer out of revenge for his having left the collective. The collectives are saddled with bloated payrolls and Soviet-era obligations, and they produce far less food than before. By one estimate, farmer productivity is one-quarter that of Chinese peasants in identical conditions. Russia imports one-quarter of its food.

Banks in Russia do not function like banks in the West. "Most were created through currency speculation in the hyperinflationary days of the early

1990's; they have survived on financial manipulations, not loans to productive enterprises. The banks siphon subsidies, hold massive stakes in the country's choicest assets and buy up high-yield government debt" (*Wall Street Journal,* 7/15/98.) A Russian friend told me she would not put money in a bank because often deposits cannot be withdrawn. When I checked with other Russians, they told the same story.

In 1996, President Boris Yeltsin ordered a top Russian bank to pay $1 billion into the federal budget (*New York Times,* 6/7/96.) In 1997 the governor of the central bank charged that a former deputy finance minister had caused a $500 million loss of government funds, siphoned through a bank of which that minister later became president. "According to an internal audit of the Russian Central Bank [in 1999], that Bank sent billions of dollars of foreign currency reserves out of the country and into a secret offshore network during the past five years" (*Washington Post National Weekly,* 3/15/99.) These are but a few of the many reported scandals; doubtless most go unreported. Virtually all banks would be technically bankrupt under Western rules; they survive only because of government loans. Analysts in Moscow call them the "living dead."

"Russia is now so webbed by official corruption that foreign businessmen, economists, and Russian analysts regard this as the largest impediment to the growth of investment and the market economy" *(New York Times,* 7/3/95). In 1998 President Yeltsin promised the Parliament that if it accepted his appointee for Prime Minister, "its members would be rewarded with bigger dachas [country houses] and faster cars paid for from the presidential slush funds" (*The Economist,* 5/2/98). "The main culprit for Russia's large budget deficit is the alliance the government has formed with powerful business interests; this alliance has raided the public treasury" (*Wall Street Journal,* 6/1/98.) Many foreign investors have pulled out, with significant losses. Others have decided to stay, losing money but hoping to gain a foothold in an economy that may be prosperous some day.

Yet the economy of Russia survives, and in some places even prospers. How? My friend Nicolai Petro, an American of Russian ancestry who has lived in and studied the city of Novgorod, writes that the ingenuity of Russian people has often found ways around the political morass. They conduct business by barter or with foreign currencies (the U.S. dollar is a favorite), they start enterprises without permission – known as the "informal" (or "black") economy - and many do not pay taxes or abide by government regulations. Because of sharp devaluations, more goods are now produced in the local economy, replacing imports. In 1997, a new regulation required all retail establishments to use only the rouble as the currency of businesses. Many establishments – realizing this would be their death knell – did not obey. If the government were to enforce all the requirements it announces, the economy would stop – and the politicians know that.

International agencies, such as the International Monetary Fund, and foreign governments have tried to "bribe" the Russian government into enforcing rules acceptable to the international community, such as improve the tax collection system, privatize inefficient state enterprises, balance the government budget, and not print inflationary money. They have failed, because the government is unable to decree a culture. All they have accomplished has been to keep the corrupt elite in power a little longer. Foreign economists have recommended policies to the Russian government, which were either not adopted or not implemented.

It was only when I studied history, political science, and economics in college that I became disillusioned with Russian socialism. Ultimately the Soviet Union became revealed to me as a concentration of power in the elite. Robert Conquest's *The Harvest of Sorrow* was a revelation, telling how farm collectivization in the thirties had caused millions of deaths, some killed outright as the army invaded the farms, many through starvation because forced sales of crops to the cities had left too little to eat on the farms. In addition, Stalin purged (killed) his enemies - thousands of them - with sham trials or no trials. The Soviet government was established with fear. How could I have been so blind?

The Soviet Union collapsed because it could not feed its people and provide them with the amenities the more developed world was enjoying. Oh yes, visitors to Moscow found enough food, but much of it was imported in exchange for Soviet raw material and manufactured exports. Since they spent on food the foreign exchange that they needed for mines, factories, and farm equipment, both industry and agriculture deteriorated to a critical point. Then the Soviet Union fell into its component parts, as independent countries.

At one city where I was speaking in Ukraine, my interpreter told me, "All our lives we have depended on the government. Now that the government has failed us, we do not know how to take care of ourselves."

Now I have a question for you. Some Quakers have told me they would seek a "humanitarian socialism" where property is owned in common but its use is divided according to humane rules. Others say that if property nationwide is not owned privately, it will be controlled by an unscrupulous few. Instead, they say, we need a society with widespread ownership of private property so that no one has too little, and with checks and balances among owners.

We do not have either society in the Western world today. We don't have humanitarian socialism. We do have private property, but many have too little. So, which kind of society do you want to work for, or do you have a totally different society in mind? Will socialism of any sort mean property controlled by the unscrupulous few, as it was in the Soviet Union? Or, can our private property society to evolve toward one in which no one has too little? How? What does Russia have to teach Quakers?

>   Yours in Peace and Friendship,
>   Jack Powelson

READER RESPONSES TO LETTER NO. 4

I hope you're wrong but fear you're right.

>   Stephen Williams, Bethesda (MD) Friends Meeting, who has lectured on law in Russia many times.

We do need a society with widespread ownership of private property so that no one has too little, and with checks and balances among owners. But we also need more property (and other assets and responsibilities) as part of the commons. We need to devote more of our resources to the physical and cultural commons.

>   Vici Oshiro, Minneapolis (MN) Friends Meeting

The University of Louisville awarded the Grawemeyer Award for Ideas to mprove World Order to Janine R. Wedel of the University of Pittsburgh for her book "Coercive Inducement." This is an interesting expose of the mistakes that were made in the attempt to remake the Soviet system. Many of them were criminal, of course, as we now know. The Grawemeyer Award is prestigious. $200,000 cash! You may enjoy reading the book.

Lee B. Thomas, Jr., Friends Meeting of Louisville (KY)

THE QUAKER ECONOMIST
April 9, 2001

Letter No. 5

Dear Friends:

Is Japan Quakerly?

Ever since World War II, Japan has appeared to be one big happy family, in which all Japanese care for each other and are unusually loyal. The loyalty operates on several levels: nation and emperor, family, *keiretsu* (or business families) and firm or government. Like the Chinese, Japanese have a Confucian history, but unlike Chinese, their primary loyalty is to the Emperor (or the nation) and only secondarily to the family. The Japanese protect their friends and colleagues. At present, Prime Minister Yoshiro Mori is widely believed to be incompetent and ought to resign.(He has said he will resign before party elections on April 24). In Britain, he would have been voted out of office long before this. In Japan, he is kept on out of loyalty by his fellow ministers. The government also protects businesses. Government money is pumped into failing firms to keep them alive. Until recently, firms have offered guaranteed lifetime employment for their workers. In a recession, they would keep their workers by putting them on to make-work jobs. If they couldn't finance this, there would always be help from the banks, which in turn would get their funds from the central bank (Bank of Japan). In the United States, such workers would have been let go.

Competition - common to most capitalist countries - is unpopular in Japan. Innovations in production are often proposed to management by a whole work group so that no one person takes credit, even if one individual thought of the innovating. The head of a department or firm usually takes an interest in the personal lives of employees, just like in a family. In a most desired situation - not always achieved - no Japanese should advance ahead of anyone else. All should move forward at the same pace. (But they compete heartily with outsiders, in the world economy, and in the Olympics).

Before World War II, businesses were formed into families, known as *zaibatsu.* Each *zaibatsu* had a bank, a vertically integrated group of industries, and wholesale and retail outlets. Supplies would be bought from a sister-firm within the *zaibatsu,* even if they cost more than from an outsider. At the end of the war, the victorious powers demanded an end to the *zaibatsu*, thinking that it had supplied power to the military-industrial complex. Ever ingenious, the Japanese re-formed it with minor changes and gave it a different name: *keiretsu.*

The Ministry of International Trade and Industry (MITI, now named Ministry of Economy and Industry) determined which exports to favor, and through the Bank of Japan, arranged that they would be adequately financed. This action might be like a father encouraging his children into professions of his choice, and financing their education if they agree. The *keiretsu* banks were kept solvent even as they made loans to less promising enterprises. Rather than drive debtors into bankruptcy, as would happen in the United States, the banks repeatedly renewed the loans. The Bank of Japan would create new money (yen) for this purpose.

Is this Quakerly? Very few Japanese are Quakers, but here I wonder whether their principles are the same as Quakers. (Hint: I used to think so). If you think "Quakerly" means taking care of your friends and neighbors, and making sure that none of them is in need, or falls by the wayside, then surely it is Quakerly. But if you think that "Quakerly" means "tough love," or having little patience with those who make unwise choices and cannot pay their debts, then it surely is anything but. The early Quakers would read out of Meeting those who could not meet their debts, since they had undertaken more than their capabilities. We do not do that today, but our capitalist society drives them into bankruptcy or receivership.

For 35 years after World War II Japan appeared to outsiders to be the world's leading economic power. In fact, however, the strength lay only in exports; the internal economy was inefficient and expensive. The Japanese worked hard but paid high prices for their food, houses, and clothing. Economists today believe that even the choices made by MITI were not the correct ones. The great industrial advances occurred in those plants opposed to central planning - Honda, for example. Ultimately, the system became too burdened by the debts of inefficient industries and agriculture. Corruption is rampant, as scandal after scandal has broken out among government officials. These scandals have led me to wonder whether, in considering Japan as one big family, the officials have failed to distinguish between what belongs to the public purse and what belongs to them personally.

Japan is now a country of failing banks, replete with bad-debt assets, propped by government. Unlike the United States, where bank reserves are held in deposits with the Federal Reserve, Japanese banks often hold reserves in equities (stocks), which have lost value in market crashes. Their loans are often secured by land whose value has also crashed. "Bankruptcies are mounting while corporate earnings, exports and asset values are falling, all of which constrain the ability of Japanese companies to repay their debts" (*New York Times,* 4/3/01).

The *keiretsu* are dissolving, as their members either fail or are forced to trade outside the family. Firms are failing, and unemployment - heretofore always low - is rising. Lifetime employment is becoming a thing of the past. Firms are merging to stay alive. Economists and diplomats are now wondering whether Japan will drag down all of Southeast Asia, where it has financed many precarious industries. If the United States also goes into recession (which some are predicting now), Japan and the United States together might drag down the world economy, since together they account for 40% of the world's output and employment.

The United States has been urging Japan to use Keynesian instruments of fiscal and monetary policy, to prop up demand. Spend, spend, spend, we have told their government (although President Bush seems to be reversing this advice). Complying with U.S. wishes, the Japanese government has built unneeded bridges, parks, and public works, just to put people to work, to give them income with which to perk up demand. Lower interest rates are proposed, to encourage businesses to borrow and invest. But - believe it or not! - the interest rate has gone down to zero, and still firms do not borrow enough, even when doing so is free. Some say Japan is in a "liquidity trap" - people and businesses hold scads of yen but are unwilling to invest them because the prospects are not good. Again, believe it or not! - prices are actually going down. Japan is deflating.

Princeton Economist Paul Krugman argues that even if the interest rate is zero, Japan should print more money to encourage spending. This (he says) would reverse expectations, from deflation to slight inflation, and cause demand to increase. Michael Porter, professor at Harvard Business School, finds this policy far-fetched. The problem, he says, lies with the ways Japanese do business. Encouraging demand will do no good, and might even be negative, if industry is inefficient and wasteful. The Japanese must change their fundamental ways, he argues, to create an economic structure efficient enough to compete with the world. (NOTE: "Efficient" means, among other things, "not wasteful.")

What do you think? Is it necessary for the citizens of any country (say, Japan) to compete among themselves to bring about the efficiency necessary to survive in a globalized world? (In a later Letter, we will consider whether globalization is a good thing or not). Is world competition necessary to prevent wasted resources, or is there some other method that may be more "friendly?"

Sincerely your friend,
Jack Powelson

P.S. A Note on the China Crisis

Quakers may be aghast to discover that the United States is monitoring the coast of China. "Everybody does it," is the usual response, "including the Chinese, who monitor us." Actually, I don't know of Chinese aircraft buzzing up and down the California coast, though the Russians have certainly invaded our space, and we theirs (remember Gary Powers, who flew over the Soviet Union in a spy plane in 1960?). But all that is irrelevant. If we want peace, we should keep our planes at home.

Just as the more modern or "Western" world is overcoming our obsession with borders, the Chinese remain territory-conscious. As the Middle Kingdom, between Heaven and Earth, in the nineteenth century, they considered themselves superior to earthly beings and would not trade internationally or open up diplomatic relations. The Western powers, wanting Chinese products - primarily tea and silk - found they had nothing to offer the Chinese in exchange. In the 1830s the British managed to get Chinese addicted to opium, so they could trade Indian opium for Chinese tea. The result was the Opium War, in which the British took Hong Kong (1840). For the rest of the century, Westerners made inroads into China, demanding special trading zones - Shanghai, Canton, Manchuria. The Chinese are still sensitive to these exploits and continue to believe that Westerners are trying to encroach upon them. The best way to treat this paranoia would be not to feed it.

At present, the Chinese need us as much as we need them, if not more. Investing heavily in China, American businesses bring new technology and capital to modernize their economy. Approximately 54,000 Chinese study in the United States. We buy $40 billion a year of their exports. The Chinese want very much to join the World Trade Organization, to get permanent normal trading relations with the rest of the world (See Letter No. 1).

All this goes against their traditional culture of border-consciousness - a dilemma of unbelievable (to us) proportions.

Under international law, our plane had every right to be where it was. But it was not very intelligent to insert ourselves into the struggle the Chinese are waging with themselves over coming to terms with the modern world.

Thank you again.

Jack

COMMENTS ON JAPAN BY AN EDITORIAL BOARD MEMBER

The extent of lifetime employment in most of postwar Japan has been, I think, overstated. Large corporations in the *keiretsu* characteristically outsourced to small sweatshops the production requiring most of their employment. When demand for their products fell, disemployment was concentrated on the sweatshops which, if composed of family members may have maintained workers but were producing nothing. It was found, for instance that Nippon Steel, a number of years ago, had 26,000 workers of which only 6,000 were actually employees of the parent company receiving lifetime employment. The rest were sweatshop employees subject to the vagaries of the market.

The major problem of the export-oriented firms financed by low interest loans from banks was that "share of market", not profits, were their objectives. Domestic producers and consumer goods distributors were highly protected and so inefficient that the standard of living for the Japanese always lagged behind that of Americans. To say that for "35 years after WWII" Japan was "the leading economic power" seems to have been based on Mercantilist criteria: they maintained the highest positive trade balance.

Krugman's basic argument was that by maintaining a believable rate of inflation, real rates of interest could be kept negative—it would pay people to borrow and consume. Recent pronouncements of the Bank of Japan seem to be subscribing to the argument.

Kenneth Boulding: "Bankruptcy was the greatest invention of capitalism."

Herbert Fraser, Richmond (IN) Friends Meeting

READERS' RESPONSES TO LETTER NO. 5

Our Friendly attitude toward others should not be restricted to just those in our family or group. We should treat all human beings with dignity and respect, no matter how distant or unrelated they might be. So my answer is that Japan should compete among themselves to become more efficient. But compete with fairness and compassion.

Virginia Flagg, San Diego (CA) Friends Meeting

Jack, I commend two recent items as an extension of your remarks on Japan and Quakers if you have not already seen them.
(1) "Our Debt to Bankruptcy" New Yorker April 16, 2001 page 32
(2) The review of "Culture Matters: How Values Shape Human Progress" Foreign Affairs, Jan/Feb 2001 p 209-211.

George Sinnott, Sandy Spring (MD) Friends Meeting.

READER RESPONSE TO HERB FRASER

Kenneth Boulding: "Bankruptcy was the greatest invention of capitalism."
The Torah tells Jews that every 7 years ALL debts are to be forgiven.
This "sabbatical year" was called "shmitah, a year of release. This practice is not followed, at this time, but I would say that this is a form of collective "bankruptcy" protection, so that folks can get back on their feet. It worked in the days when all who followed the rule were treated like "family". The new bankruptcy law, just passed by the Republicans, will make bankruptcy much more difficult to declare. What do you think of the new law?

Shalom,
Free Polazzo, Atlanta (GA) Friends Meeting

NOTE: Debt forgiveness is one of the topics on the agenda for a future Letter.

THE QUAKER ECONOMIST

April 16, 2001

Letter No. 6

Dear Friends:

What about the population problem?

Here's a popular story making the rounds of Friends. An experimenter captured a small number of fruit flies in a bottle. Soon they had doubled in number, then doubled again, then more - by geometric progression. Finally, the bottle was full, and within a day or so the fruit flies were all dead. The implication is that the bottle is the earth, and we are the fruit flies.

With a forthcoming major report of the United Nations Population Division, whose highlights were released last month, this story needs some rethinking. People are not fruit flies. Sex is only one of our urges, and we have minds that enable us to decide about our lives. We can also invent new ways of producing food, and even space. For me, a better likeness is to what Kenneth Boulding called "Space Ship Earth." We live in a space ship with resources we must nurture. And we can control what we nurture.

For decades we have been concerned with overpopulation. Now we discover that Europe, Russia, Japan, and other countries are deeply disturbed about loss of population. According to a study by the Federal Statistics Office in Germany, the population of that country is expected to drop 20% by 2050, from about 80 million to about 54 million. Italians have the lowest fertility rates in the world; each woman now bears, on average, only 1.2 babies in her lifetime. (The replacement rate is 2.1, which makes allowance for deaths). In Japan, that ratio shrank to 1.34 in 1999. In Northern America, Europe, Japan, and Australia taken together, the number is down to 1.59, by United Nations data. (I am not troubling you with references, but I have them in my file for anyone who wishes. These are reliable data, mostly from the United Nations).

Nicholas Eberstadt, probably our most learned demographer, makes the reasonable assumptions that life expectancy in more developed countries (MDCs) will rise from 71 to 85 years by 2050, that of less developed countries (LDCs) from 64 to 76; that fertility rates in MDCs will fall to 1.4

average in another decade and those in LDCs (which are now very high but falling) to 2 in 2020 and 1.6 in 2050. Given these assumptions, by 2050 the world will contain about 8.9 billion people. Global depopulation will begin in a bit over forty years, and beginning about 2050, world population will be shrinking by about 25% with each succeeding generation.

But suppose these estimates are wrong. Should we be teaching birth control now, just to make sure? Would it not be better for the world to have even fewer people by 2050 than Eberstadt estimates? I will conclude below that we should continue to teach birth control, but selectively and not in order to stabilize the world's population. If we are to influence population growth through birth control, it is essential to guess right, neither to overguess nor to underguess.

An optimal population is well distributed among age groups. Draw a Christmas tree made out of horizontal slices representing age groups: the lowest, biggest slice is age-group 1 to 10. Given that some of these will not survive, the next slice (10-20) is slightly smaller, and so on up to the top (90-100), the smallest slice of all. Slices get progressively smaller as people drop off in their sixties, seventies, and eighties. (If we all lived to 100 and then suddenly died, the Christmas tree would be like a rectangular box. Wouldn't that be grotesque?)

In a country of heavy population growth, the lower slices will be much larger than the middle and upper, but as time goes on, the "baby boom" will widen the slices in the middle, then at the top. That is happening in Asia, Africa, and Latin America now. But we may confidently expect a demographic transition, which in Europe lasted most of the nineteenth century. First, the death rate falls with improved health care, but the birth rate stays high until parents decide they do not need so many children. Then it falls. In the interim (death rate down, birth rate still high) population grows prodigiously. After the birth rate falls, it stabilizes again, as it did in the Western world.

Any society will organize itself around the shape of the Christmas tree. It must have the right number of schools for those in the younger years, the right amount of employment for those in the middle years, the right amount of health care, the right amount of food, and so on. Demographers speak of the "dependency ratio," which is the ratio of children and elderly, who depend for their care on the middle group. Whether with private or public social insurance, whether with day care centers or stay-at-home moms, workers in the middle years take care of the "dependents." If any of these ratios become out of kilter with the others, problems will ensue (unhappiness, riots, uneducated citizenry, political instability). So if we are to control population, we must know what we are doing: population should be neither too large nor too small, and it should be relatively well distributed among ages. The dependency ratio should be supportable, so that the Christmas tree looks like a natural one.

Eberstadt has detected four salient trends in the 2001 United Nations report: global aging, the decline of the West, the eclipse of Russia, and American exceptionalism. Let us consider them, in order.

(1) *Global aging:* Because of the "health explosion," average population is getting older in all parts of the world. Yes, there are scourges such as AIDS, but Eberstadt points out that "it would take a catastrophe of truly Biblical proportions to forestall this trend."

(2) *The Decline of the West [and Japan]:* This reflects the drop in population already cited earlier in this report.

(3) *The Eclipse of Russia:* "While more developed countries are positioned for decline, Russia is slated for an especially brutal descent. Today the Russian Federation displays one of the world's lowest fertility levels: an estimated rate of 1.14 births per woman per lifetime. Its appalling mortality levels, by UNDP [United Nations Development Program] estimates, currently hover between those of the Dominican Republic and North Korea" (Eberstadt in *Wall Street Journal,* 3/9/01. I have discussed the reasons for this in Letter No. 4 on Russia. (See http://quaker.org/clq/.)

(4) *American exceptionalism:.* The fertility rate in the United States is now the highest in the more developed world: just over 2 births per woman per lifetime. "The nation's population increased by more people in the 1990's than any other 10-year period in United States history, surpassing the growth between 1950 and 1960 at the peak of the baby boom, the Census Bureau reported. . . Even as many other industrial countries are suffering declining populations because of shrinking birth rates, the United States swelled by 32.7 million people in the last decade, to 281.4 million, the result of waves of young immigrants with families and a steady birth rate that outpaced deaths. The increase, which was greater than the country's population total

during the Civil War, easily surpassed the previous record growth of 28 million in the 1950's." (*New York Times,* 4/3/01).

(5) There is a fifth point that Eberstadt did not mention in the article I am quoting, but he might have. The populations of Asia, Africa, and Latin America are still growing, even though the rate of growth is declining. India crossed the one billion mark in 1999. With population growing at 1.6% per year, it will overtake China before mid-century. According to the U.S. Census Bureau, "ninety-nine per cent of global natural increase - the difference between numbers of births and numbers of deaths - now occurs in the developing countries of Africa, Asia, and Latin America. . . On average, the number of children born to a woman living in the developing world is double the number born to a woman living in one of the world's more developing regions." Already by 1950, LDC population was two thirds of the world total (and MDC only one third). By 2020 it is estimated that LDCs will reach 6.2 billion people out of 7.8 billion total.

So, is birth control needed in the LDCs, or will they stabilize themselves over time? The problem lies not so much in gross population growth, but in its distribution. All over Asia, Africa, and Latin America people are migrating to the cities. The farms do not provide enough employment for the increased population. In the cities, they live in stinking slums, with flimsy huts such as of cardboard or sometimes tin; unemployment is high, health care abominable, and begging pandemic. It is these slums that, to me, are the dirtiest part of the world.

In all my peregrinations in the Third World, I found myself drawn most to the slums, partly out of concern for the lives of their inhabitants and partly to help me understand poverty. I wandered for days at a time in the slums of all capital cities of Latin America except Havana, talking with the people there, and asking about their aspirations. Most wanted jobs and a secure roof over their heads. Population control (contraceptives especially) are badly needed, along with training. But more than that, jobs are needed. The peoples of any country do not need to grow their own food - there is enough food in all the world (and agricultural output is increasing yearly by more than population), but they need money with which to buy food.

This is something we might be thinking about, if we are disturbed by jobs moving to less developed countries. Is that not where jobs are most needed?

Peace, Jack Powelson

READERS' RESPONSES TO LETTER NO. 6

I thought "space ship earth" was Buckminster Fuller's coinage...

Kenneth B. Powelson, Berkeley (CA)

JP Comment: I think my son Ken is correct. I had only heard it from Kenneth Boulding.

What if everyone felt they were adequately fed?
What if everyone felt their house kept them warm and dry?
What if everyone felt that animals were not unduly harmed by human activity?

If the answers to those questions were yes, then no one would be concerned about population. Therefore, I conclude that there is no "population problem".

Turn it on its head. Would fewer people ensure that all people were adequately fed? Would fewer people ensure that all people had adequate housing? Would fewer people ensure that animals were not harmed by humans? The answer is every case is "maybe, maybe not."

There is a hunger problem. There is a poverty problem. There is an environmental problem. These form a set of problems that people lump together and confusingly label the "population problem". But there is no intrinsic problem with "too many people".

Russ Nelson, St. Lawrence Valley (NY) Friends Meeting

I had just finished watching a C-SPAN panel discussion featuring National Security Advisors from Eisenhower to Bush (the elder). One of them, Walt Rostow, spoke of the need for planning for the "end of the human race" which would happen because of the decrease in population that is predicted for the human race in the 21st century. I was hoping that someone in the CSPAN audience would ask for an explanation of why a decrease in population was such a disaster, but no such luck. Can you shed light on his fears? Why would a decrease in the number of humans be so traumatic?

Free Polazzo, Annewakkee Creek Friends Worship Group, Douglasville (GA)

JP Question: Can anyone among the readers answer Free's question?

Of course, we should be teaching birth control now along with sanitation and other basic health care. We do it not so much to control population in general but to assist families to make their own decisions about whether and when to have children. Your article seems to reflect an attitude that we (Americans?) should determine the future population. Not sure that is what you meant, but that is what it seemed to convey to me. We can't and shouldn't delude ourselves that we have or should try to exercise such power.

If population increases, we will learn to cope. If it decreases, we will learn to cope, and perhaps some of the other species who share this earth with us will get some relief. In parts of North Dakota bison are on the increase as number of people decreases. Perhaps some indigenous people will have a chance to regain some of what they have lost too.

And I agree that what the poor need most is jobs. I'm also intrigued with the idea that perhaps they should be given title to the land they occupy so that they can accumulate capital. I don't have your list of future articles at hand, but would be interested in your reaction to some of the more inventive suggestions for helping the world's poor cope with globalization.

Vici Oshiro, Minneapolis Friends Meeting

I have been known to ask people, "Why is a job in the US more valuable than a job in Mexico? Who needs it more?" The problem with jobs in Mexico is bad working conditions and pay too low compared to the cost of living where the factories are located. The only effective response is organizing the workers and the larger community. The micro-credit movement, which I support with cash, not only provides people with employment under their own control but encourages the development of the multiple center of power in society which both Jack and Gene Sharp argue are the fundamental sources of liberty and justice.

Bruce Hawkins, Northampton (MA) Friends Meeting

A TIDBIT FROM SINGAPORE

Here in strait-laced Singapore, it's the new patriotism: have sex.

Alarmed by its declining birthrate, this tiny city-state of just four million people is urging its citizens to multiply as fast as they can.

"We need more babies!" proclaimed Prime Minister Goh Chok Tong last fall. The world, he said, is in danger of running short of Singaporeans.

New York Times, April 21, 2001.

THE QUAKER ECONOMIST
April 23, 2001

Letter No. 7

Dear Friends:

What does the California energy crisis mean to Quakers?

The people of California want more electricity than they are willing to pay for.

First, a bit of homespun philosophy. I believe that we in the United States want more than we are willing to pay for. This explains the explosion in consumer debt. But it also applies to how we use government. We put our money into a big pot (taxes) and want to take out more, collectively, than we put in collectively. This is so whether we want to take out for national defense, for health, for public parks, or for help for the poor. We run a surplus only because we can't decide how to spend it.

Don't tear down the fence until you know why it was put up.

Regulation of public-utility rates was initiated in the nineteenth century. At that time, electricity utilities could best function as monopolies in their areas. The investment, including transmission wires and plant, was great, and one utility could usually handle the needs of its home area. Two or more would be wasteful. If one grocery were charging too much, you could go to another. Not so with electricity. But guess what? Once the investors had built expensive plants, some communities tried to force the utilities to charge rates too low to give them a fair return. (They tried to get more than they were willing to pay for.) In a famous case that all of us pre-war economics students had to learn (Smyth vs. Ames, 1898), the Supreme Court required regulators to set rates that would provide "fair return on fair value." So regulation was established both to control monopoly and to be fair to investors. (Smyth vs. Ames was later overturned as the definition of value was debated, but the principle remains).

Conditions are different now. Smaller plants have become more economical, and distribution costs have dropped, so they can cover wider areas. Two or more utilities can compete in a given area. One company may provide the lines and charge another company to use them. Because of advances in long-distance transmission, local utilities need not produce all their own power. They may buy from wholesalers thousands of miles away. Thus competition has been introduced. It is no longer necessary to regulate electricity rates any more than it is to regulate the price of bananas.

Now we can tear down the fence.

I believe the California problem could be easily solved by complete deregulation. Let the wholesale and retail producers charge what they will - just the way grocery stores do. If they charge too much, customers will buy from competitors. With deregulation, competitors will build new plants if rates are high enough. On April 5, Governor Davis proposed a 46% increase in rates, "bowing to the inevitable," as *The New York Times* put it.

In 1996, the legislature deregulated wholesale rates but not retail rates. Why not retail? Ironically, because everyone then thought the rates would go down with competition, and the retailers (mainly Pacific Gas and Electric and Southern California Edison) wanted their rates for consumers to be frozen, so they would profit by purchasing electricity at lower wholesale rates while charging the same (high) retail to their customers. They also wanted them frozen high enough to compensate themselves for the "stranded costs" of expensive nuclear plants and other capacity. What a whopping error! With Silicon Valley and other industries, California's economy was growing prodigiously, demanding ever-more electric power. Instead of going down with deregulation, wholesale rates shot up. The retailers (mainly PGE and SCE) were required to provide for their customers, but because retail rates were capped, they could not charge more to compensate for the higher wholesale rates. At this point it was the customers/voters who refused to let the regulatory commission lift the caps. PGE and SCE had to borrow prodigiously to meet their costs. PGE declared Chapter 11 bankruptcy on April 6, while SCE was forced to give up much of its assets to the California government in exchange for financial help. It is a classic case of people wanting more than they are willing to pay for, contrary to the Smyth vs. Ames principle.

Even though small, local generators are now feasible (to compete with the large wholesalers), Californians have not built any for fifteen years. Actually, California environmental laws are loose - applying only to coal-burning facilities. However, the general atmosphere of more restrictive environmentalism (than is necessary for clean air), plus NIMBY, has frightened the regulators away from awarding permits or the utilities from building. Californians now want more electricity but have been unwilling to pay its cost (in terms of NIMBY, etc.).

What about the wholesalers? Are they gouging the public, making prodigious profits? Wholesalers are organized into pools throughout the United States, which swap electricity with each other. If, for example, the Northeastern States have too much electricity but the Southwest has too little, Northeast can sell the surplus from its western edge to Central, which in turn will sell some of the surplus from its western edge to the Southwest, and so on. Although electricity cannot be transmitted economically for 3,000 miles (perhaps 1,000 is the limit), the use of these pools creates the equivalent of Californians being able to buy electricity wholesale from any part of the country. If California wholesale prices are re-capped, the utilities will buy at the (capped) California price until all California electricity is used up, then buy the excess in other states. To combat this, many Californians are urging the Federal Energy Regulatory Commission to cap *all* wholesale prices in the United States. So far, President Bush has resisted.

High prices of any commodity are essential in times of scarcity, to encourage both conservation and increased production or innovation. Historically, when *any* product is scarce or new, some people make a lot of money. Then, as competition develops and substitutes appear, their profits decline. That's what happened to hoola-hoops. So let's be patient.

New technology is on the horizon, but only if prices rise high enough. Fuel cells, which make electricity out of hydrogen (but cannot do it in infinite amounts) offer a cleaner source. Photo-voltaic cells, which make it out of the sun's rays, are also within existing technology. Right now the cost of each is too high. If wholesale rates are capped, there will be little or no incentive to develop these cleaner types and bring down costs. Ironically, the way to *prevent* clean electricity from being developed is to keep the price low.

If the price is increased, we might find ourselves spending more on electricity and less on movies, vacations, or whatever. The total amount of goods and services produced in the United States has more than doubled (inflation-adjusted) since 1950. Could we not take a small amount from that increment and devote it to electricity instead, to encourage the production of new, cleaner types?

Electricity production, distribution, and consumption is extraordinarily complex. Consider the following:

(1) Maybe it's all right for the rich to spend less on cruises and yachts, but what about the poor? I have spent many hours (days, even) wandering through the slums in every Latin American capital except Havana and in about ten cities in Africa. Most of the poverty-stricken people I talked to wanted jobs and electricity. So, why do I propose higher rates? Because I want us to create the incentive to produce more and cleaner electricity. The poor will benefit, but not right away. There are other ways to help them immediately. One is through a negative income tax (rich people pay, poor people receive). Another would be to cap retail rates but only on the first so-many kilowatt hours, and then let them rise.

(2) Capping prices causes tensions. It makes for demand greater than supply. Because the price is low, consumers waste the product - turning on air conditioners that they could get along without. (Air conditioners didn't exist when I was a child).

(3) Capping prices means that someone must do the capping. That person (Governor of California? Regulatory commission?) is subject to political pressure from those who want more because they have the electoral power to demand it. That is what is happening in California right now.

(4) I have heard rumors that wholesale producers are holding back to increase prices. Until I see real evidence, I will believe it is only rumor, because (a) power plants require heavy capital equipment, and they suffer losses if that equipment is not used, and (b) it is expensive to store electricity (as in batteries). Thus power plants lose much if they do not sell right away.

(5) The competition resulting from total deregulation would encourage the use of windmills, which are usually cheaper than all the other sources, but not enough to supply the whole country. Higher prices might also make solar energy feasible.

(6) The parent of PGE recouped much of its stranded costs. It is now rich while PGE, the utility, is going bankrupt. Had rates been deregulated, the whole PGE complex would have had to stand the losses on stranded costs,

just the way any industry takes losses when it builds plants that become outmoded.

(7) At present in California there is enough electricity in the South but not enough transmission lines to carry it to the North. More lines need to be built, but Californians do not want them in their back yards.

(8) The utilities face the problem of peak loads. They do not want to have more productive capacity than they need, yet if they have enough for peak loads, they may have idle capacity at other times. To face this problem, they make "interruptible contracts," especially for off-peak-load users. Under these contracts the customer will receive cheap electricity but knows that, in exchange, it may undergo interruptions (such as turning off air conditioners) when necessary.

(9) Despite the pooling of electricity, and the interruptible contracts for off-peak hours, it just might be that the capacity of the total United States will not meet future demand. (I believe capacity is great enough for present demand, and the main problem is delivering it to the right places at the right prices). But if the future is one of greater demand than capacity, either new transmission lines must be built or new ways to produce electricity must be found, or demand must be dampened by higher prices.

(10) Businesses are leaving California for states where electricity is more secure, usually letting their workers go. What once was the dynamic state of the future is threatened with becoming a backwater.

I submit that no regulatory authority has either the brains or the political freedom to put together an enormous jigsaw puzzle to accommodate all these forces. Only competition, with decisions made at the margin (producers and consumers negotiating with each other) will cause the right amount of electricity to be produced at the right time and delivered to the right places. Remember, this is only my outlook. I'm not trying to persuade you, but I would like to hear from you.

Let Friends seek an adequate supply of electricity at prices that approximate the cost to produce it. Let us live simply, giving up some luxuries to boost incentives for new, cleaner modes of producing electricity. Let us be generous to the poor by paying part or all of their costs. Let us not be vindictive - let us worry more about the poor getting enough than the rich temporarily getting too much.

Love and Peace, Jack Powelson

READER RESPONSES TO LETTER NO. 7

Yes, I need to learn to live more deliberately, and make choices fitting my values! When I opened my PG&E bill for 3 weeks, and it was over $500, my first thought was for those with the same bill who would choose: food or medicine - or heat! We've read about those who choose food over their necessary medicine, but having to make a third choice?

Tom and I bought PG&E stock over 20 years ago at $13/share. It's now $9+/-. Many small folks own PG&E for the dividend and count on it for their retirement income, just as many bought the 'widows and orphans' AT&T stock years ago, and held on in good faith. I guess that tells us where we should put our 'faith'! :-)

So, I'm reminded again: live my life to fit my Quaker values.

Amy Cooper, Lafayette California (but a member of Cambridge MA Friends Meeting).

PS (from Jack): Amy is the daughter of Wini Barrett, who directed the AFSC Institute mentioned in the first paragraph of the present Letter.

An article in the February 12 *New Yorker* reported that Pennsylvania did the exact same thing as California (deregulate the wholesale market, but cap the rates of the consumer market), only with different numbers, and it worked. Among the differences they cited were: more advertising to consumers about how to switch providers, and higher caps that allowed providers more wiggle room in which to compete. Definitely worth a read.

Larry Powelson, Seattle (WA).

PS (from Jack): My son Larry is correct. Pennsylvania capped the retail price well above the competitive level. Below it, firms compete just as I suggested they should in Letter No. 7.

I concur that we should not have special pricing policies for the poor, but rather work to see that welfare payments and social security are adjusted to give them adequate purchasing power to choose between spending more or less on electricity and more or less on the other items in their consumer basket. It is amazing how people sit around in tee shirts while the electric heat is set at 82F. Try sweaters in winter and fans in summer!

Jim Booth, Red Cedar Friends Meeting, East Lansing (MI)

I do not dismiss the importance of environmental concerns; but environmentalists who oppose new power plants on principle will soon render themselves impotent, since the American people WILL have the electricity they demand, one way or the other. Not a wise strategy if a cleaner environment is truly the goal.

Ken Allison, Episcopalian Church, Scottsdale (AZ)

Jack Powelson's essay on the electrical crisis in California shows more kindness towards producers than other economist, for example Krugman (NYT, April 15, 2001). Krugman advocates (temporary) price caps, mainly justified on the assumption that such would limit a huge transfer of wealth (windfall profits) out of California to a handful of out of state companies.

Publicly owned utilities such as in Los Angeles and Sacramento seem to be doing well, and have already invested in renewables and fuel cells. If I were in California, I would want to have a hard look to see if such companies could furnish electricity with greater stability, and at reasonable costs.

Jack Herring, Boulder (CO) Meeting of Friends.

THE QUAKER ECONOMIST

May 1, 2001

Letter No. 8

Dear Friends:

Protesting globalization

We stood in a friendship circle, about fifty of us, arms intertwined, and singing. It was a high school institute of international affairs, sponsored by the American Friends Service Committee, at Ferry Beach, Maine, in 1951. As we sang, we opened up the circle to face the ocean and countries beyond.

> Now wider and wider our circle expands,
> Vive la compagnie,
> We sing to our comrades in far away lands,
> Vive la compagnie.

Quakers have always opened their hearts to peoples of other lands. My international career, where I have served in about 35 countries in Asia, Africa, and Latin America, arose out of my Quaker belief in that of God in all persons. I met my future wife, Robin, in a tent camp in Paris, while she was on her way to a Quaker work camp to help rebuild war-torn Austria, and I to work in a factory in Lille, France. Later on, as I taught, lectured, or gave economic counsel in other countries, I preached the principle of "Trade, Not Aid." In a previous letter, I told you how I also wandered for days in the slums of every Latin American capital except Havana, and several African cities. I wanted to learn how I might help better the conditions of those wretched inhabitants. The answer was always, "jobs, and trade."

Imagine my shock, in 1998, to discover that many Quakers had participated in the Seattle riots against the World Trade Organization (WTO), and that much of their protest had to do with keeping jobs away from the poorest of the poor abroad, so that our much-better-cared-for workers might have them instead. The World Trade Organization, they said, was not democratic and is run by multinational corporations (MNCs) for their profit. In fact, the World Trade Organization is run much the same way as the United Nations and is certainly no more undemocratic. Both the WTO and the

International Monetary Fund reach their decisions by consensus among members. Voting is rare.

Worst of all is the anti-globalization sentiment - that we should not open up our hearts to the rest of the world. Why? Is it anti-globalization as such, or the means by which globalization is occurring, and the role of multinationals? Protesters charge that MNCs damage the poor, but I have never heard them explain precisely how.

I think I know. On a street corner in Santiago Chile in 1971, I bought a copy of *Secret Documents of the ITT.* The International Telephone and Telegraph Company had urged the U.S. Government to prevent the accession to power in Chile of Salvador Allende, who they thought would expropriate their company. The documents were leaked to the press, where they made an uproar in the United States but were not published here. When I got home I took them to the Under-Secretary of State for Latin America. "Can these be true?" I asked. They were. He was furious, because he had not been consulted (he would have opposed).

The people of Nigeria are so dirt poor they risk their lives breaking into oil pipelines to steal oil. Some have been killed by explosions. Yet the companies pay royalties to a corrupt, greedy government that cares little about the poor.

In Guatemala our government prevented a revolution that might have brought a left-wing president who would have confiscated the properties of our banana producers.

I could go on and on. Multinational corporations are no angels! So, are they all evil? Are they not managed by people, and is there not that of God in every person?

In 1976, the International Labor Office published a research report, *Wages and Working Conditions in Multinational Enterprises.* Surprise! In country after country after country, it found that MNCs paid wages higher than the domestic companies, even up to 150% higher (but sometimes only 10% or 15% higher). In very few cases did MNCs pay as little as domestic corporations. Furthermore, they offered far better working conditions - schools, housing, health care, severance pay, and other fringe benefits - than did local companies. They also provide skills, technology and training that are absorbed by the local people. So, how do we balance the good against the evil?

In my home town, Boulder Colorado, a student was murdered on the street a few years ago. But no one stereotypes all Boulderites as murderers. Those who stereotype MNCs suppose that the worst practices are done by all. In general, however, MNCs are decent citizens. They pay their taxes; they do not normally bribe, and most of the time they obey the laws. Like the rest of us, they know they would get in trouble otherwise (as they have). To me, the viciousness of MNCs should be approached just like the viciousness of anyone. (Punishment, incentives to behave well, you name it). But don't deprive the poor of the jobs, amenities, and technology that MNCs bring.

Ah yes, MNCs buy from sweatshops. I have been in sweatshops in less developed countries. Some of them are airy and light, offering pleasant working conditions. But others (where I have not been) treat their employees cruelly, insisting on 18-hour work days, punishing them by not letting them go to the bathroom when needed, and even dragging them by the hair if they try to strike. I have not seen these conditions (no one would let me), but I have read about them from reliable sources. In sweatshops everywhere, wages are low, often less than is required for a decent subsistence even in slum shacks.

Students, human rights organizations, and others in the comfortable world have been protesting conditions in sweatshops. But there is a dilemma. Sweatshops *permeate* Asia, Africa, and Latin America. Wages are low *everywhere,* and the treatment is cruel. As I visited the slums in these countries, I heard this story from all sides. Impoverished people are clamoring for jobs in sweatshops - there are not enough of them! Families will starve unless their children work in them.

If we discourage MNCs from buying from sweatshops that employ children, they simply fire the children. "In 1993, child workers in Bangladesh were found to be producing clothing for Wal-Mart, and Senator Tom Harkin proposed legislation banning imports from countries employing underage children. The direct result was that Bangladeshi textile factories stopped employing children. But did the children go back to school? Did they return to happy homes? Not according to Oxfam, which found that the displaced child workers ended up in even worse jobs, or on the streets - that a significant number were forced into prostitution" (Paul Krugman in *New York Times,* 4/22/01).

Even that is not the worst. Starving families in Asia and Africa sell their children into slavery and prostitution. Yes, slavery still exists - in Sudan, Mauritania, and elsewhere. The dealers have taken children to Saudi Arabia to beg in the streets or to become prostitutes. Children who do not fall into their hands often find work in unclean factories where their lives are in danger, the work more exhausting, and the bosses more cruel and demanding than in the sweatshops.

So, what can we do? Largely as a result of American protests, Gap was able to improve working conditions in its supply shops in El Salvador (*New York Times,* 4/24/01). The employees now have bathroom breaks and can complain to a board of independent monitors. But Gap has not been able to raise their wages.

Why not? Because there is always a long line of unemployed at the doors, and if workers complain about what they earn, or if they strike, they will be fired and replaced. If Americans insist on higher wages, the sweatshops will move elsewhere.

Every economist knows why. As Krugman writes, "Third-world countries aren't poor because their export-workers earn low wages; it's the other way around." The only way to increase wages in Third-World countries (or anywhere) is to increase the productivity (output per hour) of workers. How? By increased capital and training, the very things that MNCs bring.

Also by trade. The more we buy, the greater the demand for workers, and the higher the wages. So, boycotting sweatshops makes the poor poorer, not the other way around. As Harvard economist Jeffrey Sachs has said, "What this world needs is more sweatshops."

So, are the protesters wrong? Not necessarily. They have waked us up to the injustices and poverty of the world. Good job! Trouble is, with few exceptions they haven't studied economics or history, so many of them don't know what they have discovered - or what to do about it.

Neither do I, yet I have devoted a professional lifetime to studying and knowing people in poverty. All I can offer is a few hints. The protesters at Seattle, Prague, Washington, and Quebec have been lashing out angrily at the whole world, without focusing on the small things they can do. They can improve conditions in sweatshops (witness, Gap in El Salvador), but they can't raise wages there, nor can they order the employers to send their workers to school. They can engage in micro-credit projects through the Quaker organization, Right Sharing of the World's Resources. (More on that in a subsequent Letter). They can't make multinational corporations eschew profits, but by gaining access to the CEOs (instead of damning them) they may help persuade them that bribery and overthrowing governments is not in their best interests. The CEOs are learning this on their own, but a little "help" would do no harm.

But just raising an unfocused hullabaloo about globalization will get the protesters nowhere. (In a subsequent Letter, I will report on two globalization agents, the World Bank and the International Monetary Fund. Hint: I have serious reservations about them, but they mean well).

I am told that 80 Quakers were at Quebec to protest the meeting to form the Free Trade Agreement of the Americas. I would appreciate it very much if someone who is opposed to that treaty would write a response to the present letter.. Many thanks.

Oh yes, now for the second verse:

> A friend on your left and a friend on your right
> Vive la compagnie,
> In love and good fellowship let us unite,
> Vive la compagnie!
>
> Vive la, vive la, vive l'amour,
> Vive la, vive la, vive l'amour,
> Vive l'amour, vive l'amour,
>
> Vive la compagnie!

Jack Powelson

READER RESPONSES TO LETTER NO. 8

Vive!

Frankly my life has been so full of busyness lately, that it was a surprise to me when your Letter drew me in and I found myself at the end, vivefied. I hope to compose an item about the Letter for our Sunday bulletin before long, and perhaps also to be sent to my local Friends list. Thanks for your dedication!

Terry Hokenson, Minneapolis (MN) Friends Meeting

Jack,

I can't add anything to your article on globalization and trade, except to say I agree with you completely. Unfortunately, as you and I both know all too well, these reasons continue to fall on deaf ears among most Friends.

For a corroborating but not quite as "friendly" opinion on this subject, there is an excellent article by Peter DuPont at www.opinionjournal.com this morning (Wed 2May).

Peace, Dick Bellin, Friends Meeting of Washington (DC)

Dear Jack,

I could not disagree more with the sentiments you express here, in "Protesting Globalization." I honor your good instincts, but must correct some facts. First and most obviously, the date of the WTO protest in Seattle was in 1999, not 1998. Second, there were no "riots," unless you count the police rampages against protesters, who were overwhelmingly nonviolent. Please read my account in the March 2000 *Friends Journal;* it is as accurate as I could possibly make it, and after considerable subsequent analysis by people closer to the scene, I stand by it completely.

David Morse, Storrs (CT) Friends Meeting

NOTE (by Jack): Nowhere in the entire letter, of which the above is an excerpt, does David mention that in the May 2000 *Friends Journal,* Brewster Grace of the Quaker United Nations Office in Geneva replied to his (David's) article. Brewster found numerous inaccuracies in David's article. I have read them both, and - having followed trade agreements since their inception in the 1930s - I believe Brewster is correct. Friends may now go to their Meeting libraries, read both sides, and make up their own minds. I will not carry this polemic further.

Being part of a very active Quaker community and being committed to the community of spirit in action I observe the participation of many Friends and friends in community as a movement of spirit towards a moment of understanding that will allow the light within to permeate all daily lives. It is saddening but enlightening to observe the severe reaction of many who are not aware of the presence of spirit in our lives. In communing with those who are participating in righteous displays of their truths I am convinced that we must not be affected by fears that would suppress and distort our truths - every aversion, in my opinion, dims the light within and reduces the radiance of humankind. My community demandsmy voice be clear and my presence noteable - I comply.

Pura Vida, Bernie Macdonald, Mendocino Monthly Meeting, Albion (CA)

THE QUAKER ECONOMIST
May 7, 2001

Letter No. 9

Dear Friends:

Can we understand Asian Values?

I was once told that I could not understand Asian values because I am a Westerner. Believing that I can understand anything I want to, if the time is long enough (say, ten thousand years), I took up the challenge. Start with economic values.

Consider the Overseas Chinese, found in Malaysia, Singapore, and other Southeast Asian countries. Why do they dominate the economies wherever they are, and why have they been so successful? A popular answer is loyalty in the Confucian tradition. They have a network of relatives, friends, and acquaintances who trust each other completely, do not betray each other, and do not compete with each other. It is also suggested that Chinese who go abroad are the more entrepreneurial type. All this may be true. But a different story comes out of research by two professors of the Chinese University of Hong Kong and an economist from the World Bank.

"For many *huaqiao* [Overseas Chinese], they found, the answer lay in 'pyramids,': . . . layers upon layers of subsidiaries, as well as cross-holdings and informal links with yet more companies. Almost always, the pyramids included at least one bank with a licence to take deposits, and several publicly listed subsidiaries that could issue shares in the open market. The purpose of these pyramids was to draw outside capital into the family group while retaining control over the use of this capital within the family. . . "

"To see how this works, picture a pyramid at the top of which sits a private holding company owned by the patriarch and his family. [This holding company] owns 51% of subsidiary A, which owns 51% of subsidiary B, which owns 51% of subsidiary C, which owns 30% of company D. Separately, the family also has another (wholly-owned) vehicle, F, which owns 21% of D. In terms of voting rights, the patriarch and his family therefore control 51% of company D. At the same time, the family can claim only 25% of company D's profits (51% times 51% times 51% times 30%, plus 21% through company F) (*The Economist*, 4/14/01).

Through this arrangement, the family has greater control over the operations of the pyramid than it has investment in them. It arranges to transfer assets from (say) Company D to Company A at a price lower than market, or from any company to any other at values higher than market. Through these sales, the profits (in the form of assets valued at more than market) become moved up the chain to the patriarch and his family, while the subsidiary companies are squeezed. So their dividends are flimsy. Both the patriarch and minority stockholders lose through the scanty dividends, but the patriarch alone gains more than he loses in dividends, because the profits have really been passed upward to him through the trumped-up sales. The minority holders are unfairly squeezed.

Because the pyramids are so complex, it may take years (or decades) for the minority holders to discover what has happened to them. Meanwhile, the patriarch may have liquidated some companies and started new ones, whose reputation will not be sullied for years to come. Asian values? Judge for yourself.

Let us turn to the Mainland Chinese. Once the People's Republic had won the revolution in 1949, they declared all previous laws of China null. They would start over again. As a result, they had no legal concept of "companies" nor of "property." Ideas of "assets" and "liabilities" and "equity" had no legal standing. Bankruptcy, contract, law, fiduciary, conflict of interest, and principal and agent were not part of the vocabulary. Instead, small businesses were declared to be national property (usually under the same management, now reporting to the government), and industry was run primarily in state-owned enterprises (SOEs). Farms were collectivized into communes.

In the Great Leap Forward of 1960, Mao ordered farm families to eat in common dining halls, and women and children to plant and harvest crops. He also ordered small steel mills to be built on the communes throughout the country, and men to work them. As a result, crops died on the vine, coal and iron were hauled uneconomically across the country (steel would have been more efficiently produced in Manchuria), and hundreds of thousands of Chinese died of starvation, partly because of a drought, but more importantly because of gross bureaucratic inefficiencies.

Outrage throughout China was so great that Mao's position was threatened. To preserve it, he organized the Great Cultural Revolution (1966), in which students and other young admirers were organized into the Red Guards. The Red Guards trashed universities, burned libraries, and forced intellectuals into the country to learn the true meaning of Chinese communism on the farms. Thus Mao re-established power until his death in 1976. Those students are now known in China as "the lost generation."

Since Mao's death the Chinese economy has grown enormously, mostly through the introduction of private enterprise, but also because the communes have been dismantled and private farmers now grow most of the crops. (But they have their problems too; see Letter No. 1). Most of this growth results from starting at a low base, but much of it represents inflated statistics. Each producer (farm and industry) reports what it thinks Beijing wants to hear, and the totals become "prodigious economic growth."

The present government has laid off workers of inefficient SOEs massively, but the growing private sector cannot absorb them all. Again a quote from *The Economist* (4/14/01): "But if China is aiming for well-governed companies bought and sold on well-governed bourses, the odds appear stacked against it. For example, there is a growing suspicion that the domestic stockmarkets' stellar performance reflects nothing more than market manipulation by a few dominant brokers (colluding naked in bathhouses, according to some reports, for fear of being bugged). In February, one of the country's most respected economists, Wu Jinglian, complained that China's stockmarkets were 'worse than a casino'. Securities regulators have now begun a crackdown so fierce as to send the markets diving.

"The balance sheets of Chinese companies are, by common consent, a joke. In January, the government's official auditing body admitted that more than two-thirds of the 1,300 biggest SOEs cook their books. Johnny Chen, the Beijing head of PricewaterhouseCoopers, says that even this is an understatement. Quite simply, the SOEs' numbers are whatever the key man wants them to be. And without genuinely independent directors to chair an audit committee, that will not change."

Asian values? In fact, the Chinese - both Overseas and Mainland - lack most of the institutions that grew up gradually, over centuries, in Japan and the West. For the legal system, let me quote from a previous writing of mine (*Centuries of Economic Endeavor,* 1992: 172-3):

- The main purpose of Chinese law is to preserve state power, not the rights of the individual.
- Traditional Chinese law sees little or no distinction between criminal and civil. It is more concerned with penalties than with righting civil wrongs. Thus rules and judgments regarding trade, sales, and production were not part of the legal system before Western ways were copied after 1912.
- Inequality and hierarchy have been legalized, with different rules applying to persons of different rank.
- For much of Chinese history, only government officials were allowed to know the official law. If commoners knew the law, it was believed that they would become litigious and defy authority. This concept changed with the Ming dynasty, but the present rulers still do not go out of their way to see that their laws are widely understood.
- Codes and statutes were highly developed in the early centuries. Their principal purpose was to inform provincial magistrates on the content of the criminal statutes they were expected to enforce. Common law, or the use of precedents, has been rare.
- Unlike northwestern Europe and Japan, the basic nature of Chinese law has not changed much over the centuries. Principles from the Shang Dynasty (1766 to about 1122 BCE) still govern the legal actions of the People's Republic.

It is in the context of these principles that the Chinese government wishes to enter the economic world of the West, to accept investment from foreign companies, and to modernize its legal, corporate, and trading systems. Western businesses are perplexed as they encounter these systems. In the West and Japan, the laws of corporations, contract, debt settlement, transparency (e.g., through the Securities and Exchange Commission), conflict of interest, principal and agent, fiduciary, banking, investing, and other means of doing business evolved over centuries, through negotiations among producers, traders, farmers, financiers, and governments. For the most part, they were not imposed from on top. As all this happened, state power was diffused into the democracies we have today. In 2001, the Chinese government is attempting to impose from on top a Western set of economic institutions, while at the same time trying to preserve state power.

Do Quakers understand Asian values? Do I? Despite all my travels abroad, in which I have learned other cultures, I am still a Westerner, and I see

Asian values through a Western prism. Please let me know how you see them. If you have had different experience in Asia, please share it.

Sincerely your Friend,
Jack Powelson

READER RESPONSE TO LETTER NO. 9

Joan and I just came back from three weeks in China, our first trip there. Five days on the Yangtze, some in Beijing, Xian and Shanghai. Also just read your China piece. It seems a bit overweighted towards Chinese overseas, a special group, rather than the Chinese mainland. It is a remarkable country, and its history certainly strange to us. A professor Dali Yang from U of Chicago was with us; we came away with a strange sense that this country of 1.2 billion could be moved this way and that by a strong central leader, something that we do not understand.

Jack, you must have spent every day since we were last together in DC, many decades ago, studying, traveling and introspecting. The spirituality of your efforts (a West Coast word, now even part of the Jewish movement) come through more explicitly than in the days of thee and thine that we appreciated in your family.

Don Green, Jewish, San Francisco (CA)

I believe your critique of Chinese practices/values implicitly raises a major philosophical question regarding the very nature of values qua values: Are values, abstractly considered, created artifacts specific to particular cultures and therefore relative in nature, or are they universally inherent to all human beings and therefore culturally transcendent?

Many today in the intellectual community would argue the former , and would add that the very question I pose is itself a culturally determined artifact. Thus, an insistence on the "rightness" of individual political and economic freedom is seen as an imposition of "Western" values at best, and as an act of cultural/political aggression at worst. In this relativistic mind set, no objective judgments regarding differing value systems are possible, or desirable.

Ken Allison (Episcopalian), Paradise Valley (AZ)

THE QUAKER ECONOMIST
May 14, 2001

Letter No. 10

Dear Friends:

Zoroastrian Quakers?

Adherents to the ancient Persian religion of Zoroaster believe the world is engaged in a never-ending war between good and evil. Many religions - even Christianity - carry some of this sentiment. Therefore, calling such an idea "Zoroastrian" does not imply uniqueness; it is only a convenient handle. In its more formative years - those of the Crusades and the Inquisition - Christianity held this tradition more fervently than now. Is it time to let go of the last vestige of Zoroastrianism?.

I thought of this when I learned that Quakers had been singing "We shall overcome" at the Quebec protests. Overcome what? I first knew that song when Martin Luther King led it at the Lincoln Memorial about 1962. Racial prejudice was certainly evil, and overcoming it was a religious matter. So far as I can see, however, the Quebec singers were protesting so many different things, all under the loose rubric of "globalization," that it almost seemed that half the world is evil, and we of the "righteous" half must "overcome" the evil half.

In Letter No. 8, I told how multinational corporations (MNCs), although they do many evil things, nevertheless pay better and offer better working conditions than do local corporations. A letter from Regan Gambier, a former student of mine, now married and living in London, also puts sweatshops into perspective:

> Several of our friends participated in the Day of Action protests here in London. I know their intentions were good, no one wants to see young girls working very long hours for very little money. However, I fail to see how depriving these people of their sweatshop jobs will help them. I have not heard of an MNC going into an under-developed country and burning the land, enslaving the people, forcing them to work in the sweatshops. Instead I

read of children leaving mortgaged family farms to hire agents who help them get jobs in the new factory. The competition for these jobs is fierce, because the pay is good (compared to alternatives) and workers gain marketable skills.

When I was very young and received toys as presents, I was always disappointed by a 'Made in Japan' label. It meant poorly assembled cuddly toys or plastic dolls that wouldn't last the week. As I grew up 'Made in Japan' came to mean quite the opposite, usually still inexpensive but quality goods like my Sony Walkman. The low-skilled assembly jobs moved from Japan to Mexico to Korea and around the world. Each move signified a workforce that had gained skills and was ready for more demanding and financially rewarding work. Companies have had to move on because the workforce has improved. It makes more financial sense for an MNC to pick up and move to an entirely new country than to pay its current workers more. Heartless? I don't think so. Workers in Japan moved from manufacturing plastic toys to cars in a generation. Textile manufacturers in Mexico are now assembling computer chips and getting paid more to do so. Similarly, workers in Sheffield are now more likely to find work in an office building than a steel refinery, again earning more money.

I, too, have always thought of the world as interconnected. The jobs don't disappear, they go to someone else; someone else who probably needs them more.

Newsweek reported on April 30:

> By taunting the police, beating drums and throwing rocks, the rioters make it pretty clear that they want not a rational debate but the world's attention—and they have succeeded once again. . .

> What developing countries need more than anything else—yes, even more than new labor and environmental

> regulations —is economic growth. And yet every pro-
> posal made by the protesters would slow down that growth
> and keep the Third World mired in medieval poverty. So
> much for international solidarity. . .

> The lesson of Seattle seems to be: if you cannot get your
> way through traditional democratic methods, through
> campaigns, lobbying and legislatures, then riot and rabble-
> rouse on television. . . If this is the new left, give me the
> old stuff any day.

One correspondent has tried to persuade me that MNCs do not have that of
God in them. While every live person, from CEO to humble worker, may
embody that of God, nevertheless the MNC is only a legal being. Being
distinct from a person, this correspondent said, it may function without
God. I believe that is a rationalization, because all MNCs are managed by
people.

What are the evils we should be protesting? Certainly war is one. We Westerners tend to think of war in ideological terms, such as communism versus
capitalism. But consider the twelfth-century troubadour portrayed by the
French historian Marc Bloch *(Feudal Society*: 293): "I love to see, amidst
the meadows, tents and pavilions spread; . . . it gives me great joy to see,
drawn up on the field, knights and horses in battle array; and it delights me
when the scouts scatter people and herds in their path . . . And when the
battle is joined, let all men of good lineage think of naught but the breaking
of heads and arms . . . I find no such favor in food, or in wine, or in sleep,
as in hearing the shout, 'On! On!' From both sides; . . in seeing men great
and small go down on the grass beyond the fosses; in seeing at last the
dead, with the pennoned stumps of lances still in their sides."

Get the idea? War was beautiful, to be observed as one would a baseball
game. Learning from history, I would guess that war is still idealized by
soldiers and guerrillas of Bosnia, Serbia, Kosovo, Congo, Chechnya, Israel, Palestine, Russia, Northern Ireland, and elsewhere. Yes, there is an
ideology, and a nationalism (as there was also in twelfth-century France),
but that is only so there will be something to fight for. Perhaps war no
longer possesses inherent beauty, but it does create a surge of feeling of
power. After all, what difference should it make who is the ruler of the
Tutsis or Hutus, or whether Palestinians or Israelis or both govern their

area, so long as they do so justly? What does it matter whether Britain or Ireland is the government of Ulster, again so long as they are fair and democratic? This is an idea of the French economist, Frederic Bastiat (1801-50).

In Letter No. 11 (next week) I plan to list 39 countries (including Canada and the United States) whose violations of human rights deserve far greater condemnation than do those of MNCs and sweatshops.

If we are to be Zoroastrian Quakers - and that may not be a bad thing - let us not think of a war between good and evil - of us being righteous and others evil. Let us not think of "overcoming" multinational corporations but of controlling the evil and enhancing the good of all people and all institutions, including MNCs. Martin Luther King understood that not all Whites were racist, and one line of "We shall overcome" tells of "Blacks and Whites together." As soon as I hear us singing, "Quakers, MNCs, and sweatshops together," I might join in. Let us think of our struggle as a way of bettering the consciences of people, so we do not idealize "overcoming" others but instead seek that of God in them.

Sincerely your friend,
Jack Powelson

READERS' RESPONSES TO LETTER NO. 10

The troubador was fascinating. But you may be unfair to suggest that he saw war only as a spectator sport. With the right (meaning wrong?) ideology, people throw themselves into war with gusto.

You made a nice argument about trying to boost the good in any one, though surely Hitler or Stalin would have been a challenge (unless perhaps you got ahold them at age six or something). But your message was a great contrast to the jihads that Quakers seem to join nowadays.

Steve Williams, Bethesda (MD) Friends Meeting

The idea that because a multinational corporation is a legal being, there need not be that of God in it] is more than a rationalization. It is an error. Only individuals act in human society. Organizations cannot act. When the individual acts, they do so, more or less, from that of God within them. Organizations cannot decide. A subgroup of individuals may be empowered to make decisions for the group, but when action is taken by the group, it is individuals who accede to the decision and take the action.

Russ Nelson, St. Lawrence Valley (NY) Friends Meeting

It seems to be the baggage of cultural tradition and "heritage". People everywhere identify with a particular heritage or tradition: they feel they ARE a Jew, or Palestinian or Hutu, a certain religion, race or nationality. Is this the same as being a Quaker? Is it active belief selected by choice and reason? No, I think most is something very different, more of a feeling of membership based on history and closer family or tribal relationships (heritage).

What if Israelis and Palestinians were willing to drop these identities and see themselves as residents of a present 2001 community? (ok, it's not likely...) Such a combined group of people ARE, (in fact) members of the time and place where they actually exist. The historical traditions and dogmas are less relevant to life than the circumstances of economics, environment, society in which they live each day. If people were to acknowledge as their actual identity and citizenship being the real and present community they live each day within, together with all others sharing the time and place, would they not then feel like making their community more livable, a GOOD place to be? Would they not band together to eliminate not each other, but fix the threats to their own collective well-being? Like weapons, bombs, warfare, dangerous leadership. That is wishful thinking, since we can't even do it in the US. Nevertheless I see allegiance to these separate traditions of identity as driving the divisions and differences, traditions and heritages that are less relevant to life today than the actual circumstances of those lives than today's real concerns of economy, environment, peace-making etc.

Steve Willey, Sandpoint friends Meeting, Sandpoint (ID)

I think the people protesting "globalization" and the MNCs are basically afraid they do not and will not have the necessary skills/knowledge to move to new/better employment. "Sweatshops" in any form are what workers with even less see as a step up the ladder of success. In the early part of the industrial revolution in the U.S. and Europe the "sweatshops" were a step up. Now, from many rungs up that same ladder, we see how abusive and inhumane the system was/is. The abuses abounded and we've moved on as an industrialized civilization. We must help the sweatshop owners understand the abusiveness of the system as Quakers (and others) helped the slave owners understand the slaves were/are human who should/must be treated in a more humane manner. Lack of understanding is the evil that must be overcome by good in the Zoroastrian Quaker world concept as I understand it.

Cynthia Stevenson, Boulder (CO) Friends Meeting

THE QUAKER ECONOMIST

May 21, 2001

Letter No. 11

Dear Friends:

How do Friends feel about torture around the world?

We keep hearing of torture and other abuses of human rights all around the world. How do we feel? Are we enraged, or do we just shrug them off as everyday things far from us?

Much of the torture is inflicted by democracies, and much was witnessed or acclaimed by cheering crowds. Given our long history of compassion for the abused, what can Quakers do to relieve or protest these atrocities? I have been collecting newspaper reports on them for five years, and only a small number of my collection is reproduced below, with the countries in alphabetical order. Amnesty International will have many more cases. (NYT= New York Times, other sources spelled out):

This letter is longer than usual. One Friend suggested that I not send it, because it is too gruesome. Yes, I do appreciate the love and compassion throughout the world, but we must also face up to the cruelty. You may be too disgusted (or too bored) to read to the end. If so, please jump to the end from any point in the middle, to read the important query for Quakers.

Afghanistan

A couple accused of adultery was stoned to death. They were dropped into separate pits and covered with dirt up to their chests. It took 10 minutes to kill the man and a bit longer for the woman. Townspeople came by the thousands to witness a spectacle not seen in Kandahar for decades (NYT 11/3/96).

Afghanistan's ruling Taliban militia, along with thousands of Pakistanis lit with the fervor of jihad, went on a destructive spree this summer, killing wantonly, emptying entire towns, machine-gunning livestock, sawing down fruit trees, blasting apart irrigation canals. It was a binge of blood lust and mayhem described in consistent detail by witnesses. (NYT 11/18/97).

Algeria

Islamic militants descended on Ben Talha, a town of 8,000 shortly before midnight Sept. 22. They carried swords, hunting rifles, Kalashnikovs, fire-bombs, and iron bars. They dragged the people to slit their throats. The intruders killed 95 people by official tally or more than 300 according to villagers, whose accounts were supported by the fresh graves just outside town. (NYT, 12/28/97).

More than 10,000 civilians are reported to have been slaughtered over the past two weeks. Some were burnt alive, others hacked to death. Throats were slashed, babies hurled against walls. The savagery beggars the imagi-nation. (Economist, 1/10/98).

Argentina

An Argentine tells of dumping "dirty war" captives in the sea. Many of the victims were so weak from torture and detention that they had to be helped aboard the plane. Once in flight they were injected with a sedative by an Argentine Navy doctor before two officers stripped them and shoved them to their deaths. (NYT, 3/13/95).

1976-83: detainees were hauled into the Navy School of Mechanics, cover-ing four city blocks. They were tossed into windowless dungeons, tortured on racks, beaten with chains and pipes, and shocked with electric prods. Prisoners - some alive, some not - were taken from their holes and flung into the Rio de la Plata from airplanes. Others were incinerated on the grounds in what neighbors mistook for cadets' barbecues. (Washington Post Weekly, 1/19/98).

Bangladesh

Cruel punishments (stoning to death and whipping) for sexual "crimes" by women, ordered by the shashlish, village elders and clergy of no legal stand-ing but which have successfully resolved disputes over land and property for years. Recently more judgments seem to be directed against women. (Economist, 6/14/97).

Bolivia

In 1976, Bolivia's and Chile's ruling generals, both in power after military coups, met to exchange information on "subversives" in exile-and to detain those deemed most dangerous by their government. Many of these were handed over, and then "disappeared". (Economist, 11/7/98).

Bosnia

Muslim leaders murdered scores of Bosnian Serbs who remained in Sarajevo when fighting broke out in 1992. (NYT, 11/12/97).

Brazil

Military police and hired gunners stormed an encampment of about 500 squatters, killing them, using women as human shields and torturing, killing, and stomping on prisoners. They shot a 6-year-old girl dead as she sought safety. (NYT, 12/29/94).

Cambodia

From 1975 to 1979 Pol Pot ordered more than a million people killed as he tried to bend Cambodia to his radical Maoist vision. People were executed because they owned property, because they lived in cities, because they were professionals. Even literacy became grounds for execution. (NYT, 6/24/97).

Canada

Pictures entered as evidence in court martial show Canadian soldiers at a desert outpost with a blindfolded, bruised and bloody Somali teenager, who was tortured until he died a few hours later. (NYT, 11/27/94).

Chile

Although no accurate count exists, at least 40,000 Chileans were tortured under the Pinochet dictatorship from 1973 until 1990, people who had been members of leftist parties, unions, student groups or even merely bureaucrats in the Socialist government of President Salvador Allende Gossens. (NYT, 1/3/00).

China

Human Rights Watch charged that thousands of children have died in China's state-run orphanages from deliberate starvation, medical malpractice, and staff abuse. Pictures of starving children were smuggled out by a former doctor. Strong probability of a policy of deliberate starvation and severe abuse of orphans. Countless abandoned infants, most of them girls. (NYT, 1/6/96).

The police regularly kick and punch Falun Gong protesters in the square, often bloodying them and knocking them to the ground in full view of the public. (NYT, 1/11/01).

Colombia

The armed men, more than 300 of them, marched into this tiny village early on a Friday. They went straight to the basketball court that doubles as the main square, residents said, announced themselves as members of Colombia's most feared right-wing paramilitary group, and with a list of names began summoning residents for judgment. A table and chairs were taken from a house, and after the death squad leader had made himself comfortable, the basketball court was turned into a court of execution, villagers said. The paramilitary troops ordered liquor and music, and then embarked on a calculated rampage of torture, rape and killing. "To them, it was like a big party," said one of a dozen survivors who described the scene in interviews this month. "They drank and danced and cheered as they butchered us like hogs." (NYT, 7/14/00.)

Congo

Tens of thousands of Hutu refugees disappeared as they were being driven clear across Congo by Kabila's rebel army. The UN put the toll at 180,000. (NYT, 5/7/98).

Croatia

A Croatian's confession describes torture and killing on a vast scale. A former militiaman acknowledged that he killed 72 civilians, tortured prisoners with electric shocks and ran a death camp. He said that after awhile, killing and torture became routine. (NYT, 9/5/97).

Guatemala

Perhaps 100,000 died in the fighting; perhaps 40,000 disappeared. Hundreds of Amerindian villages were destroyed. Too often their people died with them - 350 in one single notorious piece of armed butchery. Mass graves have been excavated since the fighting stopped. (NYT, 5/2/98).

Haiti

Orphans of Haiti disappear, targets of murderous thugs. Seen as potential enemies of the state when they grow up, they are kidnapped from orphanages. No one complains, no one claims the bodies. (NYT, 9/9/94).

Honduras

During its decade-long "dirty war" against suspected guerrilla-sympathizers, the Honduran military kidnapped, tortured, and killed dozens of people. (NYT, 12/21/95).

India

Every day, year after year, women grotesquely disfigured by fire are taken to Victoria Hospital's burn ward here in India's fastest-growing city. They lie in rows, wrapped like mummies in white bandages, their moans quieted by the pain-obliterating drip of morphine. Typically, these women and thousands like them have been depicted as victims of disputes over the ancient social custom of dowry and as symbols of the otherness of India, a place where lovely young brides are doused with kerosene and set ablaze for failing to satisfy the demands of their husbands' families for gold, cash and consumer goods that come as part of the marriage arrangement. (NYT, 12/26/00).

Indonesia

President Suharto sent special forces into Aceh, a strongly Muslim province, in 1989 to put down a small separatist movement. In the process, say human-rights groups, the soldiers killed, raped and tortured thousands of people. Such was the climate of fear at the time that few Indonesians ever spoke about it. (Economist, 9/12/98).

Iran

State Department report on human rights depicts arbitrary detentions, summary executions, and widespread torture. (Economist, 7/23/94).

Israel

Case of a Palestinian prisoner of Israelis who was kept sleepless in contorted and excruciating positions with a stinking bag over his head, threatened, beaten and subjected to violent shaking until he passed out. (NYT, 5/8/97).

Korea, North

I was a doctor with a German medical group, "Cap Anamur," and entered North Korea in July 1999. I remained until my expulsion on Dec. 30, 2000, after I denounced the regime for its abuse of human rights, and its failure to distribute food aid to the people who needed it most. North Korea's starvation is not the result of natural disasters. The calamity is man-made. Only the regime's overthrow will end it. Human rights are nonexistent. Peasants, slaves to the regime, lead lives of utter destitution. It is as if a basic right to exist — to be — is denied. Ordinary people starve and die. (Wall Street Journal, 4/14/01).

Korea, South

A South Korean prisoner who has spent 39 years and 7 months in prison. Others who have been released say he is partially paralyzed from a stroke and that his teeth are all gone from decades of torture. He was the head of a military reconnaisance team from North Korea whose boat was seized when it entered South Korean waters. (NYT, 3/10/98).

Kosovo

The bodies of 15 women, children and elderly members of the Deliaj clan lay slumped among the rocks and streams of the gorge below their village in Kosovo province Tuesday, shot in the head at close range and in some cases mutilated as they tried to escape advancing Serbian forces. In village houses, three men, including Fazli Deliaj, the 95-year-old patriarch, who was paralyzed, were burned to death by Serbs who torched the buildings.

Down the dirt track a few miles at Donji Obrinje, three more elderly people lay dead on their backs in their gardens, shot in the head as they apparently came out to plead for their lives. (NYT, 9/30/98).

Liberia

When the militiamen arrived in the town of Marshall 8 years ago, they rounded up all Ghanaian immigrants they could find, marching them off with their Liberian friends and sympathizers for execution. Perhaps 1,000 were shot to death. Survivors say that children were swung by their feet by laughing soldiers as their heads were smashed against palm trees. Countless others drowned as they tried to swim across a river to the safety of a nearby island. (NYT, 2/4/98).

Malaysia

Almost every day now in Malaysia, people are reading newspaper accounts of foreign domestic helpers who have been abused by their employers. The revelations of these secret crimes have horrified a society that sees itself as kind, hospitable and soft-spoken. One young woman said she was kept in a cage by her employer. One was beaten with a heavy object that fractured her skull. One said she was poked with a stick in the gums and forced to beat herself on the thighs with a cane whenever she "made a mistake." (NYT, 2/20/00).

Mexico

Mexican rights monitor reports torture of rebels in Chiapas, contradicting the Government's assertion that it has carefully respected the law on this. (NYT, 2/21/95.)

Policemen and soldiers commonly kidnap, torture and kill people across Mexico, despite Government reforms aimed at eradicating the abuses and despite the authorities' claims that they have largely ended, Human Rights Watch said in a report issued Thursday. (NYT, 1/15/99).

Nicaragua

Arnaldo Aleman, new President of Nicaragua, vows to wipe out the legacy of the Sandinista past. In 1989, his own properties were seized and he was sentenced to 7 years in jail. While in prison, his wife, Dolores, suffered brain cancer. Despite his pleas, he was not permitted to visit her in her hospital before she died. (NYT, 10/25/96).

Pakistan

In Saidpur, just hours before the armed forces seized power on Oct. 12, 1999, Government bulldozers demolished more than 500 houses and reduced most of the impoverished village to a dusty pile of rubble where weeping children wandered in the chaos. Saidpur was largely destroyed because politicians and their bureaucratic appointees decided that it was an eyesore and a nuisance on what one official called "the VVIP route," the road where very, very important people like Prime Minister Nawaz Sharif roared past in shiny black Mercedes-Benzes. (NYT, 10/30/99).

Palestine

Hundreds of prisoners have been jailed for months without charges. In two years, seven people have died in detention. Police routinely use torture during investigations. Books critical of Arafat have been banned, and critical journalists censored, beaten, and imprisoned. (NYT, 9/8/96).

Paraguay

A mountain of records detailing repression among United States-backed military regimes throughout South America during the cold war has been brought to light in Paraguay. From floor to ceiling, five tons of reports and photos detailed the arrest, interrogation and disappearance of thousands of political prisoners during General Stroessner's 35-year dictatorship. The documents trace the creation and work of Operation Condor, a secret plan among security forces in six countries to crush left-wing political dissent. (NYT, 8/12/99).

Russia

Punishment precedes trial for some Russian inmates. One said he had been arrested and brutally beaten for stealing less than $5 and had already spent 10 months behind bars awaiting his trial. His lice-ridden, 18th century cell, built for 30, currently warehouses more than 100 men. Many detainees end up spending 2, 3, and even 4 years awaiting their day in court, in packed cells. (NYT, 1/8/98.)

Rwanda

Omar Serushago, one of the five leaders of the Hutu militia that was responsible for the deaths of more than 500,000 minority Tutsis and politically moderate Hutus in 1994, pleaded guilty to one count of genocide, and three counts of crimes against humanity. (Wall Street Journal, 12/15/98.)

Serbia

After a Serbian sweep, a Kosovo village is stunned by the carnage. 24 people killed in a brutal sweep by Serbian paramilitary units against armed members of the Kosovo Liberation Army; they bore signs of torture and summary execution, which were also the hallmarks of the Serbian forces in the war in Bosnia. (NYT, 3/3/98.)

Sierra Leone

Hacking off hands and feet of ordinary people has been a key weapon of a widespread campaign of terror and butchery waged by rebels in Sierra Leone trying to overthrow this ravaged country's president. The rebels shot thousands of civilians dead and mutilated hundreds of others. Over the weekend, scores of men, women and children, with hands chopped off or dangling limply from their forearms, have flooded the main medical center, Connaught Hospital. A few days earlier, the hospital had received so many wounded and dead that corpses lying in the driveway had drawn dogs and vultures. By the weekend, hospital officials had recorded 2,768 dead in Freetown. (NYT, 1/26/99).

Sudan

1.9 million men, women, and children have died since 1993 from the war or war-related causes. Political dissidents have been tortured. Tens of thousands of women and children, deemed "infidels," have been captured as war booty, taken from their families and forced into unpaid labor. (NYT, 12/8/98.)

Uganda

The Lord's Resistance Army, with about 1,500 followers, have killed hundreds, abducted thousands of children and terrorized by cutting off noses and ears, breaking legs with hammers and laying land mines. Many villages are so terrified that peasants hid in the fields and trees at night. (NYT, 6/21/95.)

United States

The CIA taught techniques of mental torture and coercion to at least 5 Latin American security forces in the early 1980s but repudiated the interrogation methods in 1985, according to documents and statements the agency made public today. (NYT, 1/29/97).

A truth commission report has concluded that the United States gave money and training to a Guatemalan military that committed "acts of genocide" against the Mayan people during the most brutal armed conflict in Latin America, Guatemala's 36-year civil war. (NYT, 2/26/99).

A Query for Quakers

Do we live our lives, thoughtless of the suffering of these human souls? Do we protest?

If there has been Quaker protest, I have not heard it. Instead, I hear Quakers protesting multinational corporations and sweatshops, each of which hire *voluntary* workers, pay more than these workers could earn otherwise, and teach them important skills. Has our witness turned kattiwampus?

Yes, I have some thoughts about what we can do. Please wait for them until next week, however. This letter is already too long.

> Peace if you can find it,
> Jack Powelson

READERS' RESPONSES TO LETTER NO. 11

We Quakers have really jumped on to a bandwagon labeled "anti-globalization" that lacks a driver or a long-term direction - and we seem to be without deeply considered concern for those for whom we should feel tenderness in less fortunate or truly horrific conditions. Often the recent protests for others' welfare appear to be really pleas for help from the confused, given the rapidity of global change.

I certainly look forward to your next letter about doing something about torture, but at the same time perhaps we should also consider how we may help our fellow friends/Friends who are self-tortured in their fears and anxieties. I hope in your next letter you may offer alternatives to shotgun protests to well focused, meaningful action to reduce torture. It could be an antidote for those who feel the need to do something meaningful given the gross injustices around the world.

Living outside the US, I have noticed a recent increase of anti-Americanism which, of course, is not anti-Americans. Just as individuals are feeling increasing helplessness so are smaller countries in the context of these mega forces sweeping our planet. As the last standing super power, America and its corporations will be increasingly attacked as the real or symbolic root of all evils. The Bush Administration's foreign policy actions have only added fuel to the fire and many are starting to wonder if the US has re-ignited the Cold War - particularly in regards to China. Those conclusions are hasty or at least premature if later to be proven true. In any event, I expect to hear more of the same in the coming months. Clearness is in ever increasing need.

Tom Coyner, Seoul (Korea) Monthly Meeting

As you well know many Quakers are working against violence in many ways large and small which do not make the news. This particular Friend is working to see that small children in this county are able to grow up without being abused and/or neglected - one Small step in the direction of peace. In our own Meeting many others are working for peace in many other ways.

I share your concern that many protesters fail to grant that their adversaries also have that of God in them, but I share their concern for many of the actions of MNCs and of the effects of "globalization" as it now occurs.

Vici Oshiro, Minneapolis (MN) Friends Meeting

Madhu, the government of Afghanistan, is waging a war upon women. Since the Taliban took power in 1996, women have had to wear burqua and have been beaten and stoned in public for not having the proper attire, even if this means simply not having the mesh covering in front of their eyes. One woman was beaten to death by an angry mob of fundamentalists for accidentally exposing her arm while she was driving! Another was stoned to death for trying to leave the country with a man that was not a relative. Women are not allowed to work or even go out in public without a male relative. Professional women such as professors, translators, doctors, lawyers, artists and writers have been forced from their jobs and restricted to their homes. Homes where a woman is present must have their windows painted so that she can never be seen by outsiders.

Excerpt from a much longer message sent by Sabra Newton, 57th Street Meeting, Chicago, now active with Whittier Meeting, California.

Friends do not have to re-invent the wheel. Joining existing organizations that do work against torture is as good a way to stand up to the practice as having another "Quaker" organization. Especially as Friends don't seem inclined to work together in "organizations."

Free Polazzo, Anneewakee Creek Worship Group, Douglaville, GA

COMMENT by Jack: Free and Vici Oshiro have both pointed out to me that many Quakers are protesting quietly about one or another, or more, of the atrocities mentioned in Letter No. 11.

I am appalled and outraged by the human rights abuses you describe, because for me at least, it is TRUE that human life is of supreme value; it is TRUE that torture and false imprisonment is evil; it is TRUE that fundamental human rights exist and belong to all human beings; it is TRUE that abuse of these rights is wrong. I hold these truths as basic values that, if not universal in and of themselves, at the very least point to, or are consonant with, ontologically real universal values whose ultimate source is God (to paraphrase myself again).

Kenneth Allison, Episcopalian, Paradise Valley, AZ

REPLY TO CYNTHIA STEVENSON ON SWEATSHOPS

Cynthia Stevenson writes: "We must help the sweatshop owners understand the abusiveness of the system..." I'm not sure that she's right. Do sole proprietors work under the same conditions? If so, then a sweatshop is not abusive, but instead a victim of market conditions. And Jack has done a good job describing those conditions, and how they can only improve over time, in *Centuries of Economic Endeavor.*

Russ Nelson, St. Lawrence Valley (NY) Friends Meeting

COMMENT by Jack: I tend to agree with Cynthia. As I think back on the seventeenth century, Quakers were abused in prison for other than market reasons. I do believe the abuses in sweatshops today are caused in part by the viciousness of the owners, who obtain no market advantage from them. To that extent, they can be lessened without disturbing the market prospects of the owners.

THE QUAKER ECONOMIST
May 28, 2001

Letter No. 12

Dear Friends:

Shall we trade?

A strange thing happened in the *New York Times* of May 15. It reported on Kunshan, a town that Taiwan had built in China, as follows: "About 10 percent of Taiwan's $50 billion investment in the mainland has landed here." And, "Some experts say that if the trend continues, Taiwan's government will soon be unable to afford antagonizing China, and that the cost to China of attacking Taiwan may become prohibitive." What a way to end a war! The economic integration of Taiwan and China would make war extremely costly for either of them.

This reminded me of a contrary case with Japan in the 1920's. Japan was well on its way to democracy, with the civil government gradually assuming authority over the military. Historian Edwin Reischauer wrote of "a runaway liberal movement of the urban middle classes" that shifted power away from the military, whose budgets were curbed in 1922 and 1925. But the 1929 stock market crash, the Smoot-Hawley tariff of 1930 - the highest in American history - and an overvalued yen effectively cut Japan off from world trade. Japan sank into depression and unemployment, so that many youths - with nothing else to do - joined the army. In 1931, the army commanders on their own - without any communication with either the Parliament or the emperor in Tokyo - ordered the invasion of Manchuria, and the war with China was on. Economic sanctions, and frozen assets abroad, further isolated Japan. So the military triumphed over democracy, and the new path led finally to Pearl Harbor. We will never know what might have happened had Japan been welcomed into the world of trading nations in the 1920s and 1930s, but it is just possible that its entry into World War II might have been avoided.

Trade engenders trust

In Letter No. 11, I promised a suggestion on how Quakers might react to the 39 countries listed as committing atrocities. Note that most of them were underdeveloped countries, Canada and the United States being the exceptions as they faced underdeveloped countries. Over a few centuries, the more developed countries - trading with each other - have fashioned common ways of making contracts, extending credit, settling accounts, and carrying on business transactions.

Normally, nations that become economically interdependent will not go to war. Exceptions occur when the political configurations overwhelm the economic, as with Germany and England, who traded vigorously before going to war in 1914. But why did France and England, enemies for centuries, become friends? Or France and Austria? Do you think the nations of the European Union will ever again go to war against each other? Do the United States and Canada consider war when they disagree? It is not the mere fact of interdependence through trading, but the growth of common assumptions about how to live together - *an incidental result of trading* - that makes societies want to live together in peace.

I wrote about this in my book, *The Moral Economy* (page 111), in the following quotation, slightly revised to become a Quaker message:

> Northwestern Europe was the first world area in which trade began to transcend the power of rulers, and it was private trading - less than the agreements among rulers - that brought about the high degree of trust prevalent today. Building trust through multitudes of small private transactions by relatively ordinary people, rather than having trust mandated by an elite because it is a good thing, corresponds closely to the way we Quakers seek Truth. The procedure is collective and open to expressions of doubt as well as to confirmation with reality checks. It involves respect for other parties, whom we "hold in the Light." We do not seek Truth consulting higher temporal authority.
>
> In the cattle market at Wedel, near Hamburg, in the Middle Ages, "a bargain was concluded when buyer and seller had noted the outcome on their slates . . . Good faith was the rule in the transactions themselves. The bargain would be sealed with a drink in one of the thirty inns fringing the market place . . . The rich lowland farmers . . left their purses in the inn, where the landlord looked after them in a wooden chest in his bedroom. Nobody doubted that its contents would be intact" (Glamann 1977:267). "In the

long history of human morality there is no landmark more significant than the appearance of the man who can be trusted to keep his
promises ... [Although] conscience and promise-keeping emerged
in human history ... long before capitalism ... it was not until the
eighteenth century, in Western Europe, England, and North
America, that societies first appeared whose economic systems
depended on the expectations that most people, most of the time,
were sufficiently conscience-ridden (and certain of retribution) that
they could be trusted to keep their promises" (Haskell 1985:2:551-3).

All this has led me to believe that trade among nations changed the trading
world from basically suspicious to basically trusting (oh yes, lots of exceptions). The trusting world was one of cooperation to mutual advantage.
This in turn led to opportunities for innovation and entrepreneurship, which
came to mark the difference between those parts of the world (northwestern Europe, England, and Japan) that became rich and those parts (Asia
except Japan, Africa, and Latin America) that did not.

But we need rules for trade. Northwestern Europe and Japan hammered out
rules by compromise and agreement. These rules were agreed upon mostly
by merchants and traders and only later were adopted by sovereigns. I tell
about that in an earlier book, *Centuries of Economic Endeavor* (1994).
Today we need an international organization in which representatives of
governments can meet to work out those rules. This is what the World Trade
Organization does. Why so many Quakers have opposed it (and an article
in *Friends Journal* gave them voice) is beyond me.

The idea that the WTO is dominated by multinational corporations is myth.
The WTO has made decisions that will cost MNCs plenty. For example, it
ruled against the United States for its Foreign Trade Corporations Act, an
act that gave unfair no-tax status to MNCs in Guam and other U.S. posses-
sions. If put into effect, this ruling will cost MNCs billions of dollars.

So, I am pro-choice. I believe that if any person, A, wishes to do business
with another person, B, and no third person, C, is hurt, no authority should
prevent the transaction. My understanding of history shows me that trading
and the ability of peoples to compose the rules of trade have meant the
dividing line between decent living and continuing poverty. The Free Trade
Agreement of the Americas should not be necessary. Trading should be a
human right.

What about atrocities? Whoever commits atrocities must believe the victims are worthless miscreants who do not belong in civilization. (Studies show that Germans who committed atrocities felt that way about Jews). This kind of hatred diminishes as trade occurs. True, the nationally-induced hatred against Jews was Germany's primordial event of World War II. But think also of the many persons who risked their lives to save the Jews (Schindler for example). Did they have a divine spark that Nazis did not have? I believe they had come to think of Jews as "other selfs" who needed protection just as they themselves would have under the same circumstances.

Perhaps you thought, from Letter No. 11, that I would come up with some magic kind of protest that would, if successful, cut the atrocities in half within a few years. Sorry. We can no more end the atrocities abruptly than we can jump to the moon from only our own two feet. But if we want to start changing the hearts and minds of those who commit them, we should be promoting trade, economic integration, and understanding. Maybe the atrocities will come to an end in two centuries, as they did in England with the Enlightenment.

I do not ask you to accept my theory, and I do not expect you to read my books. If my theory makes sense, you may adopt it. If it doesn't, then adopt something that makes sense to you.

> Sincerely your Friend,
> Jack Powelson

References

Glamann, Kristof, "The Changing Patterns of Trade," in Rich and Wilson, *The Cambridge Economic History of Europe.*

Haskell, Thomas J., "Capitalism and the Origins of the Human Sensibility," *American Historical Review* 90:2.

NOTE BY RUSS NELSON

I just came back from a conference put on by a couple of people trying to help the Somali people by doing business in Awdal, Somalia. We were talking about the cultural mismatch between the Somali oral culture, where a written contract is NO better than an oral contract, and an oral contract needs witnesses and a ceremony to become non-negotiable, and Western culture, where people "want it in writing".

And it seems that in most of the poorer parts of the world, it's considered acceptable and even desirable to do one's best to take advantage of your trading partners. Not so in the USA. In the USA, we presume that businessmen will be honest, from the first trade. This greatly lowers the transaction cost, and allows us to do much more business in the same amount of time.

To do business in Somalia, or India, or Peru (specific examples that were given), you must first establish trust by doing small amounts of business.

READER RESPONSES TO LETTER NO. 12

I have heard it said that war is an act of insanity because when nations go to war they usually attack their trading partners, thus doing horrific damage to themselves as well as their victims. In other words, because of his insanity, the aggressor fails to u nderstand the consequences of aggression and as a result he does what no rational person would. Thus, rational thought and action will not prevent war. This line of thinking holds out little hope that trade can overcome war. Would you care to comment?

Doug Stevenson, Boulder (CO) Meeting of Friends

COMMENT by Jack (because it is asked for): It is not so much trade itself as it is the trust engendered by trade that diminishes warfare. And it may take centuries to do so. But it has done so, historically.

Nations that allow their citizens a certain level of freedom have never fought a war against each other. There's only three caveats:
 1) "freedom" means what you think it means: freedom of speech, religion, travel, and press. In other words, a classic liberal Society.
 2) A free society must have been established for a few years before the democracy effect kicks in.
3) A war is defined as greater than 1,000 battle dead.

On employers who abuse in sweatshops: normal market competition will force these bozos out of the market (in time; good things never happen overnight). A free market doesn't tolerate nonsense like this. It doesn't abide racism. That's why the South had Jim Crow laws — because individual shopkeepers couldn't enforce racism on their own. The first shopkeeper who treated all customers fairly would have out-competed the racists, even if he didn't want to.

The free market's intolerance of intolerance, they no doubt claimed was a "market failure" which needed to be redressed by government action. Adam Smith's invisible hand forces people who are solely concerned with their own welfare to be very much concerned about the welfare of their customers. Moreover, it forces people who are actively hostile to would-be customers to grudgingly trade with them, lest their competitors do so first. And, in this context, any sweatshop which treats its employees gratuitiously poorly will be out-competed by those who don't.

Russ Nelson, St. Lawrence Valley (NY) Friends Meeting

I'm reminded of an article in the current issue of *The Public Interest.* It is a survey of leaders of business, the media, and Hollywood. The business leaders at least expressed considerably more trust in others than did the elites from the other two. Maybe they were faking, but I can't see why they would. It is at least inferential support for your point.

Your comment on favoring choice reminds me of Robert Nozick's proposition in *Anarchy, State and Utopia,* that there should be freedom for "capitalist acts between consenting adults."

Steve Wiliams, Bethesda (MD) Friends Meeting

THE QUAKER ECONOMIST

June 4, 2001

Letter No. 13

Dear Friends:

How do Friends feel about Standardized Testing?

On May 20, *The New York Times* ran a story about Jake Plumley, who had failed a standardized test, but only because the testing company had made an error. Jake had actually passed, but he had to give up a good job and go to summer school, to prepare for the test again. Many similar errors have been reported, and students' lives have been disrupted.

Errors by testing services are a minor problem, however, compared to two major ones: First, does the government lead the people, or do the people lead the government? (Who determines the standards? Federal or state government, local community, or parents?) And second, do we all have to be the same?

In *National Standards in Education,* Diane Ravitch argues in favor, "to identify a body of knowledge and skills that children should possess. Standards should be 'clear, precise, and brief, . . . they should be about academic subject matter, not attitudes or affective skills, . . . and they should be testable." (*New York Times,* 2/15/95). On the other hand, Brian Hixon, a teacher in California, writes (*NYT,* 1/25/00), "as I teach from day to day, the new expectations from the standards movement are forcing a change in my perceptions. . . I no longer see the students the way I once did — certainly not in the same exuberant light as when I first started teaching five years ago. Where once there were 'challenging' or 'marginal' students, I am now beginning to see liabilities. Where once there was a student of 'limited promise,' there is now an inescapable deficit that all available efforts will only nominally affect. . . No apologies or arguments about extenuating circumstances are going to shield me from the new state edict: Improve, or expect us at your doorstep."

In my own teaching at the University of Colorado, I never use machine-graded tests. Perhaps machine tests are all right for simple exercises like recognizing parallel lines, but not for either advanced math or the social sciences. I always ask for essays, in which the students must analyze facts they already know, put them in logical order, and reason out an opinion. There is no way to test critical thinking except through the professor's judgment. My students are all good mathematicians. They could pass the standardized tests with flying colors, but they do not know how to think critically unless I give them exercises in it.

Who decides how much math a student should learn? Milwaukee planned a test that "stressed word problems creating real-life situations. It forced students to apply math concepts, think analytically, and show their work." (*Washington Post Weekly,* 3/3/97.) Do you think such a test could be prepared by the federal government and approved by Congress?

Many other questions affect our country's education. Let me raise some of them, leaving the answers to you. At the end of this letter, I will propose a blanket answer to all of them:

(1) Should affirmative action be applied to education? Surely it has improved the prospects of minorities, but for every one given an advantage, someone else is left out. Instead, should each school or college decide on the amount of diversity it needs and set its own standards, without fear of litigation?

(2) Should teachers' pay be related to performance, or should it be determined by years of service regardless of performance, as the unions have been advocating? If by performance, who evaluates?

(3) Should political positions be taught in the classroom? (How can they be avoided?) Should all sides of political positions be discussed (as I try to do), or should certain "politically correct" positions be taught as if they are "right?" Should the history and literature of the West be ignored in favor of those of Africa and Asia? Or, can history and literature be objectively judged for quality, regardless of its origin?

(4) Tests have shown that American students lag behind Europeans and Japanese in certain subjects. But many argue that once out of school, American graduates have shown more entrepreneurship and problem-solving skills than Europeans and Japanese. (I don't have firm data on this, however). All told, has the quality of American education declined? If so, what can we do about it?

(5) Is education adequately funded? If not, what can we do about it?

(6) Harvard uses its own graduates to interview candidates for the freshman class. I know that many of my interviewees would do well there, but they are turned down for lack of room. At U of Colorado, I have many students who would excel at Harvard. Maybe they didn't want to go there, but if they did, would they have afforded it? Would there have been room? If American consumers want more SUVs, more are built (that's how the market works). If more want to go to Harvard than Harvard will accept, why do not more Harvards spring up? (Oh yes, there are other Ivy colleges, MIT, and Stanford, but these are not enough).

(7) How do you feel about social promotion? Should a student who has not completed the requirements for some grade be passed on to the next, so as not to be left behind his or her age group? Or is social promotion the explanation of ultimate failure?

(8) Do you favor bilingual education? If so, should it be prescribed by the school board, so that minorities with limited English are required to learn first in their native languages, and only later change to English? Or, should they have choice from the start? (When Robin and I lived in Bolivia, and later in Mexico, we threw our children into Spanish-speaking schools, and they picked up the language quicker than we did).

(9) In poll after poll, Blacks and other minorities have favored vouchers, charter schools, or magnet schools, to allow them to exit from decrepit, drug-infested city schools and attend quality schools instead. Opponents argue that vouchers and alternative schools would deprive the public schools of their best students. But should not those "best students" have the same opportunities as our own sons and daughters who may go to Quaker schools?

(10) Often parochial schools have much higher education standards than local public schools. Should pupils be allowed to use public money to go to them? Suppose a low-income student applied to a Quaker school, but there was not enough scholarship money? Should public money be used? More generally, should public money be applied to religious schools?

I propose that all these questions should be answered by parents and students, who would choose their schools. No one should be forced to be like anyone else. In my book, *The Moral Economy* (Michigan 1998), I propose a way. I haven't found many who agree with it (except a few way-out economists, like me). Certainly my own students do not agree with it. But I think it will happen in about 300 years. Think back to the state of Western education 300 years ago (no public schools, most persons could not read and write) and consider all that has changed since then. I also feel that any economic structure that makes sense – and I think my education plan does – will ultimately be adopted, given enough time, provided special interests or power concentrations will not prevent it. So, here is my proposal:

(1) Convert all public schools into private (profit or non-profit) that set their own education plans, their own tuition, and accept all students who qualify educationally and can pay the price.

(2) Establish a loan fund (with government or private money) from which students might borrow any amount needed for education, beginning with elementary and going as far into college, graduate studies or research as they are capable. Since educated people generally earn more than uneducated, the borrowers would use their excess earnings to pay back the loans over their lifetimes, just like amortizing an investment. They might pay back fixed amounts like mortgages, or they might pay back in proportion to their earnings. (They would decide which plan, in advance). I do not accept the argument that graduates should not be debt-ridden for life. They already are, in that we must pay education taxes (the equivalent of repaying loans) for life.

(3) Parents and students would choose the schools and colleges according to their interests. Like customers for automobiles, they would select the ones most suited to their tastes. If tastes and abilities ran toward Ivy League, more Ivy-type colleges would be created, just like SUVs. This idea is based on the proposition that parents and students have a better notion of the TRUTH in education than does a school board or government bureaucracy.

(4) Some schools would have bilingual education, some not, some would have higher standards than others. Parents and students would choose. They might take into account the reputation of the school, since potential employers certainly will.

(5) The only government regulation would be that each educational institution would be required to accept a quota of "difficult" students (however you wish to define "difficult," such as juvenile delinquents and
students with low I.Q's. Low I. Q. students would choose between
schools especially for them and mainstream schools, which would be
required to have special programs to suit their needs.

(6) The education of each generation would therefore be financed by the
paybacks from the previous generation. There would be no government finance. (With government finance, "who pays the fiddler calls
the tune.")

Please write me if you see any reason why this system would not work,
other than that it is, for the current century, politically impossible. Please
let me know if you think it is a Quakerly response to our educational problems. Above all, if is is not instituted by the year 2400, explain to my suc-
cessor why not. Thank you.

> Sincerely your Friend,
> Jack Powelson

GENERAL RESPONSE TO THESE LETTERS

I appreciate deeply the history and economics lessons which you teach with
these emails every week. I learn quite a bit from reading them. It seems to
me for the last 40 to 50 years Friends have been caught up in what many
would see as a "heroic" battle against the government and large corporations. I think the battle was morally justified as there were significant parts
of the population which were unfairly (and cruelly) kept from competing in
the marketplace, many times at the hands of governmental and corporate
forces.

But a fair amount of peace and prosperity came to the country in the 1980's
and 1990's. Now this did not eliminate all of our social ills, but a great
majority of the population experienced an increase in wealth and security
during this time. I think this fact and nothing else explains why that population has voted in a conservative manner in every election since 1976. And
I count the election of Bill Clinton within that period as no exception, if we
understand that the Clinton administration was simply less conservative
than the preceding Republican administrations.

This I believe has created a sense of ennui amongst Quakers. What attracted many outsiders into Meetings in the 60's and the 70's (the sheer heroic work that needed to be done) is no longer there. The Vietnam War, the de facto and de jure cruelties of racism, and the monolithic military/industrial complex don't hammer us anymore. Instead of huge moral conflicts, we are now faced with a thousand smaller ones that kind of nitpick at the outside of our lives and never really get under our skin long enough to push us to do anything. So without a crisis in the culture modern Quakerism, built upon activism, languishes.

If you throw the WTO and the IMF out there into this frustrated desire to fight the heroic fight, you get Seattle, an opportunity for many activists to strike at a bogus Goliath because they are unable to convince a conservative population of their views.

I hope one day to see Friends turn away from this approach. I would rather see us return to our testimony of simplicity, teaching it in our Meetings and living it in our lives. I would rather see us put our efforts into assisting the many NGO's that are doing the real work of helping poor people to gain a competing place in the market. Over time, that is where one can have an impact; providing money and volunteer and professional help to those organizations that are building schools, organizing unions, running health clinics in the developing world. We could spend our energy building up the developing world's human infrastructure and in this way help change things from the ground up, instead of trying to throw stones at a giant.

Rich Ailes, Middletown Monthly Meeting (Concord Quarter), Philadelphia Yearly Meeting

RESPONSES TO LETTER NO. 13

From Karen Street, Berkeley (CA) Friends Meeting:

I don't know numbers, and I believe that Americans have more of that prized gitgo. But, a lot of what is credited to Americans should be credited to foreigners in the US. A lot. A really large amount. It would be interesting to see a study of prized American traits vs. a country of elementary education (through 8th grade).

A fair percentage of the remaining explanation of American gitgo can be credited to aspects of our society other than our education system.

I would add to your letter that with trade comes knowledge of the "other" which reduces chances for war, but obviously does not eliminate it. In Yugoslavia, the media reports Milosevic put out on the "other" conflicted with people's personal knowledge, yet people nevertheless began to accept the media reports.

From Stephen Williams, Bethesda (MD) Friends Meeting.

As an alternative to your point #5, you might have a negative auction for the job of handling the students no one wants—i.e., each would go to the school (otherwise qualified) that demanded the smallest subsidy.

From Vici Oshiro, Minneapolis (MN) Friends Meeting:

If we are to give public funds to schools, whether directly or through intermediaries, we want to assure fiscal responsibility and assure that schools meet some standards. Do this and you end up with a government school system. The system you suggest has some similarities with the GI Bill. It worked well for those who chose Harvard (or Oberlin), but there were problems with institutions whose main purpose turned out to be enrichment of the founders rather than education of students. Sad but true.

This, like some of your other suggestions, relies on the customer having excellent information and judgment and on the provider having excellent ethics. We're not there yet and if we ever get there it will be long after you and I and our children are gone. We need systems that take into account our limitations as well as our strengths. I'm not convinced that the Quaker belief that there is that of God in everyone necessarily means we will reach that perfection.

From Virginia Flagg, San Diego (CA) Meeting:

I am very uneasy about your proposal to require all students to borrow money needed for their education, even beginning with elementary education. This seems to imply that the only value of education is to increase earning potential. I believe, however, that a well-educated citizenry is important for the benefit of all society.

I have read that part of the reason the United States was so productive after World War II was that the GI Bill made it possible for many members of society to go to college that otherwise would not have done so. Even those who did not use the GI Bill to go to college probably were better off because they could find jobs provided by entrepreneurial college graduates. Instead of a loan fund, how about a GI Bill for everyone, even starting with elementary school?

From Gordon Johnson Jr., Trinity United Methodist Church, Alexandria, VA:

I would like to see a better defense of why education should not be free to all. Perhaps the answer lies in "the more you pay, the more it's worth", but I am not sure I go along with that. The biggest problem in education is the "problem children", the delinquents and low IQ students who require extra resources. For the rest of us, the solution is simple: the better a student's performance the better should be the educational opportunities provided. The same could be applied to teachers. This would be a little tough to do well because it would require subjective evaluation on a student-by-student and teacher-by-teacher basis.

From Gordon Johnson, Sr., Episcopal, Alexandria, VA:

Our children are our future. Parents, schools and peers are all important influences, but where parents and peers are part of the problem, as in our inner cities, schools become critically important. Many of them are "failing schools." We have to find ways to mprove them. Lord Kelvin said many years ago: "If you can't measure it, you can't improve it."

National standards will allow comparative judgements between areas and schools. In addition, localities should be free to decide for themselves what they want to measure to evaluate their schools' performance. Let's even ask the schools themselves to come up with the standards they want to use. The important thing is to get started. Markets (the "experts") will then refine and improve the measuring process.

THE QUAKER ECONOMIST
June 11, 2001

Letter No. 14

Dear Friends:

Homelessness in Cali, Colombia

As Luigi and I toured the slums of Cali in his Volkswagen, we found ourselves at a dead end before a large *ceibo* tree. Ahead lay a field, about a
mile long and half a mile wide, dotted with what seemed like tents in a
campground and families enjoying a Sunday school picnic. On closer inspection they were tiny shacks framed by branches or cardboard, mainly
covered with cloth. In front of each sat a family, usually with several children. Upon spotting us, many surged out to surround our Volkswagen, threat-
ening, looking fearful and serious. They pressed so close we could not turn
around and go away. They just stood and stared at us.

Luigi was an American professor of economics at the University of the
Valley, just finishing his term, and I was being interviewed as a possible
replacement. Knowing my penchant for the poor of Latin America, he had
suggested we visit the slums. But we had not expected this fearful turn of
events.

After a few moments of standoff, a passage opened up in the crowd, and a
young man with a green armband pushed his way through. "Who are you?"
he asked in an anxious voice, "and why have you come to our land invasion?"

"I am a professor of economics from the United States," I replied, "and I
am interested in land invasions. Maybe you would show us yours?" Immediately a smile came upon his face, and when he smiled, the others showed
relief.

"My name is Reynaldo Polonía," he said. "The ownership of this field has
been in dispute by two rich families since 1820. While it has lain unused
for over a century, many Colombians do not have a place to live. That is
unfair," he went on. "So one night we decided to take it."

Polonía led us through the crowd and into the field where he introduced his
assistant, Ejidio Restrepo. They explained that they had formed a commit-

tee to study the city's development plan for this land: where to put streets and other facilities. Respecting this plan, they had assigned plots to all the homeless they could recruit – 26,000 of them – and held meetings to discuss their own plans. They would invade the land all on one night, and in the morning each family would dig a ditch to delineate its pre-assigned plot. A string would not do, since it could be moved. Then they would build rudimentary huts, which they called *chocitas.*

They had rules. No liquor. No firearms. No violence of any sort. The committee wore green arm bands. If a dispute arose, the parties would seek out the first person with a green arm band who would decide it on the spot. Any who disagreed or quarreled or disobeyed the rules would lose their plots. Outside the field, congregated under the *ceibo* tree, were over 100 "would-bes," waiting in case a plot should become available.

I came back alone the next day, to spend the weekend going from *chocita* to *chocita,* asking the families about themselves. Children would follow me, so when I took a picture of a family by its *chocita,* usually the same children were in it. The only way to know how many were in one family was to ask the parents; they varied from none to seven, with more families at the larger end.,

All were friendly, expressing concern that the American people should know of their plight. Many had lived in Cali, but most had migrated from the countryside, looking for work. About half the men were employed, earning not enough for a decent house; the women looked after the children. A few had lived in shanty towns, but most had slept under bridges or in the parks. All that I encountered were unskilled. "We do not want to steal this land," they said. "When we have enough money, we will buy it."

They had no political interests or affiliations. They were not revolutionaries. All they wanted were jobs and a place to live.

"How much will you pay for your plot? I asked." "Ten dollars (equivalent in pesos)", they replied, uniformly as if they had rehearsed in advance. I knew the market value of such land was much, much higher.

Those who had money bought food for those who had none, and these amounts were supplemented by sympathetic people from the neighboring slums. A tiny church was being constructed, with only the framework finished. A priest would come once a week to say mass. One woman showed me a box with the words, "Ayudanos en nuestra lucha, con tu óbolo" ("Help us in our struggle with your pittance").

On Sunday night, I bid them farewell. As I was about to leave, Polonía sidled up to me and said, "I want you here tomorrow at three o'clock."

"I can't," I replied. I had an appointment at the central bank in Bogotá, and my plane would leave at four.

"You must be here at three," he said. "The army will be here to rout us, and I want you to see it, to report to the American people." I asked how he knew. "We have our spies," he said.

It was a hard choice. The central bank dignitaries were to meet my plane, and I didn't even know what hotel I would stay in. The next flight (at 8 o'clock) would arrive after the close of business. Would I be stranded? But I had to stay in Cali. I would find the bank officers somehow and apologize. After all, missing a plane is not such a great sin.

At three o'clock Monday afternoon, Luigi and his wife, Silvia, and I were at the invasion site in the Volkswagen. In the center of the field Restepo was waving the Colombian flag, a signal for all to gather. "The army is coming," he announced, "and you know what to do." (They had rehearsed in advance). "You will go to your *chocitas*, raise the small Colombian flag, and sing the national anthem, to show your patriotism. When the army asks you to leave, go to the side of the field, and stand there. There will be no violence."

The army arrived, in military trucks, bayonets drawn. They went to the center of the field and ordered the families to leave. All left peacefully. One by one, the army burned the *chocitas*. One woman, tears streaming down her cheeks, approached me as I clicked my camera. "That's right," she said. "Take pictures. Show the American people how the Colombian army treats its people!"

Outside, under the *ceibo* tree, a man with a green arm band stood on a table, exhorting the "would-bes." "Don't go away," he called. "We can out-stay the army."

Twenty-six thousand people, standing several deep, silently at the edge of the field, watching their houses burn, was an awesome sight. Whoever said Latin Americans were a violent people!

At that point Restrepo approached us, holding up a newspaper to shield his face. "They have arrested Polonía," he said, "and they're looking for me. Can you help me escape?"

I looked at Luigi. It was his Volkswagen, and his call. I could imagine him thinking of tomorrow's possible headline: "American Professors Arrested Helping Criminal Escape."

But we all three knew we had to do it. Restrepo crowded himself between the front and back seats of the Volkswagen with a blanket hiding him, Luigi and Silvia sat in front, and I in back with my feet on top of Restrepo's blanket. As we drove through the military lines, I smiled and waved at the soldiers. They waved back, not knowing we were helping their quarry escape.

We left Restrepo in the center of town, and I have not seen him since. Luigi and Silvia drove me directly to the airport, to catch the eight o'clock flight to Bogotá. At the counter, the agent said, "Hurry, the plane is about to leave." I ran out to the field and up the stairs on to the plane. No sooner was I in my seat than the doors shut, and the plane took off. But it was only quarter to eight. I called the stewardess over.

"Is this the flight to "Bogotá?" I asked. After an affirmative reply, I asked why it was leaving fifteen minutes early. "Oh," she said, "this is the four o'clock flight."

The central bank dignitaries were at the airport to meet me, dressed in dark suits with neckties. It was a different world. They apologized for Avianca, the national airline. "That's all right," I said. "I have friends in Cali who kept me well entertained."

The next day we met in their luxurious headquarters to talk about national income.

All this occurred in 1963. In June 2001, while I am traveling away from my files, I will pull up some "old stuff," to help explain why I decided, in 1970, to quit consulting governments, and to study the causes of poverty.

I did get news later from Luigi. The invaders had indeed stayed until the army withdrew, then rebuilt their *chocitas*. There were other forced evacuations, in one of which a woman was killed. Finally they made peace with City Hall; they were allowed to stay and build more durable structures. They did not own the land, but they were no longer forced off it. As happens in many places in the Third World, land is occupied but unowned. Ten years later, when a student of mine was to visit Cali, I showed her the invasion site on a map. When she came home, she reported that it was a slum just like any other. No one there had heard of Reynaldo Polonía or Ejidio Restrepo or indeed that any land invasion had occurred at all!

Next week I will tell about my contacts in the Black homelands of South Africa during Apartheid, and after that my ten years conducting seminars for Latin American Marxist students who strongly criticized the United States. That will include my meeting with Paraguayans plotting the overthrow of the dictator, General Stroessner. Keep tuned!

After that, we will get back to current happenings.

Sincerely your friend,
Jack Powelson

READERS' RESPONSE TO LETTER NO. 14

Jack, PLEASE more personal stories about your experiences in the slums of the world. I had read about the poor in Cali, Columbia trying to take over unused land (or similar situations in S.A.) but reading a personal experience about that problem paints the picture in brighter colors. Thank you for sharing your knowledge with us.

Lorna Knowlton, Boulder, CO

THE QUAKER ECONOMIST
June 18, 2001

Letter No. 15

Dear Friends:

Kenya: A Turning Point

Kenya may have been the turning point, but it was only the culmination of a long-growing suspicion. Was my career as advisor to Third-World governments doing more harm than good?

First incident. Kenya, it seemed to the planning team, needed more credit to small farmers. Since it possessed a good national highway system, we proposed – for the third five-year plan – to move funds from the Ministry of Works (in charge of roads) to the Ministry of Agriculture. The team consisted of about ten Kenyan economists, representing different fields, with myself as expatriate advisor.

When the Minister of Works saw the proposed budget he stomped, furious, into the office of the Permanent Secretary (PermSec) of Finance. In the Kenyan system (copied from the British), the PermSec is the closest equivalent of our Secretary of the Treasury. The Minister of Finance, to whom he reports, is a Member of Parliament. The PermSec called me in to explain. "I have already let out contracts for more than is in my planned budget," the Minister of Works was complaining. The PermSec tried to soothe him, saying that "this is only the plan." He ordered me to take 1% off the budget of every other ministry and add that amount to the Ministry of Works.

"Only" the plan, I thought? Did my work mean nothing?

Second incident. President Jomo Kenyatta was making one of his many political speeches before a crowd, and he asked for questions. "When will the tax on *matatus* (taxis) be repealed?" a taxi driver asked. "It is repealed forthwith!" the President replied instantly. The next day the planning team was asked to delete the *matatu* tax from the budget and to jiggle the other amounts around to come out with a balanced budget. It was not that I objected to repealing the *matatu* tax – that was a bad tax anyway. Rather, I was annoyed at both the power of the President (no consulting Parliament) and the cavalier treatment of the economic plan.

Third incident. My Kenyan counterpart was assigned to write the chapter on monetary and fiscal policy in the coming five-year plan. But he wasn't interested, and I could see that if it were to be done, I would have to do it. (I knew I would share the blame if it were not done). So I wrote it.

The corresponding chapter in the preceding plan had called for low interest rates, to facilitate borrowing for capital investment. But to forecast interest rates for the next five years was ridiculous, I thought, because they must be constantly adapted to the unemployment or inflation of the time. (Alan Greenspan would never predict interest rates for five years!) But I was told to do it, so I did. (I was hired by the Ford Foundation but seconded to the PermSec of Finance, who was my "boss." I had agreed to be his civil servant.)

But low interest rates would transfer assets from the poor to the rich in Kenya, because unemployment was high. So I wrote that interest rates would be raised, to discourage the use of capital and favor the employment of labor. My Kenyan counterpart agreed. But the PermSec ordered me to find a justification for low interest rates. More sinister was that I suspected he wanted low interest rates because a small elite in the government planned to borrow money to build a tourist hotel, from a development bank they would fund with foreign-aid money. Their costs would be lower, and profit higher, if the borrowing rate were low.

Here I faced a dilemma. Being true to my calling as economist, and to my life as Quaker, called for high interest rates, yet I had promised the Ford Foundation that I would obey my "boss."

Instead of fulfilling his command, I returned the chapter to the PermSec's desk, with a note saying I could not conscientiously recommend low interest rates. He would have to order one of his Kenyan employees to write that part of the plan.

The next I heard, the Minister of Finance had called the planning team to discuss the chapter. The PermSec had been out of town, but the Minister wanted the chapter to go to Parliament right away, so he had pulled it from the PermSec's desk. The team met in the Minister's office. The Minister went over the chapter, paragraph by paragraph, saying what he liked or disliked, and asking us to change parts. He did not ask any questions, and no one on the team offered an opinion. (This has been a style to which I had become accustomed in less developed countries. The high official does all the talking; the "advisor" listens and does what is commanded).

The Minister approved the paragraph on high interest rates. So I faced another dilemma. On the one hand, it would not be proper to interrupt the Minister. On the other hand, he should know that his PermSec did not agree with that paragraph.

I broke the first rule. "Mr. Minister," I said, "Your Permanent Secretary does not agree with that paragraph." When the Minister wanted to know how the chapter had come to his desk without the PermSec's approval, I reminded him that he had called for it in the Permsec's absence. He thought for a moment, then said: "The paragraph makes sense. It is approved."

But I knew that interest rates would be kept low anyway. The plan is for show and to appease foreign-aid agencies.

Fourth incident. Through Lewis Hoskins, a Quaker professor of history at Earlham, Robin and I had come to know Sam Motsuenyane, the President of the African (Black) Federation of Chambers of Commerce in South Africa. He and Cyril Pearce, the President of the National (White) Federation, stopped for a visit in Kenya. Although these were days of High Apartheid, Sam and Cyril were close friends and often traveled together. They invited me to do a series of lectures in the Black homelands of South Africa. Knowing that neither the Kenya Government (for which I was a civil servant) nor the Ford Foundation (that paid my salary) would approve, I simply took leave time and went, along with Robin, my wife.

In the visits to the Homelands, I discovered that Black South Africans were very entrepreneurial and easily capable of governing their nation (as happened twelve years later). At the end of our week's visit, I was invited to speak at the annual banquet of the Johannesburg (White) Chamber of Commerce. I was reluctant, but Sam urged me to go, and to tell the Chamber what I thought of Apartheid.

Wearing a rented black-tie suit, I sat next to the Mayor of Johannesburg at the head table in one of the finest hotels of the city. Next to Robin sat the Mayor's wife. I spoke about economic problems of Africa, without mentioning South Africa once. At the end, however, I said:

"I want you to know that it was not easy for me to come here, and I did so only at the urging of one who is not here, Sam Motsuenyane, President of the African Federation. "In my home country I would never attend a gathering at which any of my fellow citizens had been excluded because of their ethnic origin." An uneasy silence followed, broken only when an entire table, at the far end of the hall, stood up and cheered. I found out later they were visiting Australians.

Immediately after the talk, a reporter from the *Rand Daily Mail* asked me if my presence, as a civil servant of Kenya, foresaw a rapprochement between Kenya and South Africa. I replied that the Kenyan government did not know I was there. He was surprised, and asked, "Will they sack you when they find out?" I replied that I did not know.

The next morning, a banner headline appeared on page one of the *Rand Daily Mail:* "Kenya Civil Servant May be Sacked for Visiting South Africa."

Knowing that Kenyan watchers would read South African newspapers, I decided to tell my PermSec before he heard about it elsewhere. He was furious. "Do you realize," he said, "that we are already criticized for refueling South African planes?" I had not known that, but South African Airways would fly passengers to Europe in planes marked Sabena, the Belgian National Airline. They would refuel in Nairobi. (That was the shortest route for them, and Kenya needed the money). The Kenyans tried to hush it up. Now, he said, if anyone heard that a Kenyan civil servant had visited South Africa, all hell might break loose.

The Resident Representative of the Ford Foundation was also furious. He offered to send me home immediately, but the PermSec, noting that my term was about to expire, said these things should be kept quiet.

A few weeks later the President of the Ford Foundation, visiting Kenya, asked to see me. He too was furious. "If we sent you to Egypt," he asked, "Would you feel free to accept an invitation to Israel?" "Of course," I replied. "The Ford Foundation has bought my expertise, not my soul." (I have had no more assignments with the Ford Foundation, but there may be other reasons for that as well.)

From colleagues with assignments in other countries I have heard many stories similar to my Kenya adventures. These, plus my own experiences, led me to decry the great hypocrisy and corruption of governments, especially in the Third World. It also led me back to teaching, research, and writing, to find out why, historically, a small part of the world is rich and a much larger part poor.

These incidents occurred in 1972. In June 2001, while I am traveling away from my files, I will pull up some "old stuff," to help explain why I decided, in 1973, to quit consulting governments. (Today's Letter was written at Inter-Mountain Yearly Meeting in Durango, Colorado. In early July, I will co-lead a workshop at Friends General Conference in Blacksburg, Virginia).

Next week I will tell about my ten years conducting seminars for Latin American Marxist students who strongly criticized the United States. That will include my meeting with Paraguayans plotting the overthrow of the dictator, General Stroessner. Keep tuned!

After that, we will get back to current happenings.

Please send me any thoughts you may have. Especially if you have had experiences parallel to mine, or that contradict mine, or if you know of such experiences.

Love and Peace from your Friend,
Jack Powelson

READER RESPONSES TO LETTER NO. 15

I have drawn the conclusion that it is a very difficult thing to "do good" to persons "less fortunate" who are geographically or culturally "far away" from "us," the donors.

This does't mean I'm against all such philanthropic efforts; after all, brain surgery and rocket science are very difficult too; but they also get done. All such efforts call for great skill, and our "charity" needs to be seasoned as well with generous amounts of humility. Like the person said, "be wise as serpents and harmless as doves."

If we do not study to be wise as serpents even in giving away our surplus, we may well not meet the other command to be harmless as doves; quite the opposite.

       Chuck Fager, State College (PA) Friends Meeting.

It was really interesting to read your account of the work you did and the frustrations you encountered in Kenya in the '70s. It brought back my own efforts at economic development among Quakers there in the '80s.

I raised funds from a variety of yearly and monthly meetings around the US to go to Kenya and pick up on work that had been started there by a member of my meeting, Marjorie Fox from Philadelphia, who worked for several years with Friends of Elgon Yearly Meeting, a split off from the old East Africa Yearly Meeting. (There have been many, many more splits since the '80's). Marjorie died of cancer and I felt her work should not go unfinished.

I had some years of community development experience in this country and thought that some of it might apply there. The first trip in 1986 was actually a fact-finding effort to Elgon Friends to see what was most needed and what was possible. The second trip in 1988 was one where I was accompanied by a Quaker aquaculture researcher and specialist to find out if her extraordinary achievements in aquaculture in the US could be reproduced in Kenya and become the focus of the economic development project I had hoped for there. From the very start, however, as I contacted people in Nairobi, both expatriates and Kenyans, I received communications on two levels. The top level was straightforward and very Friendly. Indeed, never have I encountered a more hospitable or giving group of Friends. On the other hand, often in whispers at the end of a hard day, I was warned about issues which would make my work difficult if not impossible.

First was the enormous animosity among tribal groups. The habits I observed involved broad accusations against those of other tribes and assurances that the tribe whose members I was speaking to weren't like that at all. Second, was the extreme oppression of women in Kenya. While it wasn't obvious at first, one soon came to notice that while all the women worked very hard in the fields, the men "supervised" sitting under a tree, or visited with other men from nearby farms.

Women, I found out, were cast off for younger wives with impunity and they and their children were then left without support. Women were legally blamed and exiled from their community if they were raped. And it was traditional that a woman could not own property and therefore her husband or father had the right to take from her anything she earned or inherited and use it as he wished. Specifically, there were no property rights or contracts which could be counted upon across tribal or sexual lines. Formally in discussions with outsiders this was all attributed to traditional Kenyans who lived in the countryside and it was asserted repeatedly that the more educated and sophisticated Kenyans weren't like that, but in reality those attributes were apparent all the way to the top of the political and organizational structures I encountered. Admittedly, many Friends did make an effort to break these traditional habits on the basis of their adopted Quaker faith but the outside pressures to conform were enormous and so they failed.

Specifically, during my first trip to Kenya, I had a lot of enthusiasm for trying to fund small women's projects but soon found that where that had been tried, the women's husbands had taken any profits that were realized and left the project penniless. Indeed the men were enthusiastic for us to give their wives some more money not admitting that they could then take it from the women and use it as they wished. In trying to develop some cooperation among groups of Friends for the aquaculture project in '88, we tried to talk with different factions of Friends about joint efforts to achieve a needed economy of scale, but found that each group wished to work only with its own people giving ample reasons why the others could not be trusted.

Jack, your conclusions in your textbook, "Centuries of Economic Endeavor", helped me put all this in perspective. Kenya, and I expect much of Africa, was a prime example of a place where the basic trust needed to ensure property rights and enforce contracts was not present. For this reason, I can see why my efforts there were doomed from the start.

I hope this narrative provides a town and village illustration of your comments about working with the top tiers of Kenyan government and helps the CLQ readership understand some of the problems of economic development in Africa.

       Janet Minshall, Annawakee Creek Friends Worship Group, Douglasville GA.

THE QUAKER ECONOMIST
June 25, 2001

Letter No. 16

Dear friends:

My ten years in Marxistland

Curiouser and curiouser. The looking glass seemed to melt, into a fuzzy substance that I could walk through to a different world. I stopped young people to ask what kind of society this was. They all spoke Spanish. So I decided I had better learn it.

My first looking-glass world was Bolivia in 1960. There I taught for one year (whenever the students were not on strike) in the University of San Andres. The students – almost all Marxists who disliked my world - were lively and friendly. Toward the end of my year, I came down with hepatitis. Students came to see me, and at the end they prepared a big *fiesta,* which I enjoyed from my bed. They were not Quakers, but I sensed Quakerly love from them. When I returned home, I wrote a book, *Latin America: Today's Economic and Social Revolution* (McGraw-Hill 1964), which contained parts of papers they had written for me or shown to me. I dedicated it to them, *con todo mi afecto . . . con un fuerte abrazo.*

For ten years thereafter I conducted an annual seminar for Marxist students from Mexico, the first one in Mexico City and the other nine at whatever university I was teaching at in the United States (Pittsburgh, Johns Hopkins, and Colorado). During that period I also traveled to all the Latin American countries except Cuba, to lecture and hold discussions with Marxist students in the major universities. Paragraphs in quotations in this Letter consist of papers written by them or are from authors they recommended. All these quotations are found in my book, *Latin America*, at pages indicated. (The book is out of print but can be found in university libraries).

The Economic Revolution

"The Alliance for Progress (foreign aid program) is but a cunning shift in the strategy of the United States. Your fundamental purpose is still economic domination in our hemisphere. But you do sense that a revolution is in the making and that it is too strong to be quelled by the blunt weapons of the past. So your only recourse is to board it and dilute it from the inside" (p.1).

Agrarian Reform

La tierra es de todos, come el aire, el agua, la luz, y el calor del sol (Inscription carved above the entry to the Ministry of Education, Mexico City. "Land is like air, like water, like light, like the heat of the sun" (p.33).

MY NOTE: In countries where Indians predominate, *latifundios* (large land holdings) have been associated with a feudal form of agriculture known as the "hacienda" system. Upon the Spanish conquest, Indians were placed under the tutelage of Spaniards and gradually became servants (peons) of the master to whom lands, previously theirs, had been given by the King of Spain. They met their obligations through labor and sharecropping. After World War II (earlier in Mexico), agrarian reforms ended the hacienda system in country after country, but the reforms themselves have confiscated rights of the peasants wholesale. (I wrote about these reforms in *The Peasant Betrayed,* by Powelson and Stock,1960.) Such is the situation in Chiapas, Mexico, about which I plan to write a future Letter. Mostly, these peasants still live in poverty. Despite what my students thought, most of the haciendas were owned by Latin Americans, only a few by American corporations. All of these have by now been sold or "reformed."

"The representative of the United States of America (in a conference on agrarian reform in 1959) did not approve one single proposal that might signify the expropriation of land, because he was thinking of the enormous *latifundios* exploited in Latin America by businesses and private persons of his country. Nor did he approve the creation of an Inter-American Agrarian Bank, because he understood that an institution of this nature would be, as indeed it would, a constant invitation to all the peoples of Latin America to accelerate or undertake their respective agrarian reforms. Such an occurrence would constitute a menace to the territorial interests of the United States" (pp.33-4).

Monopoly

"The economy of the United States displays pronounced monopolistic traits. The large enterprise is the typical economic unit in the American union. Groups of two, three, or four big companies dominate the most important activities. Their power does not derive from the fact that there are no other enterprises operating in each activity, but to the great magnitude of the "small group" in charge of each branch's operations. Thus the economy of the United States is characterized by a concentration of giants in each important activity" (José Luis Cecena, Mexican economist; p. 69).

Primary Products

"He who has no trade, no skills, and cannot read or write is a poor man. He lives by his 'broad and sinewy hands' and his strong back. He splits rails, and society pays him verbal homage for his humble beginnings. When rail fences are supplanted by wire (which he cannot make), he digs ditches. When giant excavators can do his day's work in a few seconds, he polishes boots. When depression comes, people do not have their shoes shined, and even with prosperity they never wear more than one pair at a time. For years he alternates between the breadline and a meager livelihood, for – unlike other people – none of his occupations provides him with skills to cope with an ever more complex society. One day he wakes up to find that continuous charity alone will keep him alive" (p.99).

NOTE: This is my paraphrase of what many Marxist students told me. The students believed that dependency on primary products (agriculture and mining) kept Latin America poor. It was in the interests of the United States to perpetuate this dependency, because then the U.S. could buy primary products more cheaply.

Sugar and Cuba

"The trouble with the economy was sugar. A warning of the danger of monoculture, of the trend toward a one-crop economy, had been given as far back as 1883 by the greatest of Cuba's heroes. In that year José Martí, revolutionist, orator, poet, philosopher, sounded the alarm: 'A people commits suicide the day on which it bases its economy on a single crop.' . . But in Cuba's case it wasn't suicide. It was murder. In 1883 Cuba was on the road to the top of the cliff, but it was the United States that pushed it over the top." (This was written by two US economists quoted wherever I went in Latin America). (p.138).

Free trade

"Capitalist economies were protectionist in their earlier days but became free traders upon maturity as a means of expanding their power over weaker ones. Contrary to the wishes of the powerful, protectionism is necessary for less developed countries in their fight against political vassalage to the great powers." (Paraphrased from Iván Anaya, Bolivian economist). (p.195).

Why the United States opposes Economic Development in Latin America

"The fear of . . . vacuum causes the country to the north to look askance at our development. Only machinery and capital goods would be exported to Latin America, and fewer consumer goods – this would represent a loss for the United States. This explains why the North American government emphasizes consumer goods in its aid to underdeveloped peoples, and small quantities of money insufficient to push their growth. If American aid were given in capital goods, it would be much more effective and would meet the desires of our peoples. In consumer goods, however, it serves only to kill off national industries" (by a student; p.222).

"The intimate dependence of the economy of our country on that of the cyclic center is revealed in relations of interchange. It is a dependence taking on political and cultural aspects as well, influencing in decisive form the backwardness of Bolivia. It is expressed not only through the imposition of prices by the United States but also in the "American aid," which destroys incentive to produce within Bolivian territory and serves to dump excess North American production in Bolivia" (by a student; p. 222).

What should I say to them?

All this was a looking-glass world because it carried a certain resemblance to my world, yet my world was different from that one. My experiences were different, too. I had walked through the slums of every Latin American country except Cuba, talking to their inhabitants; the students were mostly from middle-class families who had never known the poor except as servants. I had sat across the table from presidents, ministers, American ambassadors, and CEOs of multinational corporations. These were all imaginary figures to the students, who could only form their own images of them. The best I could do (I thought) was to bring my students the viewpoints of the world where they had not lived. I did not try to persuade them of the "correctness" of that world, or of any world; I just wanted them to know what it was like.

One rule I have applied in teaching is: "Never tell a student he is wrong." (Well, hardly ever). Instead, ask the student where her opinion comes from or how he obtained the facts. Carry on the conversation from there. This I applied to the Marxist students, and they appreciated the respect I showed for them. In return, they began to treat my world with respect.

To overthrow the government of the dictator, General Stroessner, of Paraguay?

Readers may be surprised that it was not the Marxist students, but the American Embassy, that arranged my visit with Paraguayans plotting the overthrow of General Alfredo Stroessner. Wherever I went, I found the embassies eager to keep in touch with the opposition. "We might have to deal with them some day," they explained.

Of course the plotters did not tell me their strategy. But they did explain all the crimes committed by General Stroessner, and they objected to our government supporting him. They knew that I, as a professor, and the student officer of the embassy who accompanied me, could not influence our policy in any other way except through our voices, so their aim was to influence that. Why did they not think we might be C.I.A. officers ready to report them to the military? I don't know.

Stroessner was overthrown, not by the students but by a military coup in 1989, which sent him into exile.

                        Sincerely your Friend,
                                Jack Powelson

COMMENTS ON LETTER NO. 16

The comment (from Minshall) was fascinating.

            Stephen Williams, Bethesda (MD) Friends Meeting

I was struck by Janet Minshall's comments about Kenya and their lack of ability to trust each other. Years ago I took a course on development of East Africa and was struck by the deliberate strategy of the British to play one group off against another - divide and conquer.

The British and other colonial governments can't be held totally responsible for current cultural hatreds - but unfortunately they were a contributing factor.

Vici Oshiro, Minneapolis (MN) Friends Meeting

THE QUAKER ECONOMIST
July 23, 2001

Letter No. 17

Dear friends:

The World Trade Organization

At FGC, I co-led (with Carol Blotter of Chelsea MI Meeting) a workshop on globalization. Let me share some of the findings of this workshop on the World Trade Organization (WTO).

Misinformation about the WTO that is currently making the rounds is (1) The WTO is operated by, and in the interests of, multinational corporations. It is designed to transfer the operations of MNCs to countries of cheap labor, and (2) The WTO attempts to excuse MNCs from their responsibilities toward the environment. Therefore, it promotes environmental degradation.

The correct information is: (1) Some of the major findings of the WTO would harm the bottom line of some of the largest MNCs, and (2) The WTO has no jurisdiction over a nation's environmental policies, which are entirely within the sovereign power of governments. In fact, the WTO has no sovereign power at all. It cannot order any government to do anything. It does not have an army or police force, and it cannot put President Bush in prison if the United States does not implement its findings. Both the United States and the European Union have refused to put into effect major findings of the WTO.

So, what does the WTO do? Two things, mainly: (1) It provides a platform in which governments may negotiate a level playing field for the trade of member countries. Member governments have agreed that their own citizen traders, and traders from other member countries, will all operate by the same rules. Thus, if a tariff concession is made to one country, it must be made to all member countries. No government may place a restriction on the trade of other countries that it does not apply to the trade of all. (2) It attempts to negotiate reductions in the overall level of trade barriers (tariffs and other restrictions) among nations.

Suppose a member government violates its agreement with the WTO, by granting preferential terms to some countries' traders that are not granted to all. Any government discriminated against may appeal to the WTO. Upon finding a violation, the WTO does not order the offending government to stop. Instead, it gives the offended government the right to retaliate (reasonably) against the offender, without itself being called for a violation. Thus the European Union has given preferential treatment to former European colonies in the import of bananas. The United States, whose companies sell Latin American bananas, has complained. The WTO found against the EU, but the EU did not correct its violation. Instead, the US was given permission to institute penalty tariffs against EU exports without being called for a violation.

In another example, the United States requires tuna fishers to use special equipment to limit the accidental kill of dolphin. Since Mexican tuna fishers are not required to use the same equipment, they can produce tuna more cheaply. The US therefore restricted the import of Mexican tuna. The Mexican government complained, and the US was found in violation. (It is cases such as this that cause the belief that the WTO is anti-environmental). But the WTO did not order the US government to change its policies (remember, it cannot order any government to do anything). Rather, it told the Mexicans they would not be charged with a violation if they retaliated (reasonably) against the US. So far, the US has not changed its policies, and so far, Mexico has not retaliated. Instead, the two governments are negotiating to see how the Mexicans can reduce the dolphin kill. This is hard for them, since Mexico is a poor country, and tuna fishers have some political power.

I do not know of a single case in which a government has reduced its environmental protections because of a WTO decision. If you know of any, please tell me. (I am a general international economist who does not study the WTO in the details of all its decisions – only the most important).

Now consider the bottom line of MNCs. The United States gives preferential tax treatment to "foreign sales corporations" (FSC). These "are shell companies in offshore tax havens through which American firms channel foreign income to avoid tax. They benefit some 6,000 American firms. Among them are Boeing, whose FSC saved it $130m in tax in 1998, and General Electric, which saved some $150m. They also benefit American subsidiaries of foreign firms, many of them European. In 1998 these included Britain's BP, ICI and Unilever; Germany's BASF, Daimler Benz and Hoechst; and France's Elf-Aquitaine and Rhône-Poulenc" (*The Economist,* 3/4/00). The European Union complained that these tax preferences constituted illegal discrimination. The WTO found in the EU's favor, giving them the right to retaliate against the US. So much for the fiction that the WTO is a "tool" of multinational corporations!

Rather than do environmental harm, it seems to me the WTO has forged a platform on which the governments (e.g., Mexico and the United States) can negotiate their differences. The environment does not belong to the United States, and if we want to clean up the world, we must do it in conjunction with our fellow human beings.

Negotiating reductions in tariffs is, however, the most important WTO function. One of the principal barriers to employment and prosperity in the less developed regions is their inability to export to the more developed world. They have complained about this for decades. Just recently, however, a "panel of financial and development experts has called for a new round of international trade talks devoted primarily to helping countries too weak to reap any benefits from the growing global economy. The panel - which included Robert Rubin, the former United States Treasury Secretary, and Ernesto Zedillo, the former president of Mexico - recommended that a ministerial-level World Trade Organization meeting planned for Qatar in November 'should set an objective of making trade as free between industrial and developing countries as it already is among the industrial countries.' The matter is urgent, the experts said in a report commissioned by Secretary General Kofi Annan, . . . because many poor countries are suffering from a slump in the prices of the commodities they produce, and rich countries are dragging their feet on promises to help open more markets to them. Mr. Zedillo, the panel's chairman, said at a news conference here today, that richer nations should see the intractable poverty of so much of the world as an issue of self-interest" (*New York Times,* 7/1/01).

How does the WTO function? Here the workshop participants and I had some friendly discussion. Suspecting that the WTO panels might be dominated by multinational corporations, one participant felt it very important to know who constituted their membership. I thought, on the other hand, that if we dwell unduly on their membership, we tend to stereotype, such as: "Executives of MNCs find in favor of MNCs." Rather, I thought, we should examine the results to determine whether findings do in fact favor

MNCs. I believe that mainly, the decisions are designed to level the playing field, and whether they help or harm MNCs depends on where the chips fall. In the FSC case, for example, the decision would harm many MNCs.

The WTO consists of a Director General appointed by the governments (currently Mike Moore of New Zealand, whose background is mainly in government), a Secretariat, and 550 staff members of about 60 nationalities. The professional staff is composed mostly of economists, lawyers and others with a specialization in international trade policy. When a member government complains about another's actions (as in Mexico complaining about the US tuna rule), the WTO offers its services for negotiation. If negotiation fails, a Dispute Settlement Body appoints a panel of three or five specialists in the field under consideration, to prepare a recommendation. The recommendation may be appealed to a higher body; otherwise, it stands.

I have told you in earlier Letters how I have wandered among the slums of all Latin American capitals (except Cuba), about ten in Africa, and some in Asia. During these wanderings, I have talked with the poorest of the poor. What they want most of all is *jobs,* and jobs will be possible only if the rich countries buy their products. Negotiating this – which the WTO does – is probably the best thing we can do for the impoverished of the world.

So, who ever said that the WTO is the big bad wolf?

Peace and friendship,
Jack Powelson

READER COMMENTS ON LETTER NO. 17

I challenge your assumption that reducing restrictions on trade creates a level playing field. Often, as with NAFTA, the consequences are quite the opposite. Small farmers in Mexico are being buried in cheap imports of rice, corn, milk and coffee. In a global market, the cheapest producers (regardless of true environmental costs, intensity of petroleum use, labor standards, etc.) have the capacity to destroy small ones.

It's worth pondering, isn't it - those of us who are interested in the plight of the global poor. As I know you share my concern, I am curious how you would answer.

David Morse, Storrs (CT) Friends Meeting

RESPONSE Though it is not my custom to answer readers' comments – I had my turn – nevertheless when asked, I might consider it. David's point is another Bastiat example. What is not seen is that poor Mexicans, for whom corn is a major part of the diet, are forced to pay higher prices than they would when allowed to buy corn from across the border. And there is mal-nutrition among poor Mexicans!

True, the Mexican farmer faces a crisis. It is a crisis brought on by decades of mismanagement by the Mexican government, as well as "protection." To "protect" the farmer further merely prolongs the poverty. The lasting solution is (1) to help the Mexican farmer increase productivity on the farm, with new methods and new machinery, so he can compete with imports. Small farming *can* compete with large-scale farming if the large-scale farmer insists on US wages (as he does). And (2) help the Mexican farmer move into new jobs in which his productivity (and wages) will be higher (as American farmers have been doing for the past century and a half). Until this happens, his misery will continue. Sorry, but I believe your proposal, if adopted, would immiserate him further.

Jack Powelson, Boulder (CO) Meeting of Friends

No, WTO is not the big bad wolf, but neither is it innocent Little Red Riding Hood.

WTO is the creation of governments and its policies and actions reflect the economic power of the various goverrnments. OECD countries have the experience, the wealth, the knowledge and the ability to influence the work of the WTO secretariat and the negotiations more than the LDCs can. But little bit by little bit that seems to be changing.

Seattle negotiations broke down not just because of the protesters. Some LDCs protested in their own ways.

Vici and Seiki Oshiro, Minneapolis (MN) Friends Meeting

ANOTHER NOTE from Jack: One Friend commented: If the negotiators are an ant and an elephant, what good does a level playing field do? My answer: The WTO might pass a rule that neither is allowed to step on the other.

But would it? Well, it has passed many analogous rules. If there were no WTO, however, the elephant would surely have his way.

THE QUAKER ECONOMIST

August 2, 2001

Letter No. 18

Dear friends:

What is Seen and What is Not Seen

Frédéric Bastiat died of tuberculosis at age 49. But in the two hundred years since his birth (1801), his simple philosophies of economics have turned up time and again. In one parody, he concocted a petition by candlemakers for protection against "the ruinous competition of a foreign rival who works under conditions so far superior to our own for the production of light that he is flooding the domestic market with it at an incredibly low price." The rival was the Sun, and the suggested remedy was mandatory shuttering of all windows, so candlemakers might thrive.

Perhaps his most famous essay, which has relevance today, is "What is Seen and What is Not Seen." Bastiat was one of the first to point out that many "obvious" solutions to economic problems turn out to aggravate the very same problem when the unseen part is factored in. This observation is so modern that we talked about some of the cases at the workshop that I co-led (with Carol Blotter) at Friends General Conference just last month.

The Minimum Wage

One of these is the minimum wage, currently $5.15 an hour in the United States. A "living wage" movement is afoot, to mandate increases. "Everyone" (me too) would like poor workers to earn more. What is not seen about the minimum wage is:

> (1) The law can force employers to pay the minimum wage *if they employ*, but it cannot enforce them to employ. The minimum wage was increased almost yearly from 1961 to 1981. During that period the unemployment rate for black teen-agers increased every year, to 40.7%, or four times its 1950 level. This unemployment is what is not seen. Newspaper delivery boys or "fill-'er-up" teen-agers at gas stations are also not seen.

(2) As employers cut hiring because they prefer mechanization to paying the higher wage, they select from the available pool of workers the ones they believe are the "most desirable." These tend to be White Males, which is a probable reason black teen-age unemployment rises with the minimum wage. The same applies to women just off welfare. Thus the minimum wage is sometimes said to be "racist" or "gender-biased." This again is the part we do not see.

(3) Because more skilled workers insist on their places in the hierarchy, a higher minimum wage leads to higher wages at all levels. This in turn leads to higher prices (inflation), until soon the minimum wage "has to" be increased again.

If increases in the minimum wage will not raise the real (inflation-adjusted) wage in full employment, how do we bring about a "living wage?" If Bastiat were here today, he would have the answer. The only way is to increase the skills of workers, through education, training, and culture change.

Sweatshops

Friends are deeply concerned about sweatshops in less developed countries – long hours, unhealthy and unsafe work conditions, cruel punishments (such as flogging and not letting workers go to bathrooms), and above all, very low wages. Many Westerners are calling for boycott of sweatshops that do not meet minimum requirements for health, safety, and wages.

What we do not see is (1) sweatshops are found *everywhere* in the less developed world, not just in the producers of our clothing, and (2) sweatshop workers come mostly from families whose very subsistence depends on their keeping their jobs. Employers have sometimes fired them in order to please the American buyer. "As a result of American pressure, perhaps 30,000 children have been thrown out of their jobs in [Bangladesh's] textile industry in the past two years. A study by Oxfam found that far from going to school, many of these children have ended up in far more dangerous employment, in welding shops or in prostitution" (*New York Times,* 2/20/00). Other studies have found them being sold as sex slaves in Saudi Arabia.

So, what can we do? We can demand that purchasers of sweatshop products (Gap, Nike, etc.) monitor the work and safety conditions, as Gap did in

El Salvador. But we cannot demand that employers increase wages or provide education for their workers, as some have proposed. Why not? Because sweatshops are a way of life in the Third World. No producer can operate much in advance of general conditions everywhere. One cannot be an island in a sea of poverty.

American wages, health, and safety conditions are the result of centuries of struggle, innovation, and rising productivity. We cannot impose the rich person's way of life upon the poor without adverse unseen consequences. What we can do, is join the centuries-long struggle to improve standards of living all over the world. (That's another subject).

Debt forgiveness

Third World governments are swimming in debt. This debt must be forgiven, or so pronounce the advocates of "Jubilee 2000." What is not seen is that the debt is primarily owed by corrupt politicians who have used the money to pad their own bank accounts abroad. The poor, by contrast, do not have debts, because they do not have satisfactory credit ratings.

The debt is so great that it will never be repaid. Yet forgiveness would tell the corrupt debtors that they got away with it, and maybe they can do it again. Being forced to repudiate the debt, on the other hand, would bring them shame and possibly force them out of office. Many governments have defaulted on their debt, but we do not have an international court of bankruptcy. Steve Williams (of Bethesda MD Meeting), a jurist, responds by saying: "No procedure, paralleling domestic bankruptcy, exists for compelling creditors to accept some uniform percent of the debts of bankrupt governments (e.g., 25 cents on the dollar). with the debtor free to contract new debts. This is an area where international law and institutions could make real and important progress."

The corrupt borrowers should be pushed to repay, just like any borrower. When they cannot, the lending agencies will learn a lesson.

Bastiat's Lesson

Applied today, Bastiat's lesson is that we cannot solve the terrible economic conditions around us by manipulating wages and prices, by excusing corruption, or by boycotting the poor if they do not live like the rich. For every economic policy, we must examine what is not seen. If we do that, we will find that we cannot change the world all at once. We must work, patiently and persistently, toward those solutions that will better the world as the way opens.

Can you think of other economic events where the unseen reverses the benefits of the seen?

Peace and friendship,
Jack Powelson

PS Research showing that the minimum wage has no effect on unemployment usually selects an extraordinary boom period when the increase in demand eclipsed the minimum-wage effect (e.g., 1996-1999). When longer periods are chosen and adjustment made for extraneous forces, increases in the minimum wage virtually always accompany increased unemployment of low-income workers.

READER RESPONSES TO LETTER NO. 18

For debt, The Oxfam report targeted independent funds for the indebted countries, that can only be used for education, combined with debt relief. They also give some examples of it working. It's interesting as an idea to be used in conjunction with an international bankruptcy court.

Geoffrey Williams, Bethesda (MD) Friends Meeting

We had over 100 people at our Southeastern World Affairs Institute last weekend to discuss "Understanding Globalization". I think you will agree with Janet Malkemes when she says, "It's a fact of life in the developing world today, that children are working because if they don't, then the whole family starves."

Some attenders were concerned about the environment and labor issues, but John Fobes, retired UNESCO staff, pointed out UNESCO and other UN organizations are working on this and we should use the UN rather than the WTO.

George White, Charlotte (NC) Friends Meeting

When I purchased Universal Woods, they were paying just over the minimum wage. They were getting just about what they paid for. Our CEO is Paul Neumann who is also a member of our Louisville Friends Meeting. He is now part owner. He has worked with management to increase the skills and the participation of the shop to the point that, with benefits, the shop people are earning close to $30,000, and they are on a guaranteed 40 hours the same as management. They are earning it. As we have increased our technology level, the percentage of cost in labor has gone down. This also enables us to spend more on worker quality.

Lee B. Thomas, Jr., Louisville (KY) Friends Meeting

I don't believe there is any way the small farmer in Mexico or any other country can compete with the big farmer unless she too is using genetically engineered seeds and confined animal feeding operations, which are spoiling the soil, air, and water.

Deb Garretson, Fall Creek Meeting

For most people the idea of becoming an economist presents an insuperable, depressing burden, to which they may well react in a hostile manner. It also sounds as if they're not OK the way they are and that they are being labeled uneducated. This is all part of the "Unseen " to which they are reacting.

At this point in my life I have very little ego invested in my ignorance, and I think it's possible for people with the very best intentions to make grave mistakes. It suits my current attitude to want to review things, and perhaps learn a little bit here and there.

Faith Williams, Bethesda (MD) Friends Meeting

THE QUAKER ECONOMIST
August 13, 2001

Letter No. 19

Dear friends:

Results of the Questionnaire

Russ Nelson (publisher) has sent me the data from 60 questionnaires, including the comments without names of respondents (that's the way I wanted it). How often should *CLQ* come? Thirteen said weekly, eighteen biweekly, and sixteen monthly. So, I have decided to send it when the spirit moves me. I will not feel compelled (as in the past) to get it out weekly.

Most read it right away, some save for later, and a few select, not having time to read all. Twenty-seven found it "very interesting," and twenty-four "stimulating."

Almost all who wrote remarks were encouraging and want *CLQ* to continue. One, however, said he or she had expected a journal with many authors, replies and rebuttals, carrying many points of view. I sympathize with this desire, and if I were thirty years younger I might undertake that. At age 81, however, I am not about to launch a new career. Nevertheless, I owe an explanation of why *CLQ* is as it is.

When I joined Friends fifty-eight years ago, we were a diverse Society. Republicans sat in the benches in about equal numbers to Democrats. Men in uniform came to Meeting, then went off to war. Others went to CPS camps or ambulance service. Some loved Roosevelt, others hated "that man." If this atmosphere existed today, anti-abortion Friends would sit next to pro-choice, and Bush Republicans next to Naderites. All would be accepted as having God within them, and all would be inspired by the Quaker spirit.

Instead, over the past five decades, the "Liberal Left" has gradually taken over our Society, so that others (such as me) have not felt comfortable. As older Friends died and younger ones replaced them, the Meetings took on a leftwing political complex. They favored Sandinista Nicaragua, the Cuban Revolution, even the Soviet Union, all of which I believe have seriously damaged the welfare of their peoples. Friends condemn multinational corporations and world trade, both of which I believe will be major forces lifting the poor from their poverty. Many want to protect dying industries, such as textiles and steel. I believe we should shut them down and buy these products from poor countries where the jobs are truly needed.

Three years ago I wrote a book that I wanted to call *The Quakerly Economy,* meaning a hypothetical world economy based on Quaker business practices of the seventeenth century. The publisher (University of Michigan Press) thought it should have a wider audience, so we re-named it *The Moral Economy*. When I presented its ideas at a week-long workshop at Friends General Conference in 1999, ten Friends (out of twenty) walked out at midweek. The pity of that is the vast majority of economists and leaders of the Third World hold views similar to mine rather than to the "Quaker line." Deregulation and economic freedom are the direction the world is heading. Like it or not, we should understand it.

I do not aim to persuade Friends of my opinions. Rather, I want them thoughtfully considered. Five decades ago, Friends conducted active discussions on social questions, examining all sides, in institutes of international affairs (high school and adult), shipboard orientation programs (for students going to Europe after the war), Young Friends, and Pendle Hill conferences. In all of these I was a leader or participated actively. I find nothing like that among Friends today.

Kenneth Boulding (my friend and mentor, whose loss I feel enormously) once said, "It is not that Quakers do not know economics. Rather, the economics they know is wrong."

I have wondered why there are not nearly so many economists in Meeting today as there were fifty years ago. Perhaps the reason can be found in the following message, written by one Quaker economist to another, with copy to me:

> "One always hates to give up something that seems quite logical and compelling, in this case what seems to be a potentially fruitful linking of classical liberal thought with contemporary Quaker concerns. But, there may be times and situations that simply do not work out, and it is my feeling that this is the current reality. I am scaling back my Quaker activities because many of the things that I care about passionately, and which I believe are consistent with Quaker insight, simply do not resonate with the majority of Friends.

"One hopes that the objectives that Jack has worked for through his writings and dialogs with Friends will in some way surface in the future in a manner and context that leads to more acceptance and open debate — Seeking Truth Together. Jack cannot be accused of being frivolous or of not having gone the extra mile. I look back at my discovery of his *Holistic Economics* Pendle Hill pamphlet, and all that has come after, as being a wonderful and informative voyage of the intellect and spirit."

Here are some examples of how I have felt unwelcome among Friends.

(1) Chuck Fager (a well-known Friend) invited me to a conference on Peace at State College, PA, last April. When he reported to the committee, they vetoed me. I was told that my economics does not lead to peace.

(2) One reader of *Seeking Truth Together* wrote me the following:

"I must say I found *Seeking Truth Together* to be among the most dishonest works I have read. What I found most offensive was your use of 'the manner of Friends' as a disguise for indoctrination. To pretend that everyone's view is given a fair and even ear and then to conclude with your dogmatic pronouncement, as if that is the consensus, is so objectionable that the word 'obscene' comes to mind." (MY NOTE: *STT* reports all positions, and when there was no consensus, it says so).

(3) In the midst of the overwhelmingly positive comments to the *CLQ* questionnaire, the following appeared:

"Please remove me from Jack's mailing list - Jack's views of Global issues are extremely uninformed and opposed to the Quaker intent of world peace. I believe further dissemination of his larger view is beyond a mis-service (sic) to the Society of Friends and particularly to FCNL's missions." (MY NOTE: So, it is a "mis-service" to hear ideas other than one's own?)

If the unidimensional nature of Quakers today were everything, I would have left the Society of Friends three decades ago. But, other values overwhelm that temptation.

Chief among them is that I am held tight by the original Quaker spirit. I am committed to silent worship and Friends' ways of doing business. I believe in that of God in every person.

Next, I feel loved in Boulder Meeting. It is my home. So long as I don't mention economics, I get along very well with Friends here.

I see two rays of hope. At Friends General Conference two months ago, I co-led a workshop with twenty participants who understood my dilemma and even felt it themselves. They too wanted a more open, less biased Society of Friends. At worship sharing the final day, one by one they expressed appreciation that I had continued to "hang in there." The other ray of hope is you, readers of the *Classic Liberal Quaker*. I am overwhelmed by your positive responses to the questionnaire, and I am encouraged to hang in a bit longer, God willing.

What about the commentator who "expected a journal with many authors, replies and rebuttals, carrying many points of view." Try *Friends Bulletin,* 5238 Andalucia Court, Whittier CA 90601, whose editor, Anthony Manousos, is committed to just that. If you want the "modern Quaker line," however, you have a variety of Friends' publications that present little else. *CLQ* is my only medium to help bring Friends back to their spiritual origins. It is the vast majority of Friends who have strayed, not the few of us who still want an Open Society, welcoming all political viewpoints. We are all children of God.

I leave with Friends two lines from my college alma mater:

> Let not moss-covered error moor thee by its side
> As the world on truth's current glides by.

Sincerely your friend,
                    Jack Powelson

READER RESPONSES TO LETTER NO. 19

Referring to the Society of Friends 58 years ago:

A most moving, charitable and inspiring note. A wonderful summary. What it must have been like to be in a loving circle of Friends with diverse interests and views and the Love to share them in constructive and open ways! I was simply 40 years too late, or possibly just not up to the task.

J. D. von Pischke, Herndon (VA) Friends Meeting

I feel considerably enlightened by the explanation contained in your last email, which described the questionnaire results, and I look forward to reading future CLQs with that knowledge. Regardless of any difference in our views, it is always good to understand where the other person is coming from. Thank you very much.

Michael Jack, Alexandria (VA), Friends Meeting of Washington

Compassion, empathy, Christian love, and egalitarian society will tend to appeal to those holding to a liberal religious view that says we are bound by a spirit that cares for all. Those holding fundamentalist religious views tend to see a stern and judging God of rigid rule, favoring some nations and individuals and approving conquest of other nations. Sure, this is a hasty generalization, but politics and religion do seem to line up in those rows, don't they? No wonder then that Quakers, given the content of the testimonies and queries (that tend toward caring and compassion and responsibility for each other), land on the liberal side of that field. And I am thankful for that fact.

Steve Willey, Sandpoint (ID) Friends Meeting

QUESTION by Jack: Do you really believe that anyone who fails to adopt a modern liberal view cannot be among "those favoring compassion, empathy, Christian love, and egalitarian society?" Are only those of the "liberal religious view . . . bound by a spirit that cares for all?"

I felt moved by your biography and analysis. I have thought the same things for several years, that the Society of Friends was taken over by our left wing "revolutionary" 1960's culture. I include myself in that takeover because I was drawn to Friends because of its left wing quality. Now I see that the "left wing" quality has really eroded any sense of a tradition which can be passed down to other generations of Quakers. Our present Quaker culture emphasizes a highly individualistic orientation towards values while at the same time supporting the notion that "society" is at fault for individual behavior (and is responsible for correcting those faults!). It is probably the reason why we have taken God out of our lives and out of our worship, because God makes demands on us and we are loathe to see ourselves under the jurisdiction of anyone; let alone a deity whose existence cannot be physically proved. What we have tried to do is substitute a political philosophy for a spiritual way of life.

The other day I was thinking how strange not many of our children were drawn to doing missionary work in "hot" or destitute spots overseas, like Africa, the Middle East or the Balkans. There are not a lot of liberal Quaker services that the Quaker young flock to these days. Why? Because we have concentrated for so long on doing "activist" things which lift up those who do non-violent civil disobedience, we no longer see it as our individual duty to go and help others less fortunate in the world. We are drawn to the heroic rather than to the mundane and the heroic better have quite a lot of "kick the butt of the powers that be" in it for us to give it our support.

Rich Ailes, Middleton (PA) Meeting

The irony is that both the far left and the far right in this country want the government to solve the social ills that they perceive. It is no wonder that you find yourself under siege a good deal of the time—as a (dare I say) traditional Liberal you come at issues from a point of view that is outside the current framework of what passes for political/economic debate. Your belief that individual human beings are capable of determining for themselves what is in their own best interest without the dicta of those who think they know better remains a radical idea in this world of ours. But, as I say, there are hopeful signs. I suspect that you reach more ears, and accomplish more, than you know.

Kenneth Allison, Episcopalian, Paradise Valley AZ

I agree completely with your assessment of the attitudes among "liberal" Friends today. While we accept and encourage a virtually unlimited scope of spiritual beliefs, when it comes to economics and politics, most FGC Friends seem to demand a rigid, "politically correct" lock-step conformity.

My Meeting, Friends Meeting of Washington, was created out of two other meetings so that then-President Herbert Hoover could have a place to worship. This is now somewhat of an embarrassment to many of our members, because Hoover was, heaven help us, a REPUBLICAN! As were many of the Quakers of his day.

Like you, I despair that anything will change or improve. It took me over twenty years to come to clearness that I could join my Meeting in spite of this attitude. It was only when I realized that my own beliefs are what really matter, and that no one can tell me what to believe either spiritually or politically. But it does make it very difficult quite a bit of the time, especially when certain Quaker organizations claim to speak for all Friends. Unfortunately, this seems to be a phenomenon which affects all organizations.

Dick Bellin, Friends Meeting of Washington (DC)

Your experience with the critics — your sense of unwelcome among some Friends who describe your thinking as "dishonest" or "obscene" or a "misservice" — reminds me of John Adams, the Adams portrayed in David McCullough's recent and feted biography.

When Adams bluntly questioned the revolution in France in 1789, for example, Philadelphian James Callender, championing the opinion of Thomas Jefferson, was not content to disagree with Adams on the merits of his case. Callender wrote instead that Adams was a "repulsive pedant," a "gross hypocrite," and "in his private life, one of the most egregious fools on the continent," McCullough reports.

Roger Williams, Ft. Myers (FL)

RIGHT ON, Jack! Although not an official Quaker (only in heart and mind) I agree with you completely. The Bouldings first interested me in getting involved in Peace Protests and efforts here in Colorado. I was a bit more active in Wisconsin before retirement. Please don't give up! Our world needs you.

> Lorna Knowlton, Boulder (CO)

With reference to the changed meaning of "liberal:"

It's all part of the theft of the term "liberal". Freedoms are lost not through direct government action against the idea of freedom, but instead by rede-fining "liberal", "freedom", or "rights" to have a meaning opposed to the traditional ones. People oppressed in this manner think they _are_ liberals, that they have freedom and rights. But instead of having freedoms to and rights from, they have freedoms from and rights to.

> Russ Nelson, St. Lawrence Valley (NY) Friends Meeting

I enjoyed reading your letter—all of which I read. Back in Dunster House [where you and I lived in college] I was convinced that Keynes had the right view of our sick economy—lately I have come to the conclusion that I should have learned more from Milton Friedman. You support giving people the help they need for them to use as they see fit.   Stay with it!

> Dick Wolf (college classmate of Jack's)

THE QUAKER ECONOMIST

August 27, 2001

Letter No. 20

Dear friends:

The International Monetary Fund

Back in 1950, the gag was "How do you get to Washington?" Answer: "Go to Harvard and turn left."

So I did just that. Back then, the International Monetary Fund (IMF, or just "Fund") was a darling of the Lefties. I was a Lefty, so I joined the Fund with my freshly-minted PhD. Now the IMF is the scourge of the Lefties, and I am no longer a Lefty. I do not work for the Fund any more, so I can speak of it dispassionately. I join the Lefties in thinking the IMF should be abolished, but I have my own reasons.

The IMF was created in 1947 to solve the problems of the 1930s. These problems had vanished by the 1950's, after I had left the Fund, and the Fund itself gradually evolved into a different creature. Its main purpose has always been to help member countries solve their balance of payments problems, but those problems fall into a different pattern from when I used to work there.

Here is the current pattern. The government of Country X spends more than its people are willing to pay in taxes. It "buys votes" by paying subsidies to many sectors, often including education and health services for the poor. It sets up state enterprises to sell gas, electricity, and transport to the people at less than cost, then bails them out when they suffer losses. It lends to private businesses so they can pay wages higher than their sales revenues allow, but it is politically reluctant to demand repayment. It puts money in the pockets of politicians, who deposit it in Swiss banks. To cover the excess of spending over taxes, Country X prints money, which causes inflation. Since X's prices become higher than those of the rest of the world, foreigners buy less of X's goods, while X-residents buy more abroad. As demand for X's goods falls, unemployment leads to full-scale depression, much unrest and riots. Foreign investors, who have been supporting X's economy, withdraw their funds at the first inkling of crisis, and available jobs plummet further. This pattern has been taking place mainly in Asia, Africa, and Latin America – more recently in Russia and former Soviet countries.

Fearing for its existence, the government of X runs to the IMF for a loan. The IMF will lend on two conditions: (1) X should devalue its currency to bring local prices more into line with foreign. (If X-currency prices are higher than dollar prices, the mismatch can be made up by giving more X-currency for the dollar. This is a devaluation of X-currency.) (2) X must agree to stop overspending its budget, so the situation will not recur. These requirements are known as "conditionality."

By the time the problem is recognized, however, so many individuals and groups have vested interests in the federal budget that the budget cannot be balanced suddenly, without a political upheaval. So the IMF lends dollars to the government to cover its balance of payments deficit until the budget can be reduced gradually, under the two requirements just mentioned. To see that the government behaves, the IMF usually sends "advisors," who are really monitors. Aha! The IMF is now looking over the shoulder of the government, monitoring its financial behavior.

In 1960 I was asked by the United States foreign aid program to be financial "advisor" to the Government of Bolivia. Bolivia had spent much money wastefully and had a triple-digit inflation, but they had now agreed (after a devaluation) to balance the budget. Not only the IMF, but the US foreign aid program, had loaned funds to tide the government over, so both the IMF and the US sent them advisors.

One day in the office of the Governor of the Central Bank, I saw a sign (in Spanish), "Don't be afraid to ask for credit. It will be cheerfully refused." On another occasion, I was sitting around the table with President Paz Estenssoro and his cabinet. The President was proposing some expenditures that I knew would violate the agreement. So I reminded him. He sloughed off the question, saying, "Oh we know all about that." He had ways of getting along with the US Ambassador. But in general, the agreement was kept, the inflation conquered, and the IMF was paid off.

Since the poor always suffer most in inflation, I felt I was doing my part to help them. Since the government had been corrupt, I didn't mind monitoring its newly-good behavior. I felt good about my job and proud of the IMF.

Since then, I have had assignments all over the world. As I associated with presidents, governors of central banks, and ministers in Asia, Africa, and Latin America, I became more aware of their power and their greed. For example, a "land reform" would really benefit the Minister of Agriculture rather than the farmers. (Later on, I co-authored a book on the perversion of land reforms everywhere, called "The Peasant Betrayed.")

As I met high officials of multinational corporations (sometimes CEOs), I found them more benign to the poor than were their governments. They paid their workers better than other employers and provided more health care, education, and housing. (These personal observations have been confirmed by scholarly research, including studies by the International Labor Organization). So I ceased to be a Lefty, believing that governments that "take care" of their poor generally take care of their own power first – this includes the United States – but that private businesses are more compassionate, not because they want to be, but because the market forces them to be. MNCs treat their workers better because they want the pick of the crop.

Conditionality did not work (in my opinion). Governments were still wasteful and corrupt. State enterprises have been lining the pockets of their officers and putting the money in Swiss banks, knowing the state would bail them out. China and Russia have been notorious for this.

Curiously enough, the IMF often did not enforce conditionality. After all, the IMF had to look out for its own existence. If it kept trying vainly to enforce its terms it would have to cut off the disobedient governments. If it didn't make loans, it would go out of business. So, when conditionality was not met, the IMF would often extend the period, making another loan (this happened several times in Russia).

Instead of demanding that borrowing governments simply balance their budgets, the IMF began to insist that they balance them in certain ways that the IMF would stipulate. The principal causes of the budget deficits were corrupt state enterprises and subsidies to private enterprises enabling them to pay wages higher than their income would allow. So the IMF began demanding that state enterprises be privatized and wage ceilings be enforced. (In many countries, such as Argentina, the government oversees annual bargaining and sets the allowed wage increase).

These stricter requirements became known as "structural adjustment." Structural adjustment often requires the government to cut down on social services and keep wages low. But the horse is already out of the barn. The rich have made off with the loot, and now they demand that the poor pay. Still, no one on earth can make the rich pay, so if the poor do not pay, no one will.

One famous news picture showed the Managing Director of IMF, arms folded, standing over the President of Indonesia, who was bent over a table signing the agreement for structural adjustment. This picture caused great resentment throughout the Third World, but the IMF's position always has been (from the beginning): "You got yourselves into this mess. If you don't like our conditions, you don't need to borrow."

Here are two scenarios, in either of which the poor suffer:

In the first, the government puts the IMF conditions into effect. Education and social services are cut, and employers cannot borrow the money to pay excess wages. State enterprises are privatized and can no long employ redundant workers. The inflation is stopped, but the government no longer supplies the services to which the poor had become accustomed. (It also has nothing for the rich to send to Swiss banks).

In the second – the one preferred by the Lefties - the government defies the IMF and continues to print money for social services, education, and the like. The cycle is repeated, inflation erodes away the social services that were kept, and the poor suffer even more from higher prices for their necessities. The ultimate result is joblessness and violence. So in this scenario also, the poor suffer.

What a dilemma! The poor suffer either way, because the rich have already made away with the loot, and there is no way a foreigner can make them pay it back, short of invading the country and running it ourselves, as we did with Germany after WWII. So long as the rich remain in power, they can work around any conditions foreigners place on them. They know the territory better than we do.

Therefore, structural adjustment should not be imposed by foreigners (read, IMF). Instead, the IMF should be abolished, an international bankruptcy court established, and governments should go bankrupt in hopes they would be replaced by honest ones, even though that is not assured. Lenders would lose. Yes, the poor will suffer, and we should help them directly with cash – but not help or excuse their corrupt governments.

Finally, is the IMF a tool of multinational corporations and banks? I believe the IMF errs in continuing to finance countries like Russia, Argentina, and Country X when, time and again, these countries have not mended their profligate ways. In supporting them nonetheless, the IMF bolsters financial markets so that foreign lenders and investors do not lose, or lose less (and the IMF survives). Do they do this because they are tools of the investors, or because they honestly believe they are saving the economies of the borrowing countries? I vote for the latter. My successors on the Fund staff believe they are doing the right thing for everyone. I disagree, but I do not question their integrity.

LAST MINUTE NOTE: Since I wrote the preceding paragraph, the IMF has agreed to lend Argentina $8 billion, on conditions yet to be worked out. They argue that a depression in Argentina would spread to the rest of Latin America (as indeed it would). Is the IMF a tool of foreign banks that fear that their holdings of Argentine debt would be defaulted, or is the IMF trying to preserve the entire Latin American economy from depression and unemployment? I believe the latter. But my "what-to-do" would be different from theirs. Mine would be: No IMF money. Let the Argentine government default; let bondholders take the consequences. In this, I agree with the Lefties. But mostly the Lefties have not figured out that the cycle would be repeated, and after the inflation takes hold again the poor will be without jobs and maybe without food. If that truly concerns us, we will think of programs to help Argentine workers directly, without going through the government.

My regret now is a personal one. Friends say I am not "compassionate" because I no longer march to the Lefties' drums (see letter from Steve Willey, below). But I could not live with my conscience if I did.

> Sincerely your friend,
> Jack Powelson

READER RESPONSE TO LETTER NO. 20

Here's my preferred scenario [for the IMF].   Yes, stop making the disastrous and ineffective, even harmful big loans to corrupt governments.   Stop

the structural adjustment programs which harm the poor, and by some accounts have led to millions of indirect deaths of the poor (e.g. privatized
water systems that the poor cannot afford).   Instead, direct the wealthy
nation monies to build up undeveloped countries from the bottom up. Do
this by massive, decentralized and non- governmental banking programs to
create the dispersion of economic power you speak of in the Moral Economy,
Centuries of Economic Endeavor, and elsewhere.   The main institutional
vehicles to accomplish this would be self sustaining banks issuing non-
usurious interest micro- loans to individuals and small businesses.

Rich Andrews, Boulder (CO) Meeting of Friends

that on dollar obligations because the peso is distrusted (devaluation feared). This difference also reflects a distrust of the Argentine government itself. (Consider Argentina as Country X in my Letter No. 20).

Question: Should the western hemisphere adopt the U.S. dollar as a universal currency? What are the pros and cons of this? Does doing so imply a new brand of U.S. imperialism, even if the Latin governments themselves make the choice?

An international court to try war criminals

Should the United States join other nations in favoring a court to try accused war criminals such as Slobodan Milosevic and Saddam Hussein, if he is ever captured?

How about dictators who abuse their own citizens, like Augusto Pinochet of Chile?

Did you favor the Nuremberg trials? If Germany had won the war, would Roosevelt have been tried instead of Hitler? (Of course, they were both dead, but you get the idea).

Suppose the court were dominated by countries hostile to the United States, and Clinton and Kissinger were kidnapped and tried before it for crimes in Libya and Kosovo. Suppose lesser figures, like ordinary American soldiers, were tried for "peace keeping" in Somalia and Kosovo. How would you feel about that?

Do we require the poor to live like the rich, when they cannot afford it?

A farm I know of in Colorado was housing legal Mexican migrant workers in huts that were substandard according to our building codes, but that were much better than the housing they were accustomed to in Mexico. The authorities required the farmer to upgrade the houses. He could not do so economically, and the farm was closed, the workers thrown into the streets, and I do not know what became of them.

If the codes on maximum occupancy in New York City were strictly enforced, thousands of people would be thrown into the streets. Is it proper to have laws that we do not enforce because doing so would create intolerable conditions?

An architect friend of mine wanted to build affordable housing for the poor. He designed an electrical socket that could be operated by a string extending from the upper floor to the lower. It was rejected by the inspectors, who insisted on three-way switches in both locations – which would have made the house more expensive. How do you feel about that?

Would homelessness be alleviated if people were allowed to double up more? Do our housing codes cause homelessness?

This raises a broader question: Do we require the poor to live like the rich when they cannot afford to do so? This question applies to sweatshops abroad, debt repayment, conditions of foreign aid, and other. It applies to Canadian foreign aid to Tanzania, in which roofs were required to withstand three feet of snow.

Other questions

What other questions shall we consider in future Letters?

Current plans

As you receive this letter, Robin (my wife) and I will be on a river cruise from Amsterdam to Vienna. Then we will fly to Frankfurt and entrain for Heidelberg, where I will participate in a conference, giving a paper on Japan. (You didn't know I was an expert on Japan, did you? Well, neither did I. But I am not going to turn down an opportunity just because I am not the most qualified person.)

Right after World War II, while employed as an auditor (living in Paris), I was assigned to a three-month audit in Frankfurt, which lay in ruins. Not wanting to live in the expatriates' hotel, I found a German Quaker family to take me in. I slept on the couch in their living room in a partly bombed building. The stairway to their floor had no wall on the outside, so I looked out on ruined buildings across the street. I paid my "rent" with food they could not buy but to which I was entitled in the post exchange.

The American Friends Service Committee had organized a Neighborhood House (*Nachbarschaftsheim*) to bring some semblance of community life in a bombed-out neighborhood. I taught folk dancing to young Germans there. A hiking club, called Naturfreunde, met there, and, wearing Lederhosen, I joined them for some of the best hikes of my life. (An American soldier once threatened to shoot me because I walked too close to a military rest resort). One of the Germans, named Klaus, became my special friend. Now, 54 years later, Robin and I will visit Klaus and his family in Frankfurt, just before we return home. (P.S. The *Nachbarschaftsheim* still exists).

Sincerely your friend,
Jack Powelson

THE QUAKER ECONOMIST
September 17, 2001

Letter No. 22

Dear friends:

Pacifism in the Face of Terror

As a conscientious objector in World War II, I told my draft board I would rather be killed than kill. I would lie down in front of an approaching German tank and hope its driver would have the conscience to stop. Bold words, but never put to test. How do I feel now that Terror has come to our shores?

Why do I feel more strongly about the Terror of September 11 than I did about Hitler's concentration camps? Not knowing about them in 1941 is no excuse. I feel more strongly because I identify more with the victims in the World Trade Tower than I did with German Jews or the victims of Hiroshima and Nagasaki, who were also people, families with children, just like us. Not very Quakerly, is it, or consistent, for someone who affirms that everyone, everywhere, is a child of God? At least, it is the truth.

I have tried to rationalize. World War II had goals – to win – and bombing innocent victims was an accepted part of it. In 1948 I stood in the rubble of Frankfurt with my 19-year-old friend Klaus, speechless as Klaus told me of the horror the Germans had suffered. Too young for war, he had served on the bucket lines. Last week I visited Klaus and his family in a rebuilt Frankfurt, and he said to me, "At least in this war we are on the same side."

I shuddered. Are we at war? If so, this is not a war in which the Terrorists have any goals other than to spread chaos to the Western World. They must be stopped. Am I still a conscientious objector?

Yes. I will not support military action against any country or its people. I would not bomb Afghanistan (if I were of draftable age). But I have always supported the use of force to bring criminals to justice. Force may also be used on those who hide or defend the criminals. The only "revenge" for the victims of the Tragedy should be every effort to make sure it does not happen again.

This is my stand, but it is a blurry one. Wasn't Hitler a criminal? I cannot reconcile my logic, only answer to my heart.

Love and Peace,

Jack

P.S. Robin and I have just returned from our river trip through central Europe. It rained every day – no sitting on the sun deck – and the water on the Danube was so high that our ship could not fit under the bridge at Regensburg. So we were bussed to Vienna. At Passau on September 11, news of the Tragedy arrived. Then my conference at Heidelberg was called off. For five hours yesterday we stood in security lines at the Frankfurt airport (Klaus, my friend of 53 years ago, and his daughter stood by us all the time.) Now, after nine hours in the air we are thankful to be home. I will have more to say in the next Letter, when comments on previous Letters will also be published. Right now, I am tired.

COMMENTS ON LETTER NO. 22 ON PACIFISM FACING TERROR

A good letter. I feel that there are bonds or proximity that are important, that views change over time, and that initial reactions become either tempered or reinforced.

It seems clear to me that pacifists and Libertarians and Quakers are placed at a tremendous disadvantage in times like these. We have nothing new to offer, while those who want retaliation carry the day. What we can offer is better over the long run, I believe, but in the short run our "alternative service" is relatively feeble, however noble.

J. D. von Pischke, Friend from Reston (VA)

If a murder is committed it is appropriate for the police to seek out the murderer. The law and most people's moral standards also recognize that reasonable force could be used to effect an arrest. But the hunt for the murderer would (should?) be carried out with regard for the civil rights of others — including, even, those of the suspect. It would also be carried out with regard for the safety of others. For example, police forces have guidelines about when to call off a car chase because it is endangering innocent civilians. Or let's try a better example. Suppose after the Oklahoma City bombing, McVeigh fled to a city — say, Detroit — and we didn't know where he was except that it was somewhere in Detroit. Would anyone think it would be appropriate to bomb Detroit into ruin because, in the process, we most likely would have gotten McVeigh?

May God protect us all.

Frank Perch, Central Philadelphia Monthly Meeting (PA)

I too was a conscientious objector.

Killing innocent folks is NOT acceptable, any time, any place, for any reason. In fact this is precisely this, (terrorism), which we are determined to see ended. Engaging in the same is not, in my humble opinion, the way toward that end.

Steve Willey, Sandpoint (ID) Friends Meeting

Your stand on the use of force to bring criminals to justice is one which has always been accepted by Quakers. William Penn and others, in their arguments for tolerance, claimed (as has turned out to be true) that government did not need to concern itself with forcing a common faith - it only needed to protect the common good. And that common good included protecting the innocent in their persons and property.

Gusten Lutter, Mountain View Meeting (Denver CO)

My concern about our reaction is whether it will be wily enough. I think we have to be as selective as we can (without being ineffective). And my impression is that we are letting the war for "the hearts and minds" of non-lunatic Muslims be lost be default; Safire in the Times calls for getting moderate Muslims clerics to speak out. They should—and to do more than whine about how not all Muslims are terrorists.

Steve Williams, Bethesda (MD) Friends Meeting

One way of dealing with this situation is to insist (how?) that the countries accused of harboring terrorists allow an international inspection of suspected activities, reporting to an international body (like Interpol?). One would start with the obvious suspects: Afghanistan, Pakistan, Libya, Iran, Iraq, Saudi Arabia, but will have to include Canada, France, England, etc. and the USA as well.

Tom Selldorff, Weston (MA)

As I have told Friends many times, one of the principal reasons it took me over twenty years to come to clearness about joining the Religious Society of Friends was and remains my doubts about pacifism and the Peace Testimony. "Work to remove the causes of war?" Certainly. Take every step to avoid it? Definitely. However, I am afraid I unite more with the statement from the Torah above. Maybe you are willing to be killed rather than kill, but I am not that self-sacrificing, and neither are my children. My son keeps a rifle in his house, and I can't say he is totally wrong. Which, along with my dismay expressed to you and others about the general economic and political views which pervade "liberal" Quakerism, leads me to keep asking again and again the question which has no clear answer - why am I a Quaker?

Dick Bellin, Friends Meeting of Washington (DC)

Clearly action is called for. We as a Society will be more effective in directing that action if we are providing realistic alternative initiatives, instead of just saying, no don't do that.

Friends need to concentrate on A Quaker Action Plan to stop terrorism, and put that forward as an alternative to policies that we disagree with.

Kruskal Hewitt, Tokyo (Japan)

I can't speak to the goals of the terrorists. However, I think we will not be safe until our conversations talk about the US's bombings of Iraq over ten years, our arming of Israel against the Palestinians over 50 years, and countless other acts that have caused endless suffering of innocent people. That is the context in which this disaster was perpetrated.

My great hope is that now that innocent people have died on our shores, we will begin to openly discuss this history and see, once again, that there is no peace without justice.

Patience A. Schenck

We appreciate your feelings about the tragedy. We have told in detail how it was on December 7, 1941 to so many younger members of our family and friends. They are eager for every detail. We tell them that day changed our lives forever in every way, and the lives of all Americans, but that it was not nearly as awful and scary as this event. However, our efforts and our feelings are the same as they have been; urging caution by our government but seeking out and demolishing the terrorists without condemning a whole country and culture. We have plenty of terrorists in our own culture. It would all be so easy if we could isolate evil in one person, one movement, one country, one culture and eradicate it, but that is not possible. Evil resides in the hearts of all of us and raises its ugly head at inopportune moments.

Tom and Lorna Knowlton, Boulder (CO)

THE QUAKER ECONOMIST

September 24, 2001

Letter No. 23

Dear friends:

Pacifism in the Face of Terror (Continued)

Quakers especially have been doing a lot of introspection about the responsibility of the United States for the Tuesday attacks. Since World War II our Congress has abdicated to the President the initiative to invade or bomb many places around the world, on his own say-so alone. Especially we are conscious of the bombing of Iraq and the foreign aid and support for Israel as it continues to encroach upon Palestinian territory. While our government has officially disapproved of Israel's new settlements, we have not told them emphatically **NO,** we will not support you if you do that. I believe the Palestinians should have a separate state with a firm boundary, probably the one approved by the United Nations in 1947 (which the Palestinians rejected, but they might accept it now). Our government should insist upon that.

However, those who call us "The Great Satan" have other complaints, many of which – unlike the above - are not true. Those who say "Great Satan" generally do not understand the values of Western society – freedom of speech, democracy, freedom to travel, and the rest. We encourage this misunderstanding when Quakers repeat the statements reproduced below, which were collected by Janet Minshall, co-editor of "The Friendly Woman" and a member of the CLQ editorial board. She heard all the following statements by prominent Quakers, investigated them, and published her findings this year in "The Friendly Woman," vol 14:5. We re-publish them with her permission:

1. "The Capitalist system under which we now live has created a great disparity of resources between rich and poor."

Not so. Capitalism, throughout its more than 300-year history, has steadily narrowed the gap between rich and poor. Merchant capitalism, the precursor of our present-day Capitalism, arose out of the breakdown of feudalism in the 13th and 14th Centuries. Merchant capitalism was not Capitalism, but there were relations established between owner and worker which eventually evolved into Capitalism and created the possibility of accumulation of capital by ordinary, untitled people as well as upward financial/social movement which produced the middle class.

From 1973 to 1996 the increase in population in the United States and the demographic bulge it produced augmented the supply of workers. Not enough new jobs were created, so the growth of wages was suppressed. In the boom years of '97, '98 '99, however, all of the shortfall in job creation and wages from the previous 23 years was made up so that we reached very close to full employment at markedly higher wages. In addition, computers produced great increases in efficiency in a short period of time. This has created a concentration of wealth that the market has not yet absorbed by providing super-high salaries for technology workers and an astounding increase in the number of new technology millionaires. Thus innovation, and a fortunate turn in the business cycle, has held the overall relationship between rich and poor in this country relatively steady.

2. "Another significant trend has been the increased poverty of women."

Actually, over the course of Capitalist history, the poverty of women has been steadily decreasing, not increasing. Fundamentalist Islamic societies like Afghanistan's, which have actually gone backwards by restricting the ownership of property by women, are far outweighed by the world's developed and developing economies which, over the past hundred years, have specifically granted women the right to work for pay, to retain control of that pay, and to retain control of any property bought or inherited.

What is increasing (and this is an important point) is population, making it extremely difficult , even with all the economic changes which have benefited women directly, for them to remain above the poverty level. All the additional resources, for example, appropriated for maternal and child health must now be spread over a much larger and still rapidly expanding number of women and children. The world's explosive population growth can be seen as comparable to an epidemic. In countries experiencing an alarming increase in the number of HIV infected persons, even significantly increased allocations of funds for health care cannot keep up with the rapid spread of the disease.

3. "Corporations, especially multinational corporations, are predominantly malevolent and are engaged in illegal practices which do harm to their workers, consumers, and the general public."

In "The Criminal Element", a paper circulated among Quaker e-mail groups about a year ago, Russell Mokhiber and Robert Weissman spoke of "pervasive criminality in the marketplace" and listed one-hundred corporations found guilty of illegal activities worldwide. However, nearly half the corporations listed were not US- based. There are many, many corporations based and originating outside the US which have been or could be charged with illegal activities. To take 50 of them and combine them with 50 US-based corporations found guilty of illegal practices to show "pervasive criminality in the marketplace" is dishonest. What US anti-capitalist and anti-corporate activists have claimed in their writings was that US-based global corporate capitalism was criminal in its activities. Lacking evidence to prove this, they lied with statistics by creating the pool of 100 corporations cited.

In fact, of the 500 largest and most profitable corporations based in the US, represented by the index called the Standard and Poor's (S&P) 500 , slightly more than half can pass a social responsibility screen indicating that they neither make weapons nor parts and supplies for weapons, that they do not make or supply ingredients for alcohol or tobacco products, that they are not involved in any way with gambling or with the nuclear power industry, that they have good records on product quality, consumer relations, environmental performance, employee and community relations, AND that they have positive policies and performance on the hiring and promotion of minorities and women. Think about it, fifty or so US corporations found guilty of illegal activities and more than two-hundred and fifty of the largest and most profitable US corporations which can pass a social responsibility screen. I think that comparison is impressive!

Through socially conscious investing, in which we buy stocks or mutual funds comprised solely of companies which pass a social investment screen, Friends can actively support the many, many good corporate citizens among us.

4. "Friends should not invest or do business in markets in countries with a history of significant human rights and/or women's rights violations."

Actually, there is evidence that investing and doing business in such markets has a significantly positive effect on both the level of human rights in general, and the level of women's rights in particular in those countries. Investment always carries with it the values of the investor. If a foreign company pays women and minorities less for work done, and treats them poorly according to custom, US investment forces them to face the reality that such differential treatment costs the company potential profits. (We've all known ever since we first started talking about prejudice that it is counter-productive and costly. Business has made that realization a part of "good business practices".) Thus positive social changes which would ordinarily take decades or even centuries to evolve are speeded up and reinforced by the introduction of values of equality in the workplace, and those values of equality then spill over into the economy and the society as a whole. While we, living in the US, may not think of US workplaces as particularly egalitarian, by comparison with workplace relations in many other countries, ours are exemplary.

This point touches on another very controversial concern. Often anti-development activists speak out harshly about the need to preserve "traditional beliefs, values and practices" in other societies. Friends have to decide, however, whether they can support those traditional beliefs, values and practices if they involve the subjugation of one group or sex by another, as is often the case. Do we insist on equality only in our own culture and turn away our eyes from the racism, extreme sexual inequality and related oppression in many traditional cultures?

5.   **"The World Trade Organization (WTO) is an elite organization composed of representatives whose participation is determined by how much their governments pay. The WTO meets together periodically to find ways of moving companies and jobs out of the US and circumventing US environmental standards. The WTO should be dismantled and its policies exposed."**

The first sentence of the quote is quite true, but the rest is false. The number of representatives to the WTO is determined by how much a government pays to support the organization. The WTO does not set environmental standards. Each country sets its own standards and chooses how to enforce them. Neither does the WTO suggest the relocation of companies and jobs outside the US. Individual corporations make those changes on the basis of their internal production needs.

Throughout our history monumental changes have occurred as a result of organizational structures developed by and favoring the wealthiest and most powerful men of the dominant culture. The Magna Carta eight hundred years ago, and the Declaration of Independence/US Constitution more than two hundred years ago are but two examples. These dramatic declarations and the organizational structures that developed from them began a process of democratization which eventually resulted in extending to ordinary people rights previously granted only to the privileged. What a mistake it would have been if those initial efforts and organizational structures were overthrown because they did not immediately enfranchise and fully support the interests of the poorest and least powerful.

As for globalization and its effects, Quakers have been very active in promoting globalization and improved trade relations between all the countries of the world at least since WWI. The process of globalization and the acceptance of common standards for trade were seen by Friends as necessary steps toward world peace. But we have recently forgotten our own history and are now following the lead, primarily, of narrowly focused union representatives who care, first and foremost, about preserving the jobs and wages of American workers.

In order for the rest of the world to share in the material advantages and standard of living we have come to enjoy, the kinds of jobs American workers do will have to change. If the unions and their sympathizers spent their time, energy and money retraining American workers in dying "old economy" industries to fill the many unfilled jobs in the "new economy" technology and communications industries the fear level among displaced American workers would diminish dramatically. They would no longer be prompted to demonstrate against globalization and change. Indeed, they would welcome globalization as an expansion of the markets they serve.

Young people graduating from our high schools are not prepared to learn the new skills and more difficult functions required in the jobs actually available now. If the unions and their sympathizers made improvement of the US educational system their highest priority, the US would not have to import huge numbers of highly educated people from other countries. We are, in effect raiding the brain power of the rest of the world in order to make up for the serious inadequacies of our own educational system.

6. "We, as Friends, must support the initiative, called Jubilee 2000, whose focus is to forgive the debts of countries around the world."

It is clear that loans to many Third World or Less Developed Countries (LDCs) were made inappropriately as a result of intense political pressure and/or inaccurate information obtained about the countries' ability to repay. Those loans should most certainly be written off by the lenders as "bad debts" and lending policies should be thoroughly reviewed to preclude repeating the same mistakes in the future. This reality has already been recognized in the highest echelons of global Capitalism as the only practical alternative to resolve the ongoing problem of trying to collect debts which are actually uncollectable.

If a country does not meet the requirements to become a borrower of funds for development, they should have ready access to development grants which do not have to be repaid. Friends need to be strongly supportive of the increased availability of such grants to the poorest countries.

However, if a country legitimately qualifies and applies for a loan, for whatever purpose, that loan should be honored and repaid. Think about the process followed to teach people financial responsibility in this country. Credit is granted in small amounts and then a person's credit limit is increased on the basis of timely and reliable repayment. Is that unfair? Do we encourage young adults just starting out to take on as much debt as possible because the debts they undertake will be "forgiven" anyway? No, that isn't the message we want to send – that isn't the example we want to set.

What happens when well-intentioned people apply for and take on too much debt? We have a process called debt consolidation which allows people to receive free counseling and help on how best to pay off the debts they have contracted. Does it work? People who have been through that process tell me it works very well. If these are the standards that we hold for honoring loans contracted among ourselves, are they not the standards we wish to share with other countries in process of development? Anything less would be patronizing!

In addition, holding countries to their contracts to repay the debts they owe will work far better than wars to unseat exploitative leaders who divert resources aimed at bettering the lives of their people into their own pockets. Already, several less developed countries have arrested former leaders and officials and confiscated assets to regain control of their economies.

MY NOTE: The above was written by Janet Minshall. I add only that those Friends who, in all good conscience and spirit, repeat these falsities unwittingly encourage the enemies of our way of life.

> Love and Peace,
>> Jack

READERS' COMMENTS ON LETTER NO. 23

One of the truly disturbing after-effects of the September 11 bombing has been the efforts to "piggy-back" upon a horrible tragedy, and to use what happened as an opportunity to forward a separate, and unrelated agenda. I was extremely disappointed to receive this month's installment of the CLQ precisely because your later comments are so grossly unrelated to the tragedy or your introductory remarks, which reference "Pacifism in the Face of Terror" and "introspection." It is not so much that I disagree with your views (although I do disagree with some), it is that I disagree with using September 11th as a platform to raise all of your previous views and disagreements with others. If you want to simply reiterate your views, than do it honestly without reference to the bombing or introspection. If you wish to address the bombing, do so by sharing authentic reactions based upon the event, as I thought you very effectively did last letter [No. 22], rather than trying to squeeze a square peg (your economic views) through a round hole (pacifism in the face of terror).

Ben Barton, Knoxville (TN)

You asked, "What would you do?" For the first time ever, I am holding a public figure in the light, namely, George W. Bush. As of this writing, he has not ordered anything terrible, and I suppose it has been necessary to send out the military to convince the masses that he is doing something. But he has slowed down from his first pronouncements, and I heard him use the word "patience" twice. He showed a capacity for change by stopping his drinking when he became a born-again Christian.

Now he is hearing other points of view of the world, as dignitaries from other countries parade through the White House—people he never had to consider when he was governor. Maybe he will learn that slow, patient, nonviolent methods will triumph in the long run.

Virginia Flagg, San Diego (CA) Friends Meeting

You say: "Those who say "Great Satan" generally do not understand the values of Western society — freedom of speech, democracy, freedom to travel, and the rest." For some, yes, but I think that many see these things as a threat. That underlies fundamentalist Christian rejection of them as well. There are opposing world-views at work here: 1) the view that humankind is basically evil and can't be trusted without rigorous guidance and magic salvation (adhered to by many fundamentalists), 2) the view that humankind is basically good and can work things out with the help of intelligence (adhered to by many liberal Quakers), and 3) the view that humans have the potential for either good or evil and often need healing from the latter (adhered to by some people I know, including myself). Discussions that don't acknowledge, as most don't, these differences, get mired in incredulous misunderstanding and the view of the other as an evil person.

On the WTO: I am less sanguine about the good results of elites than you are, and point to your own "Centuries of Economic Endeavor" (Michigan 1992) for support. The peasants, whom one would hardly describe as an elite, got leverage from the struggles of opposing elites. It was vital that the viewpoint of non-elites was somehow represented. And I think that is what is going on here too. The protesters play a vital role, and they are affecting the thinking of the elites.

Bruce Hawkins, Northampton (MA) Friends Meeting

Jack, may I have permission to reprint this [Letter No. 23] on an Internet newsgroup for discussion there? I've been called to task as a Quaker the past few weeks (as have we all) and I'd like to use your essay as a point to begin discussion, if I may.

Tracy Vanderhoop, Boulder (CO) Meeting of Friends

On Fresh Air, (NPR Interview Program), Terry Gross asked Richard Reeves (a regular sojourner in Pakistan as well as reporter and commentator), "Why do they hate us?" I was surprised by his answer - "The first thing America does when it comes into a country is try to educate the women." If this is an important reason for hatred of the US - and it was the ONLY reason he gave - then we may have to admit that people may hate us because of beliefs and practices that we can't give up without ceasing to meet our own ideals, and our own sense of what really is right.

Is educating women and raising their status the same as requiring indigenous people to give up their religions and practices to become "Christian?" Is this the same as asking people in tropical countries to dress in European clothing? We had better answer this question.

Gusten Lutter, Mountain View Meeting, Denver (CO)

Do these teachings [Christian and Jewish] require us to suffer abuse without defending ourselves? The answer, I believe, comes from the Jewish tradition. A friend sent me this quotation from Chockmat Halev that seems to chart out what it means to take strong and determined action that is in line with spiritually developed consciousness.

"The Torah path is not a pacifist path, it is a warrior path. We are permitted to fight. But we are forbidden to hate."

Dick Bellin, Friends Meeting of Washington (DC)

The day before the attack on the WTC and the Pentagon I was putting together a piece for the upcoming issue of *Friendly Woman*. It was about the experiences of a 77 year-old Quaker woman from Yellow Springs, Ohio, who is presently serving time in federal prison for her protests against the School of The Americas (SOA), renamed this year Western Hemisphere Institute for Security Cooperation (WHISC), at Fort Benning, Georgia.

She provides graphic and terribly disturbing eyewitness accounts of what troops from Central America have done to their own people after training at the SOA. SOA training has included instruction in political assassination and counter-insurgency tactics used to keep protesting people from overthrowing the repressive governments of their countries.

Janet Minshall, Anneewakee Creek Friends Worship Group, Douglasville (GA)

The action by Israel since the 1967 war to place outposts of its people and army in areas where invasions occurred was a minimal step taken to provide more warning time and defense in the event of other attacks. Since the peace process began and land and cities were returned to the Palestinian Authority, the issue of abandoning settlements has been on the negotiating table. There is substantial support in Israel and abroad to remove settlements. To have the US government dictate terms on settlements would be the height of presumption; it would represent the kind of imperial attitude that other nations must do what we want or else. I do not believe that is the Quaker way.

You object to Israeli incursions into neighboring cities under Palestinian control from which terrorist organizations have continually terrorized Israel; and you object to protecting the rights of Israelis to live in settlement areas controlled by a neighbor state. What would you have the Israelis do: give back the settlements and hope for the end of Palestinian attacks in Israel? Or would you insist on credible evidence that such peace would prevail? Do we have such evidence?

Donald Green, San Francisco, a pacifist during the Korean War, too young to be drafted. I worked with my friend Jack Powelson in Bolivia and have loving memories of our families' longer time together in Washington DC. My son's family in Israel will soon be waiting for their father's return from annual military service. He and we want a peaceful resolution to the conflict there more than anyone I know. Cutting off aid to Israel will not help.

In general I agree with Jack. I was a combat infantry soldier in WWII. I did some unspeakable thing. I saw Hiroshima a couple of weeks after it was bombed. I saw the awful suffering. When we put our garbage cans out, the Japanese would dive in and eat raw garbage. I made friends with Japanese individuals. I came home and joined Friends. The suffering of those in New

York is no different. We must bring people to justice. We must change attitudes, and mine was changed. A huge challenge. Violence will not do it.

Lee B. Thomas, Jr

The U.S. military budget proposed for FY2002 is about $345 billion (not including the "black or unseen secret budgets"). For illustration, if one takes as half the world in poverty or severely economically stressed condition, or about 3 billion people, that U.S. military investment is about equivalent to $115 per each of those people. If we could ever redirect our "investment" that would equate to somewhere around $600-$700 per poor family (per year). Given that many families in undeveloped country don't make even that much in a year, think of the boost that could be provided to individual sustainability or starting of family owned businesses through micro loans of this magnitude. It would be tricky in actual implementation because there are many national governments that don't really want to empower the poor. This simple example does illustrate what I believe to be our overall misallocation of wealth. If we invested in building peace even a portion of what we invest in military dominance (and waste), I firmly believe we would have a more secure world.

Rich Andrews, Friends Meeting of Boulder (CO)

In the seventies I was on the Regional board of the AFSC and I remember hearing the young people reporting on their encounter with the police during a peace march. I was surprised that the attitude they displayed was no more loving for their neighbor, the police, than the police's attitude toward them. As I thought about this I came to the conclusion that it wasn't politics or economics that would change people into peaceful neighbors but a fundamental change of attitudes and motivations. It was in trying to imagine how such a change could be brought about that I arrived at the basis of my concept of how a world community could be built on love.

Lyle E. Smith, Motor Friends Church, Milo (IA)

Most are touting the numbers killed as the reason to be so upset. But to me, a single soul's journey that is ended by another's violence is violence against us all.

Free Polazzo, Anneewakee Creek Friends Worship Group, Douglasville (GA)

THE QUAKER ECONOMIST
October 3, 2001

Letter No. 24

Dear friends:

Why Do They Hate Us?

The Christian Science Monitor (9/27/01) tells why:

All the way from Jakarta to Cairo . . . a mood of resentment toward America and its behavior around the world has become so commonplace that it was bound to breed hostility, and even hatred. And the buttons that Mr. bin Laden pushes in his statements and interviews - the injustice done to the Palestinians, the cruelty of continued sanctions against Iraq, the presence of US troops in Saudi Arabia, the repressive and corrupt nature of US-backed Gulf governments - win a good deal of popular sympathy.

Here is a quotation from USA Today (9/27/01):

One student's vow: "I will get your children!"

Peshawar, Pakistan — Morning at the Dar-ul-uloom Haqqania madrassa, or religious school, begins with a prayer and a defiant chant: "Oh Allah, defeat the enemies of the Muslims and make Islam and the Taliban victorious over the Americans in Afghanistan," the 3,500 students say in unison in the school's courtyard. Then they break into a chorus of "Jihad! Jihad!" or "Holy War! Holy War!" Their words bring a smile to the face of the school's chancellor, Maulama Sami ul Haq. . . "Osama and the Taliban would be proud," he says.

Have you seen the pictures of crowds of happy Middle Easterners, faces bursting out in smiles, as they cheer what to us was an overwhelming tragedy?

Are there any other reasons?

Long before the tragedy of September 11, I have been aware that we are hated from all over the world. I spent ten years communicating with

Latin American Marxists who hated America, and who said that if they had the chance they would have joined Che Guevara to promote guerrilla actions against the Capitalist system. The points in Janet Minshall's essay in Letter No. 23 are the very ones they raised. (See Letter No. 16, "My Ten Years in Marxistland," at http://clq.quaker.org.)

Universities in Latin America (in their economics, sociology, and political science departments anyway) — and I presume the Middle East as well — are full of students who hate America. I have taught them and discussed with them. Our economic might is hated all over the world, and it is this hatred that we must overcome if we are to be secure.

One reader of CLQ chided me for using the tragedy to propagate my economic views (see Readers' Comments, below). But I truly believe they are related. The hatred stemming from our actions in the Middle East is but another layer built upon the solid base of hatred because of our economic and military power.

A complex hatred

The main thread linking all these reasons for hate is the wealth and power of the United States. If it were solely the arrogance with which we flaunt our power, the Islamic countries would be even more guilty: consider how the Taliban has brought Afghanistan to abject poverty and stoned women to death for disobeying their creed; how clerics have denied democracy to Iranians who cry out for it; how Saddam Hussein invaded Kuwait; and - farther back in history - how the Islamic peoples conquered from Poitiers, France through Spain, North Africa, into India, and all the way to the Philippines. They have been just as arrogant as we have, much more oppressive, and much more imperialistic. The main difference is that we have been successful economically, and they have not.

This is the first time in our history that we have felt hated. In the next Letter (No. 25), I would like to offer some thoughts about how this complex syndrome was brought about.

What to do about it?

In the short run, we must (1) Bring the criminals to justice, by the usual means of doing so. With international cooperation, infiltrate their ranks, and keep them on the Most Wanted List. (2) Draw on the many peace-loving Muslims to support us in rooting out the terrorists. (3) Tighten security in the airlines; follow El Al's example. (4) Prepare for an entirely different attack - not on an airplane.

Still, remember: The Islamic empire, during its heyday, offered most or all of the freedoms we are accustomed to in the West, including freedom of religion and freedom to trade. Islam is a religion of peace. Most of the world - including Muslims - does not want to live by the rules of terror. Therefore, the long run is on our side.

For the long run, we must teach our children humility. We must expand our trade and contacts with those who hate us. Student exchanges, living abroad, and all those. But most of all, we must trade with them. Drop our barriers against less developed countries. Support the World Trade Organization as an international body in which these barriers may be negotiated away.

What would you do?

> In Peace,
>
> Jack Powelson

READERS' COMMENTS ON LETTER NO. 24

When you mention the schoolkids in Peshawar screaming " Jihad!, Jihad", my mind wandered back to the the times of the *Hitlerjugend* and their Satanically-gripped mentors who learned in the saddest, most destructive manner the wrongness of their beliefs. We must all pray without ceasing that some of these children are not placed with Kalishnikovs before Abrams tanks. And don't think that something like this can't happen.

Maurice Boyd, Friends Meeting of Washington (DC)

In a society whose all-male power structure regards women as chattel to be treated in any way the whims of her male superiors lead them, it would not surprise me at all that they would find the egalitarian, democratic, secular Western society unsupportably offensive. So it is all very fine to hear that Islam as a religion is gentle, nonviolent abhorrent of murder, etc., etc... But, I think the place of women can't be anything but a nearly unbridgeable chasm between their world and ours. The upshot is that the posture of the West and the USA in particular should be to mend ways the Muslim world finds offensive wherever possible, but to be prepared for a long face-off resulting from almost irreconcilably different values, particularly as they relate to the place of women in society.

Tom Todd, Jamestown (RI)

One of the corollaries of living in an economically and politically unsuc-cessful region is powerlessness. Another is being ruled by unscrupulous bastards who have inordinate power over you. Both these things tend (I suspect) to make people less likely to compromise, and more likely to seek violent solutions. I think this holds even for the wealthier individuals like bin Laden. Because it has less to do with the individual's wealth or poverty, and more to do with the overall "social capital" of the system, the simple transfers of wealth from our regions to theirs that some are suggesting will do nothing (I believe that support for educational institutions and health care could help, however).

Geoffrey Williams, Bethesda (MD) Friends Meeting

The arrogance the US is accused of is entering other territories and creat-ing death and harsh conditions when they could have done that better for themselves unmolested. The Taliban creates their own misery in the belief they are enforcing fundamentalism. A great difference, though the end re-sult at ground zero may be alike.

Steve Willey, Sandpoint (ID) Friends Meeting

I believe the WTO's ability to reduce hate through trade is mixed at best. A large part of the fundamentalist's complaint is the westernization of their culture, which the WTO promotes through increasing access to markets for Hollywood and McDonalds.

Larry Powelson, Seattle (WA)

THE QUAKER ECONOMIST
October 11, 2001

Letter No. 25

Dear friends:

American Imperialists.
Is Quaker Righteousness - Away from Home - also Imperialism?

Just when Americans and British began bombing Afghanistan, I received the following from J.D. von Pischke, my good friend and editorial board member. It made me wonder how our incursions into the cultures of other nations - including incursions by Quakers - may have affected their liking (or hatred) for us.

J.D. writes: "Little by little, through peaceful official intervention (USAID and its servants the NGOs and the consulting firms, the World Bank, etc.) and through military adventures (Lebanon, Dominican Republic, Granada, Panama, Sudan, Iraq, Afghanistan, Libya, Haiti, Somalia, Serbia, Kosovo and still counting) the West, with the US at the top of the pile, has made extraterritoriality a reasonable proposition in the popular mind here at home. Is this contemporary imperialism?

"What is being promoted by the US and by much of the rest of the West? That women should have the same rights all around the world, consistent with our standards. That everyone should be able to vote in free elections. That you should live up to our fair labor standards or we won't buy from you. That family planning should be an entitlement. That debts of corrupt rulers should be forgiven. That everyone should have health care. That all should have healthy diets, often supplied by others.

"Still more: That structural adjustment engineered by technocrats in Washington can improve your poor economy. That sanctions are acceptable and even patriotic responses. That making certain types of narcotics illegal in the US gives us the right to intervene in controlling the crops farmers can plant in the Andes, and to help determine the size of the military in Colombia. That all banks of any reasonable size around the world have to meet our standards and report to our authorities. On and on the list goes.

"While each of these efforts has a certain logic and may in certain cases - or even frequently - be just and useful, why do we make it our business? How are we, in these dimensions, promoting the do-it-yourself efforts of ordinary people that Jack credits as the one and only historical basis of prosperity? In his book, *Centuries of Economic Endeavor,* Jack attributes the remarkable development of the Western world and Japan to the fact that they not only did it themselves, they *thought* of it themselves.

"By trying to make other nations model themselves after the United States and its values as suggested by the examples given above, are we changing their hearts and minds, or do we cause them – or those in authority - to hate us all the more? In all the above, I have intermingled ideas that come from Quakers (and the "Liberal Left") with those that come from our government. So, do not many Quakers and our military come from the same culture of extraterritoriality, equally insistent on imposing our ideas (good or bad) upon the rest of the world?

"Exercising extraterritoriality is not at all what the Founders had in mind when our rights as Americans were defined. According to them, the President needed a Congressional Declaration of War to engage troops against a foreign state, whereas today a call from the White House to the Pentagon can do the trick. The original idea seemed to be that an independent nation open to trade with all on the same terms would be regarded as a good citizen among nations, and this would enable it to function peacefully without maintaining a large defense force. It would not attract others to attack us, nor would it attack except in extraordinary circumstances, which would be retaliatory (e.g., against the Barbary pirates). In short, the Founders wanted to take away the occasion for foreign wars and were quite clear on how to go about it.

"Switzerland may be the closest to this model today. Canada likewise, but it may be a free rider in North American defense. New Zealand may be another approximation, and Costa Rica, too. Although the comparison can be overdrawn, the ideal role of such countries in the global community may be similar to the original role of Quakers: voices of conscience, providers of humanitarian assistance, searchers for peaceful means of conflict resolution, protectors of innocent fugitives, etc.

"Would it be possible for us to remain a free nation (or to hold on to whatever may be left of it) by trading peacefully, without using official means to tell others how to live, and without having to bomb and invade? Could this be a Quaker vision, even though we as a nation (but not necessarily we as individuals) would have to stand by as innocent people in poor countries suffered? Or, are we willing to accept the use of force if force alone seems to protect innocent people? Under what conditions might some of these concerns be acceptable or objectionable to us?

"If we could disengage from our current, taxpayer-funded, adventures in extraterritoriality - including those advocated by the Liberal Left and the Quakers among them, as well as the Pentagon – then I should think the hatred against us would diminish over some reasonable period, such as a century, i.e., roughly the length of time it took the US to forget about the Civil War. This period could also permit civil society in poor countries to move ahead through power diffusion and crafting institutions they could call their own, just as Jack calls for in *Centuries of Economic Endeavor.*

"Please note: I advocate humanitarian assistance, at a level that keeps people alive, in all cases in which it can be delivered to ports or air fields by commercial or other private carriers and distributed by unarmed volunteers whose violent deaths would not constitute a reason for retaliatory military action, i.e., they would be a sort of suicide bomber in reverse, causing no harm except to themselves. This approach would constitute a minimalist extraterritoriality that attempts to impose no particular values while of course implying some very particular ones."

(End of message by J.D. von Pischke, a Friend from Reston, VA.)

Yours for Peace,
Jack Powelson

READERS' COMMENTS ON LETTER NO. 25

JD's proposal is both inviting and thought-provoking, but a few questions bother me: (1) While a lot of trade has, I think, the beneficent effects that Jack and others mention, our purchases of oil to a large extent line the pockets of kleptocratic foreign regimes. There is little or no favorable spillover in terms of development of civil society. May we not have some responsibility to undercut the adverse effects of this (e.g., as manifested in Iraq's invasion of Kuwait)? (2) JD mentions the Barbary pirates. This seems to have been an early form of state-sponsored terrorism. (At least John Adams negotiated with a sultan who purported to be ready to prevent the pirates from attacking US vessels—for a price.) While the Barbary pirates seem to have been equal-opportunity thugs, unlike al Qaeda, the experience suggests that there may be quite a lot of international predation that in the natural course of events would threaten us (and others). I'm not sure that the current version is so different from that example. And, given our (and others') oil purchases, there is a lot of money floating around in ways likely to flow into the hands of the predators.

Stephen Williams, Bethesda (MD) Meeting

Thanks for sharing von Pischke's letter. Some useful different perspectives on old questions and offering of some new ones.

Don Marsh, Seattle (WA)

Maybe I am naive to think that extraterritoriality can also bring understanding between cultures. Maybe I am naive to think that this shouldn't necessarily mean Imperialism, but can also mean stepping closer to a one-world mentality. Maybe this is a bad thing, but I'd like to think we are one community. For example, I don't feel the need to make my neighbors become Quakers any more than they expect me to convert to Judaism, but I do expect that we learn from one another and practice respect for one another's faith, and I do expect that we will on some basic level of safety and decency, look out for one another. I'd like to think the same is true when we venture out into the world at large. And I'd like to think that basic human rights apply to everyone.

Tracy Vanderhoop, Boulder (CO) Friends Meeting

I have a long list of policies on which I would urge the USA to "mend its every flaw" and most of them are probably the same issues you and others would also change. Regardless of how full the a gunny sack of USA misdeeds is, as our critics emphasize, the basic liberalization of life the USA has assisted over the centuries is a welcome breath of fresh air, and it's a record I'd take over any other country's.

Jim Booth, Red Cedar Meeting, Lansing (MI)

Surely there are situations where intervention is necessary and just, regardless of the beliefs/culture etc on the other side: genocide, for example. International terrorism of the scale we are seeing today would seem to be another. Our problem as a democracy is that things have to get very bad before we are roused to action, and by then it is often too late. (U Thant said, when he retired as UN SecGen, that he felt the biggest problem for the world and the UN in the years ahead would be international terrorism — that was 1972.)

Gordon Johnson, Episcopalian, Northern Virginia

I think to a certain extent, the key question I have about the proposal is: Are we expecting brutality to obey some form of reason (i.e., is America hated because of its interventions, or is it hated because bin Laden's got a screw loose? Would Hutu militias be brought to bear by non-violence as well or better than by a swift military strike at the local radio stations and armories?).

Geoffrey Williams, Bethesda (MD) Meeting

1.) A Saudi prince interviewed in "Frontline" explains that in his country a King must be balanced in his actions and rule fairly or he will (literally) lose his head.

2.) In an interview with a young Arab member of al Qaeda, the bin Laden organization, we are asked sincerely "OK, the US is now the world's super power so why can't you play fair?" Another good question.

Now that the cold war is over and capitalism has proved itself to be the most successful economic system in history — now that we have clearly won — why do we continue to back certain regimes and governments one-sidedly and thus perpetually create very real feelings of unfairness and resentment in those we do not back or back only nominally? Why do we continue to play the old and outmoded form of power politics that is no longer appropriate to our position? Why can't we become the balanced and fair-minded leader that both the Saudi prince and the young terrorist seek?

Janet Minshall, Anneewakee Creek Friends Worship Group, Douglasvillle (GA)

In response to Jim Booth, who wrote: "Think of populations being left behind in some countries rather than being made poor by free trade, multi-national corporations, the WTO, IMF and World Bank as the whipping boys the radical voices usually put forward."

"Left behind" seems to me an optimistic view for Africa, where in many places the lifespan has been going backwards since the spread of AIDS.

Lynn Gazis-Sax, Orange County (CA) Friends Meeting

In my opinion, these poor countries cannot overcome their poverty unless they have a government that promotes the institutions that have to be in place to make the economy work; we have producers, wholesalers, retailers, delivery systems, lending institutions, free markets, small and large businesses, government friendly to the free markets, all the local institutions, access to capital, stock markets, etc, etc. If these poor countries can't understand our system, how can they change their situation??

Herb Clark, Homewood Friends Meeting, Baltimore (MD)

In "Who Says It's Not About Religion?" (*New York Times,* 10/14/01), Andrew Sullivan argues that we in the West may think that this episode through which we are going is only about terrorism and the events that may have fomented it, but that that view is probably not widely held in the Islamic world, and that we had better be prepared for something vastly more difficult.

Tom Todd, Jamestown (RI)

I don't (and didn't) favor many of the actions mentioned in CLQ-25, but I am willing to be enough of an imperialist to have both NGOs and the U. S. government oppose such things as

1. Imposition of criminal sentences without some kind of due process.
2. Denial of education to anyone

I do not ask that they do everything our way.

With respect to banks and other economic institutions, I think it is fair to say, "If you want to do business with us we need a certain amount of transparency and confidence that you adhere to certain standards. If you cannot adhere to these standards our business will probably be limited to cash transactions."

Vici Oshiro, Minneapolis (MN) Friends Meeting

I am in general unity with your proposal for peace in the Middle East, with one small but important point to offer for consideration. The 1947 boundaries were not accepted by the nascent Jewish state's Arab neighbors. In fact, they (Lebanon, Syria, Iraq, Saudi Arabia, Egypt, and Jordan) declared war and attempted to destroy Israel. So, when you write, "they didn't have to go there in the first place", this is a bit misleading. In fact, to maintain a militarily defendable posture in the region, they did have to do some "going there".

1967 is a different story, and Israel has in fact since the 1967 war occupied territory not needed for its survival — in violation of international standards of conduct, and a constant provocation. I thus would use the pre-1967 boundaries as the norm for any Palestinian state.

It is interesting (and frustrating) to imagine: Had Israel's Arab neighbors simply accepted Israel and made a true peace (i.e. formally recognized and had normal commercial and diplomatic relations with Israel) after the 1949 ceasefire, chances are the next 50 years would have looked a lot different (and almost certainly more peaceful).

John Rich, Bethesda (MD) Friends Meeting

Dr. Meeks, a theologian, author of *God the Economist* writes that pure capitalism is severe and "amoral" and that religious values need to be developed to temper it. Hence the reason for doctrines or codes like the Ten Commandments and the Beatitudes which should be viewed as a type of broad economic provincial. He attributes rising international contempt for America to the world's increasing awareness of its general poverty through ever-expanding media and communication, perhaps similar to the racial violence that erupted in this country in the mid to late 1960s.

Joseph Mills, Kalamazoo (MI) Friends Meeting

THE QUAKER ECONOMIST

October 20, 2001

Letter No. 26

Dear friends:

Is Life Sacred?

When Henry V of England besieged Rouen in 1418-19, the starving French inhabitants pushed the noncombatants out of the gates, thinking the English would let them by. But Henry was adamant. He watched women, howling children, and elderly men slowly die of sickness, cold, and starvation in the moat.

In 1572, on St. Bartholomew's day, Charles IX of France ordered the massacre of all Huguenots in France - 3,000 in Paris alone, many thousands killed by mobs elsewhere.

Terrorism abounded in Europe in the Middle Ages. Ships and passengers were massacred by pirates, villages attacked and inhabitants murdered, roads to towns were destroyed and harbors silted to divert commerce from another city to one's own.

Five centuries ago our ancestors dealt with terror daily. So how did it come about that by the end of the twentieth century we trusted our fellow Americans not to terrorize? Haven't we always assumed that competitors would not send us anthrax? (Wasn't Timothy McVeigh an exception?)

But we have learned this year that to many people life is not sacred. However, we suspect such people are not mainly from Western Europe or America. Why?

I believe the sanctity of life comes in degrees. Some find it not sacred at all; they kill for robbery or for hate. At the other extreme is the Buddhist who will not kill any sentient being. In between are most Americans, who would kill to win World War II but who abhor murder. Farther up the scale are Quakers (not all of us) who oppose any use of violence.

How did it come about, that for some people life is more sacred than for others? I think I have some ideas, which are byproducts of quite a different quest. After teaching economic development for thirteen years, in 1970 I cast aside my economics (without forgetting it) and delved into history to seek an answer to why a small portion of the world is rich and a much larger portion poor. Only fifteen years later, after extensive reading, did I sense a reason, and for the next seven years I wrote the book (and five supporting books).

Along the way, I deduced that trust is the essential element in both economic wealth and the sanctity of life. People who trust each other work together for mutual prosperity. They do not kill each other. After undertaking professional assignments in 35 countries of Europe, Asia, Africa, and Latin America, and after reading widely in history, I have concluded that both trust and prosperity are greater in the Western World and Japan than they are in the less developed areas. I believe this is part of the explanation why so many in the world hate us when we do not hate them. How did Europe evolve from the St. Bartholomew massacre to the European Union? Here is how I believe it happened:

First, power was gradually – over centuries – taken away from rulers (kings, emperors, church, shogun, nobility) and made to rest in "lower" classes (merchants, traders, farmers, manufacturers), who seized the opportunity to invent and innovate, and to save and raise capital. The rulers tried to confiscate their product and their capital, but they did not usually succeed. Keeping the profits for the producer was a prime incentive.

Second, power diffusion occurred because the elite classes were in conflict with each other, and the lower classes could swing the balance one way or another, always demanding a share of power in return. If their side lost, they would bide their time until the next occasion. I found many, many such instances in northwestern Europe and Japan, and very few in the rest of the world.

Third, the innovators of northwestern Europe traded widely. They negotiated the rules of trade, debt repayment, and property ownership among themselves, not allowing the ruler to impose them. By practicing these rules, they developed trust for each other.

Fourth, except for Japan, this power diffusion did not occur in Asia, the Middle East, Africa and eastern and southern Europe. It did not occur in Islamic countries. Power is still concentrated in the elites of these regions, who not only treat their people brutally but suppress innovation by workers, teachers, and farmers. They are afraid innovators would take power from them. Social classes are hierarchical and do not trust each other up and down the ladder.

This is a brief summary, from which I have omitted many qualifications. I do not encourage you to read my book, *Centuries of Economic Endeavor* (Michigan 1992), which contains more history than most of you want to know. I only ask you to understand that my beliefs spring from historical research and experience. (If you insist, however, I will send you a copy for $15, plus $2 shipping – that's at author's discount of 40%. See address below).

Did we become rich through imperialism?

The greatest imperialists of the last twenty centuries were Rome, Russia, Spain, Portugal, Ottoman Turkey, Mongolia, the Incas, the Aztecs, and Islam. Africa and the Middle East employed slave labor as far back as history goes. None of these areas became wealthy. On the contrary, it was the Europeans who ended official slavery in Africa (though it continues today in Mauritania and Sudan.)

Europeans were imperialists, but that is not how they gained their wealth. In the now-more-developed countries, wealth accumulation correlates far more closely with inventiveness, innovation, saving, and capital building than it does with imperialism. They did not get rich by stealing from the poor. Northwestern Europe was well on its way to economic success long before Africa was colonized. (Some historians put the beginnings of European ascendancy as far back as 1000 CE).

If not for plunder, why did northern Europeans colonize? Mainly because Asia and Africa did not live by European rules - piracy abounded, contracts were not honored, property was seized, and so on. (It was different for Spain and Portugal; they did plunder the Americas). But northern Europeans wanted to trade, and only part of the world lived by their principles. The French colonized Algeria in 1830 to get rid of the Barbary pirates; they did not foresee the bloodshed of the next century. The British colonized

India for trade, and Kenya to secure their trade routes to India. (How do I know? I have read the works of historians who examined the documents of the time.)

ITTSL - innovation, trade, trust , and the sanctity of life - go together. They are the principal elements common to more developed countries. They are not found significantly in the less developed. ITTSL are also associated with increasing equality in income distribution, increasing acceptance of other ethnic groups, increasing attention to the environment, increasing compassion for the less-well-off, and increasing desire for peace. From this, I conclude that ITTSL are the forces to be concentrated on, if we wish also to promote the higher incomes, fairness in their distribution, and pro-tection of the earth.

What can Quakers do?

The rest of the country is raising flags and repeating the war cries. I am patriotic, but I will not raise a flag or sing about bombs bursting in air. What is the Quaker counterpart of all this?

Quakers must understand that our country is not evil (compared to the rest of the world), that we did not gain our wealth by exploitation but mainly by inventiveness, that our wealth is more evenly distributed than in the less developed countries, and that our freedoms, including the freedom to trade, are associated with both our wealth and our trust for each other. I do not say we never plundered (our record with Native Americans is abysmal), only that we are far from the worst in world history and our wealth did not come from colonialism.

After the September 11 tragedy, we must also understand that - except in wartime - the sanctity of life is more highly valued in the West than in the less developed world. I will gladly come and talk with any group that wishes to question these points. (This month I will discuss them at Swarthmore College, probably Pendle Hill, and at World Learning in Vermont.)

We must understand that other parts of the world are not as wealthy as we are and cannot afford our luxuries. We must drop our extraterritorial de-mands (see Letter No. 25) by which we demand that others live by "Ameri-can" standards. We must be patient while they gradually think up work rules, rights for women, environmental protections, and other ways of life that are practiced by the rich. We must teach our fellow citizens to be humble about our wealth, to be willing to sacrifice so that jobs may be created in other parts of the world, and to trade with other nations, to create international trust. Above all, we must value the sanctity of life.

Let us criticize our country freely, remembering that most of the world would risk torture and death for criticizing theirs. But where our country does not deserve criticism, let us not invent it. Quakers must overcome our need for guilt.

In peace,

Jack Powelson
4875 Sioux Drive #001
Boulder CO 80303
Phone 720-304-7175
Email: jack.powelson@colorado.edu

READERS' RESPONSES TO LETTER NO. 26

On an African development mailing list, yakub2222@hotmail.com writes "..most of the upper class in Africa do not know how to reach out to the poor. Both the poor and their rich patrons soon find out that the reward system relies largely on connections and restricts the lower class' social mobility and entrepreneurial success, even after having been equipped with education and technical skills."

It was once that way in Europe as well. What is different about Africa? I think this question is answered well enough by Jack Powelson's book *Centuries of Economic Endeavor,* which is described in CLQ Letter No. 26. In northwestern Europe and Japan, for geographic reasons the rich and poor could not escape each other, so they had to cooperate.

In Africa, and Asia, the population was more mobile, and the poor could simply walk away from trouble. They didn't need the elites, and the elites didn't need them. The power-sharing opportunities didn't occur, and so no middle class has arisen.

Russ Nelson, St. Lawrence Valley (NY) Friends Meeting

It is unclear exactly how diffused power was in these [early] societies, but the October issue of National Geographic repeated an indicative fact I'd heard previously: the tax rate on "peasants" during the Han Dynasty was only 3%. This is not surprising from an elite whose Taoist motto roughly translates to "rule as unobstructively as possible". Such a policy seems to put more economic power in the hands of the lowest classes than any nation in "the west" ever did.

Patrick Koppula, Golden Gate Lutheran Church in San Francisco, graduate of Moorestown (MJ) Friends School

NOTE by Jack: It is my understanding that "peasants" during the Han Dynasty (206 BC to 220 AD) lived under the strict authority of the central government. According to the Encyclopedia Britannica, "the Han adopted a Confucian ideology that emphasized moderation and virtue and thereby masked the authoritarian policies of the regime." When one responds to an authoritarian ruler, the nominal tax rate does not matter.

THE QUAKER ECONOMIST
November 5, 2001

Letter No. 27

Dear Friends:

Pacifism in the Face of Terror (Continued)

When I wrote Letter No. 22 on Pacifism, I was too shocked by the Tragedy of September 11 to express myself clearly. Now I have had time to give some thought to my position as a Pacifist.

I believe that whoever is a conscientious objector when his or her country is at war ought to have an alternative plan - something beyond "Don't bomb Afghanistan." Pacifism means "make peace." from the Latin, Pax (peace) and Facere (to make). I emphasize the "make."

Let us begin with common objectives. I think virtually all Americans (and surely all Quakers) believe in the following:

(1) The perpetrators of the crimes of September 11 should be captured and punished.

(2) Precautions must be taken so that similar actions do not occur, in so far as is possible.

(3) Promote all means of communication. For example, World Learning (in Brattleboro VT), which I visited last week, brings young Israelis and Palestinians together to become friends and discuss their problems. They do the same for North Ireland Catholics and Protestants.

Beyond these points, we may not agree. Here is my proposal:

(1) Stop bombing Afghanistan. (We never should have begun).

(2) The common objectives should be agreed as binding by as many governments as are willing to accept them.

(3) Any attack on civilians shall hereafter be illegal under international law. (I hold this as absolute. Some, believing the bombing of Germany and Japan was legitimate to win World War II, will wish to confine it to a nation with which one is nominally at peace). It should apply to all guerrilla actions in the Middle East and North Ireland, no matter which side commits them. These attacks should be just as illegal, and just as much

prosecuted, as the attacks of September 11 in New York and on the Pentagon.

(4) Any nation agreeing to these principles shall have the right to apprehend, try, and convict those who commit such acts, when evidence of their guilt is agreed by an international assembly acting as a grand jury (deciding whether to indict). This principle applies whether the suspect is an ordinary citizen or the Prime Minister or Leader of any people. (The Milosevic case is a precedent.) But in so acting, no nation shall have the right to harm any civilian.

(5) Covert action by intelligence agencies would be an appropriate means of detection, just as covert action may be used within a nation to apprehend a suspected criminal.

(6) The United States, Western Europe, and Japan should promote the development of solar cells and photovoltaic cells as rapidly as possible, to rid ourselves of dependency on oil for energy (and on Saudi Arabia in particular). The technology for both of these is available now; we are just unwilling to pay the price (but we seem willing to pay the price of war).

(7) All mail in the United States should be subject to irradiation to kill anthrax and other bacteria. This will not be cheap, but life is not cheap either. Private services such as Fed Ex might begin this on an optional basis as "good business."

(8) When a means of terrorism (hijacking, anthrax, etc.) is found to be not cost effective, we can count on its being stopped. Our major effort should be toward making terrorism more costly to the terrorists.

Still beyond these points, I propose the following:

(1) Despite denials by the Israeli government and many Jewish citizens in the United States, American support of Israel is a principal focus of the current crisis. (Not all feel that way; there is a peace movement in each country). We should no longer send arms to Israel (or anywhere else, for that matter). Likewise, our support for governments that commit crimes against humanity should be withdrawn, and our military presence in Saudi Arabia should be removed. (As Steve Williams pointed out in his response following Letter 26, buying oil provides funds passed on to terrorists.)

(2) Israel and Palestine have had over fifty years to reconcile their controversy. The United Nations should agree that this is long enough and impose its own solution. This would include the declaration of a Palestinian state and international supervision of elections. It might - though as a Pacifist I shudder at this - include sending U.N. soldiers to monitor and

protect the boundary between Israel and Palestine.

     (3) Non-military sanctions against Iraq should be ended. They have done no good. (Readers probably know that I oppose sanctions in principle, anywhere, since depriving people of their livelihood is to me only one step away from killing them in war.)

Obviously, my proposal will not be widely accepted. My only justification for it is that I would not be true to myself if I am only a conscientious objector to this war. To validate that position, I must hold in mind an alternative, whether it would be widely accepted or not. (I had an analogous alternative in mind during World War II).

President Bush is conducting World War II all over again, when the object was to win - to occupy the territory of the enemy. Whatever "enemy" we have now cannot be defeated in the same way. The terrorists' purpose may be to destroy our society, but I believe they do not want to govern our territory. Such a "war" demands a totally different approach (the one I just outlined) from the one we are taking.

Surely you will find reasons why my proposal would not work. That is all right. If so, however, please suggest something better. If you are a conscientious objector to bombing in Afghanistan, what is your pacifist alternative? Let us use the pages of CLQ to discuss these questions (though not exclusively; the world has other problems as well).

                    Yours in Peace,
                        Jack Powelson

READERS' RESPONSES TO LETTER NO. 27 ON PACIFISM

I have just read your letter 27, and was delighted to see a written expression that was very close to my thinking, plus adding some new insights. The only missing element was a stated objective to achieve our former position in the world enjoyed briefly after World War II when all other peoples thought we were great benefactors and leaders. Despite bombing civilian populations in Germany and Japan, we then went in and helped them rebuild their countries so that they became effectively working democracies and our best friends. Ever since, we have been arrogantly bombing where we pleased, and then leaving the population to rot in the ruins. And most of our "Foreign Aid" has been US weapons.

Joe Willits, Los Altos Hills, CA

The image that sticks with me is the fighter jets that scrambled after the jets hadbeen hijacked. If I had been in one of those fighter jets, or in some other way had had the potential to destroy one of the planes before they hit their target, I would have done so. I think the killing of innocents would be counterbalanced by the opportunity to save the lives of others.

If you agree to that choice, then you are admitting that there are circumstances that justify lethal force - to paraphrase Shaw, the rest is simply discussing the price. Even in the case of your proposal for international legal action, the need for lethal force would remain.

I still believe that moral and ethical persuasion should be used whenever possible with any person or persons who threaten us, sometimes it simply is not possible. In some of those cases, I think it may be moral to move beyond moral persuasion and to use physical violence to thwart the goals of people who would cause damage to others, and to risk the lives of innocents to protect some larger good. But I'm still conflicted and unsure what is the best way.

Geoffrey Williams, Bethesda (MD) Friends Meeting

NOTE by Jack: How would you know whether it was about to hit a target, and which one?

By jolley, Jack, you are full of surprises. Your statement of 11/5 puts it together superbly. You are becoming a radical liberal after all.

I support your proposals. Not just because you mentioned solar electric generation, my work. The absolute prohibition or illegality of purposely doing harm to individuals for any reason, any time or place is what the world needs to stop terrorism in all its forms. Most citizens of every country would not want to harm their neighbors, and would attempt to rescue a neighbor from drowning or house fire. When these same majorities everywhere see someone making or preparing to use a bomb or other preparation to do harm, and feels the personal responsibility to get help and get it stopped, and when that help is available, only then can we get control of terrorism. And it matters not whether the bomb maker is a "crazy" man down the street, or wears the uniform of your own country.

Steve Willey, Sandpoint (ID) Friends Meeting

QUESTION for Steve: Thanks for your support. BUT: Are pacifism and radical liberal thought melded? Can one be a classic liberal and a pacifist at the same time?

Your ideas on peacemaking all rest on the assumptions (1) that the sides in conflicts are morally equivalent, and (2) that the sides are equally likely to be brought to justice. Both of these assumptions are mistaken. To take the most controversial example of number (1), the position of the Arabs is that Israel should not exist; their goal is to end its existence. Israel's position is that is should coexist with its neighbors. It is difficult to see how more communication is going to change this, or how a UN solution would change the minds of the Arabs. It reminds me of a compromise with Hitler: Hitler wants to kill all the Jews, I want none to be killed; so Hitler gets to kill half the Jews. (I do believe that a prolonged effort to show the Arabs the benefits of freedom will work in the long run, but not in the short term we are dealing with.)

Judy Warner, Lutheran, Rohrersville, Maryland

Your point #4 (of the second batch) is fraught with booby traps. I can see Iraq, for example, arresting and trying an American citizen on whatever "war crime" they might conjure up to fit the situation, and the U.S. being unable to come to the aid of its citizen because it is party to an international agreement that countries can arrest and try individuals they deem to be terrorist criminals. It gets close to home. I, for example, after the revolution in Iran, was tried along with my partners (in absentia I hasten to add) in an Iranian court, found guilty and condemned to death for "defrauding" the State of Iran of large sums of money. Needless to say, I never expect to go to Iran. But, suppose they had the right, by international agreement, to demand the extradition of the citizens of another state to stand trial in Iran? I shudder to think of it. While I agree in principle with almost all of your proposals, the terms of their execution would need to be studied with cautious and careful attention.

Tom Todd (Jack's brother-in-law), Jamestown RI

I liked Letter 27 so much that I have copied it to reread and share. I believe I am in 100% agreement! Maybe on closer study I'll take exception to something - but not at this point!

Lois Jordan, New Castle Friends Meeting, Indiana

Why would a pacifist object to a permanent U.N. peacekeeping force in Palestine if they would do it, which is dubious anyway? Isn't that the purpose of the U.N.? Perhaps the best solution is to admit any and all Israelis to Florida, and cease funding of the current Israel by the U.S. Exodus III.

Maurice Boyd, Friends Meeting of Washington (DC)

I agree with your proposals. I have been thinking along the same lines. We should pursue and prosecute the terrorists in the same way that we would pursue any international criminals. After all, one murder by one individual, for whatever the motivation, is a kind of terrorist act. But by bombing Afghanistan, we are recruiting more terrorists.

Virginia Flagg, San Diego (CA) Friends Meeting

I find this so helpful, Jack. Especially living as I do in an environment where not everyone agrees with this proposal. And many feel more bombing would be better.

Sigh. At school, almost all the children have been told to hit back and hit back harder. Such advice does not produce a peaceful atmosphere.

Faith Williams, Bethesda (MD) Friends Meeting

NOTE: Faith is librarian at an inner-city school in Washington, D.C.

What the people under Osama are doing, are what they feel is right. They are not guilty, by any means. They have grown up in a world that has taught them, and shown to them, that extreme measures are required to achieve their goals. They are fighting against the evil United States, in their eyes. They are doing the just and right thing, by killing Americans. And we have our own beliefs, from what we have experienced in our society and the world.

Tony R.

Here in Louisville there is to be a Thanksgiving dinner for the "Children of Abraham." Thus Islamic, Jews and Christians will break bread together. I wish the Buddhists, and Hindus had been included, but it is oversold. A positive step. I have been told that 60% of the think tank participants at the Council on Foreign Relations are now opposed to the bombing and the % is growing. Please let us observe Ramadan. A big fault of many Americans, particularly those in power is arrogance. As a business leader, I finally learned to listen. It is remarkable how many great partnerships can be formed and strengthened that way. Of course, it is also the way Friends find unity with the Eternal Spirit.

Lee B. Thomas, Jr., Friends Meeting of Louisville (KY)

THE QUAKER ECONOMIST
November 19, 2001

Letter No. 28

Dear friends:

The Disintegrating Corporation

Peter Drucker tells us that the corporation is disintegrating. Drucker is a widely consulted management expert, possibly the brainiest in the world. Since disintegrating corporations will be of great interest to Quakers, in the next section I quote key paragraphs from his article in *The Economist* (11/3/01). In the next one following, I will comment on the relationship of Drucker's thesis to Quaker values. Finally, I will ask readers to express yourselves on the likely future.

Drucker's thesis

"The next society will be a knowledge society. Knowledge will be its key resource, and knowledge workers will be the dominant group in its workforce. Its three main characteristics will be:

o Borderlessness, because knowledge travels even more effortlessly than money.

o Upward mobility, available to everyone through easily acquired formal education.

o The potential for failure as well as success. Anyone can acquire the 'means of production', ie, the knowledge required for the job, but not everyone can win."

"The 20th century saw the rapid decline of agriculture. In volume terms, farm production now is at least four or five times what it was before the first world war." Because other sectors have grown even more, however, the relative contribution of agriculture in rich countries has dwindled, and the farm population is down to a tiny proportion of the total. In short, we produce much, much more food with only a tiny fraction of the farmers we had a century ago.

"Since the second world war, manufacturing output in the developed world has probably tripled in volume, but inflation-adjusted manufacturing prices have fallen steadily, whereas the cost of prime knowledge products - health care and education - has tripled, again adjusted for inflation. Manufacturing employment in America has fallen from 35% of the workforce in the 1950s to less than half that now, without causing much social disruption." As in agriculture, we now produce as much, or more, manufactured goods as before, but with a smaller number of workers.

"Knowledge workers are the new capitalists. Knowledge has become the key resource, and the only scarce one. This means that knowledge workers collectively own the means of production. But as a group, they are also capitalists in the old sense: through their stakes in pension funds and mutual funds, they have become majority shareholders and owners of many large businesses in the knowledge society.

"Effective knowledge is specialised. That means knowledge workers need access to an organization - a collective that brings together an array of knowledge workers and applies their specialties to a common end-product. The most gifted mathematics teacher in a secondary school is effective only as a member of the faculty. The most brilliant consultant on product development is effective only if there is an organised and competent business to convert her advice into action. The greatest software designer needs a hardware producer. But in turn the high school needs the mathematics teacher, the business needs the expert on product development, and the PC manufacturer needs the software programmer. Knowledge workers therefore see themselves as equal to those who retain their services, as 'professionals' rather than as 'employees'. The knowledge society is a society of seniors and juniors rather than of bosses and subordinates."

My comment: It is the organizations bringing knowledge workers together that possess fluid boundaries. Knowledge workers form new organizations, or they flow from one to another or offer their services to many at a time. (End of my comment).

"The multinationals of 2025 are likely to be held together and controlled by strategy. There will still be ownership, of course. But alliances, joint ventures, minority stakes, know-how agreements and contracts will increasingly be the building blocks of a confederation. This kind of organization will need a new kind of top management."

My comment: Think of a multinational corporation as a jigsaw puzzle, with divisions and departments as pieces, and a hierarchy with management on top, responsible to stockholders. Now break the puzzle apart, and combine it with pieces from other corporate puzzles. These are the "alliances, joint ventures, minority stakes, and know-how agreements" of which Drucker speaks. These groupings will produce health care, education, computer software, web pages, and other knowledge-based products that become the greatest part of people's consumption. Who will own the producing groups? More and more, it will be the knowledge workers, who may however have obtained funds from outside investors, some of whom will also become owners. (End of my comment).

"For most of the time since the corporation was invented around 1870 - [My note: corporations have been known for centuries, but they came to dominate American production only about 1870] - the following basic points have been assumed to apply:

     o The corporation is the "master", the employee is the "servant". Because the corporation owns the means of production without which the employee could not make a living, the employee needs the corporation more than vice versa.

     o The great majority of employees work full-time for the corporation. The pay they get for the job is their only income and provides their livelihood.

     o The most efficient way to produce anything is to bring together under one management as many as possible of the activities needed to turn out the product."

"Every one of these assumptions remained valid for a whole century, but from 1970 onwards every one of them has been turned upside down. The list now reads as follows:

     o The means of production is knowledge, which is owned by knowledge workers and is highly portable. This applies equally to high-knowledge workers such as research scientists and to knowledge technologists such as physiotherapists, computer technicians and paralegals. Knowledge workers provide "capital" just as much as does the provider of money. The two are dependent on each other. This makes the knowledge worker an equal - an associate or a partner.

     o Many employees, perhaps a majority, will still have full-time jobs with a salary that provides their only or main income. But a growing number of people who work for an organization will not be full-time employees but part-timers, temporaries, consultants or contractors. Even of those who do have a full-time job, a large and growing number may not be employees of the organization for which they work, but employees of, eg, an outsourcing contractor."

"One thing is almost certain: in future there will be not one kind of corporation but several different ones. The modern company was invented simultaneously but independently in three countries: America, Germany and Japan. It was a complete novelty and bore no resemblance to the economic organization that had been the 'economic enterprise' for millennia: the small, privately owned and personally run firm. The tide turned around 1970, first with the emergence of new institutional investors such as pension funds and mutual trusts as the new owners, then - more decisively - with the emergence of knowledge workers as the economy's big new resource and the society's representative class. The result has been a fundamental change in the corporation."

What should be the response of Quakers?

I believe Drucker is right. So, if al Qaeda does not destroy our society (and I don't think it will), Friends must adapt our vision of economic society and the multinational corporation. Many Friends have negative sentiments toward the multinational corporation. Although MNCs have committed heinous acts in the past, trying to overthrow governments, nevertheless most of them behave like decent citizens, pay their taxes, do not bribe governments, pay their workers more than they could earn elsewhere, and provide more social services - health, education, housing - than the workers could otherwise receive. (This was explained in Letter No. 23, section 3). Atrocious though their situation is, even the *maquiladoras* on the Mexico-US border pay higher wages than their workers could earn elsewhere (the workers are free to go elsewhere in Mexico if that were not so).

Little or none of this would have happened except in a society of flexibility, where individuals have freedom of choice over their employment, and in which companies decide what to produce, whom to hire or contract, and what technology to use. Inventors have free rein to invent, and innovators to select new forms of organization. In most less developed countries, one cannot start a new enterprise, or modify an old one substantially, without a zillion government permissions and probably more bribes than one can afford. Creative ideas stem from below - they do not belong to government - and only when they are allowed to emerge does development occur. The stodgy state enterprises of China, India, most African countries, and Latin

America are more the subject of power struggles than they are conducive to innovation. This, I believe, is the principal reason for underdevelopment in these regions, in contrast with the freedom-allowing (well, mostly) societies of northwestern Europe, Japan, North America, and Oceania.

Perhaps you are alarmed by the number of mergers you hear about, such as Enron and Dynegy. Every business wants to be a monopoly, and we must be careful about allowing this. However, many mergers are last-resort operations by companies such as Enron, that have suffered great losses. Many are proposed in order to lower costs and prices through more efficient combinations of management. How do we tell the difference between "good" and "bad" mergers? Only by studying them separately and not jumping to ideological conclusions.

Whatever you think about multinational corporations - whatever your concept may be - all that is changing. So, what will happen?

First, regulation may be more difficult. Steve Williams (Bethesda MD Meeting) writes: "My own sense is that the more mobile resources are—workers, capital—the harder it is for government to impose regulation that doesn't yield benefits equal to its costs or taxation that exceeds the value of the government services provided in return." Steve's comment implies that "good regulation," whose benefits exceed its costs, will still be possible, but excessive regulation may not. I think this is difficult to forecast, but I hope it will be so. What do you think?

Second, will the world now be divided in two: between wealthy knowledge workers (the new capitalists) and the poverty-stricken left-outs? Or will there be new opportunities for all, and will the wealth spill down (that's more than trickle down) from the knowledge workers to the rest? On the other hand, will more opportunities open up for the underclass, so that they too may become knowledge workers (as Drucker predicts)? Will uneducated people become social outcasts? I have some ideas on these questions, but before I express them I would like to hear yours.

Yours in friendship,
Jack Powelson

COMMENTS BY READERS ON LETTER NO. 28

This "new" way of thinking about knowledge workers is already happening in the mental health field where HMOs and other insurance companies are contracting with smaller groups and individual professionals to actually do the work on site. This may be one sector to look at for one type of history of the emergence of this type of organization. So far, for me as a therapist who does not want to be the enterpreneur organizing the system, it has been frustrating, resulting in more paperwork (even if it is online) and a pay freeze from the companies involved. At the same time, my referral sources have changed from medical doctors to insurance companies. All of it is in flux. To me, the ability of a company to handle massive quantities of information and to disseminate information quickly and efficiently has given the insurance companies more control than is useful to consumer and provider. But even that is still in flux. We are definitely in the midst of this change that Peter Drucker is talking about and have been in flux for about 20 years. So at the moment it seems that corporations in my workplace are still able to look at the bottom line and dictate a lot, for better or worse. And the key word here is ...for the moment. Questions that still need to be answered include: How do the individual knowledge workers organize to deal with the larger corporation? What are alternatives to anti-trust laws for the independent knowledge worker? How do the independent knowledge workers gain power to influence lawmaking decisions during the transitions? These are the kinds of things my sector has been dealing with to date. Thanks for the Drucker information.

Barb Seidel, Gwynedd (PA) Meeting

A most thought-provoking letter, with a long view ahead. Thanks!

Roger Conant, Mt. Toby Meeting, Leverett (MA)

Hi Jack, Thanks so much for your comments on Drucker's article. I have been reading his books with admiration for years.

Janet Minshall, Anneewakee Creek Friends Worship Group,Douglasville (GA)

You didn't say quite why the corporation is disintegrating. Ronald Coase showed that a corporation exists to reduce transaction costs.* If you need to keep a machine busy all day long, you need a reliable source of labor to operate the machine. It has been much cheaper to hire a worker for a year at a time. As the nature of production (in the U.S.) has changed to require more skill of employees and less capital invested in machines, people can be hired and fired as they are needed. That's the pessimistic view. A more optimistic view of this trend is for people to view themselves as an independent business, with a varying set of customers. This is the life I live. It's scary sometimes, but rewarding as well, and nobody tells me I can't take ten days off to go to the FGC gathering.

Russ Nelson, St. Lawrence Valley (NY) Friends Meeting

*Transaction costs are the cost of making a transaction, e.g., hiring labor, finding and buying a product, etc., which may be reduced if the labor and product are within the walls of the company.

A recent conference that I attended emphasized that the number of liberalized telecom markets in Africa, and the number mobile providers, has jumped tremendously in the last few years. In 1995, only 7% of African countries had competitive mobile markets. Now more than 50% do, and the number of mobile operators, continent-wide, has gone from 33 to 100. The trends show no sign of slowing, either. Excellent news all around.

Geoffrey Williams, Bethesda (MD) Friends Meeting

Steve Williams's comment implies that "good regulation," whose benefits exceed its costs, will still be possible, but excessive regulation may not. I think this is difficult to forecast, but I hope it will be so.

The problem may be that good regulation isn't possible. Much of the opposition to multinationals centres around their avoiding regulation. Some of the treaties threaten to make it difficult to regulate; a company's preferences seem to override local law. If a company can escape to where it can poison the atmosphere, pay wages less than minimum at home, and so forth,

it can use this as a lever to overcome environmental regulation and decrease wages where it is.

Jim Caughran, Toronto (Ontario, Canada) Monthly Meeting

It is hard to imagine Drucker's scenerio happening in our corporate controlled society, and yet I do see small signs of it beginning to happen here in
Boulder and Denver. Perhaps the recession will move it along. Since corporations control our government and most of our judicial system, if it
happens, it will take some time, and over-regulation (strangulation) will be
an ever present danger. Some regulation would certainly be necessary.

You ask about the spread between the haves and have nots in such a world.
It would seem that the current wide spread between the two will grow greater
until EVERY child receives a good education. Since we continue to talk
about the education problem instead of correcting it, it seems to me it would
take a good many years to narrow the gap if it
could happen at all.

Lorna Knowlton Quaker at Heart Boulder, CO

THE QUAKER ECONOMIST
November 30, 2001

Letter No. 29

Dear friends:

The Skeptical Environmentalist

In his new book of this title (Cambridge 2001), Bjorn Lomborg of Denmark begins with a quotation from Julian Simon, Professor of Business Management at the University of Maryland, who died in 1998 (just after I had met him):

"This is my long-run forecast in brief:
The material conditions of life will continue to get better for most people, most of the time, indefinitely. Within a century or two, all nations and most of humanity will be at or above today's Western living standard. I also speculate, however, that many people will continue to *think and say* that the conditions of life are getting worse."

Lomborg was an environmentalist, a member of Greenpeace. Then he met Julian Simon, and - convinced that Simon was wrong - he parceled out Simon's many statements about the environment to his students, asking them to do the research to prove Simon wrong. Instead, the students reported that they had found Simon correct in case after case. So Lomborg became skeptical about his former beliefs. As a scientist, he makes up his mind on the basis of evidence (not hearsay or ideology), and he will change his mind if the evidence shows he was wrong. Not many of us will do that.

Let me quote from a review in *The Economist* (8/4/01):

"These environmentalists, led by such veterans as Paul Ehrlich of Stanford University, and Lester Brown of the Worldwatch Institute, have developed a sort of "litany" of four big environmental fears:
  • Natural resources are running out.
  • The population is ever growing, leaving less and less to eat.
  • Species are becoming extinct in vast numbers: forests are disappearing and fish stocks are collapsing.
  • The planet's air and water are becoming ever more polluted.

> Human activity is thus defiling the earth, and humanity may end up
> killing itself in the process.

"The trouble is, the evidence does not back up this litany. First, energy and
other natural resources have become more abundant, not less so since the
Club of Rome published 'The Limits to Growth' in 1972. Second, more
food is now produced per head of the world's population than at any time in
history. Fewer people are starving. Third, although species are indeed becoming extinct, only about 0.7% of them are expected to disappear in the
next 50 years, not 25-50%, as has so often been predicted. And finally,
most forms of environmental pollution either appear to have been exaggerated, or are transient—associated with the early phases of industrialisation
and therefore best cured not by restricting economic growth, but by accel-
erating it. One form of pollution—the release of greenhouse gases that causes
global warming—does appear to be a long-term phenomenon, but its total
impact is unlikely to pose a devastating problem for the future of humanity.
A bigger problem may well turn out to be an inappropriate response to it."
(END OF QUOTATION FROM THE ECONOMIST).

Furthermore, all the trash that the entire world will generate over the next
century would (according to Lomborg's estimates) fit within a landfill eighteen miles square and 100 feet deep. In 1997, the Worldwide Fund for
Nature stated that two-thirds of the world's forests are lost forever. The
truth is nearer 20%, and much of this occurred in Europe during the first
millennium CE. The land covered by forests has actually increased since
World War II.

Let me now quote from myself:

For decades we have been concerned with overpopulation. Now we discover that Europe, Russia, Japan, and other countries are deeply disturbed
about loss of population. (See Letter No. 6 for the rest). Population is growing
in the Third World, where however the growth rate is decelerating and is
expected to reach zero by 2050.

The *Washington Post* is enthusiastic about Lomborg. Here is a quotation
("Book World," 10/21/01):

"In a massive, meticulously presented argument that extends over 500 pages,
supported by nearly 3,000 footnotes and 182 tables and diagrams, Lomborg

revisits a number of heartening breakthroughs in the life of the planet. Chief among these is the decline of poverty and starvation across the world. Starvation still exists, but there is less of it than ever, as our capacity to produce abundant quantities of food continues to improve. Likewise with other dire scenarios of resource depletion: We are emphatically not running out of energy and mineral resources, the population bomb is fizzling, and, far from killing us, pesticides and chemicals are improving longevity and the quality of life. Neither need we fear anything from the genetic modification of organisms." [Maybe you won't believe these statements. But please hold off, until you read Lomborg's evidence.]

Lomborg also "traces the urban legends of the green movement back to their sources." For example, he "traces the oft-repeated claim that 40,000 species go extinct every year . . . back to an offhand and completely unfounded guess made by a scientist in 1979. It's been repeated endlessly ever since - and in 1981 was increased by arch-doomsayer Paul Ehrlich to 250,000 species per year. (Ehrlich also predicted that half the planet's species would be extinct by 2000"). (END OF QUOTATION FROM WASHINGTON POST).

I have read Lomborg and find his data compelling. They either fit with what I had already known (as in population growth) or his sources are scholarly. But I do have some caveats. Everything we do or do not do, that impacts upon the environment, involves risk. Without the green revolution, millions might have died from hunger. At the time of the green revolution, however, we did not know the environmental consequences (which turned out to be benign). The same may be so today on genetic engineering and global warming.

Why do many Americans - especially Quakers - continue to believe the litany? Maybe the story of the five monkeys will help us understand that. Start with a cage containing five monkeys. Inside the cage, hang a banana on a string and place a set of stairs under it. Before long, a monkey will go to the stairs and start to climb towards the banana. As soon as he touches the stairs, spray all of the other monkeys with cold water.

After a while, another monkey makes an attempt with the same result: all the other monkeys are sprayed with cold water. Pretty soon, when another monkey tries to climb the stairs, the other monkeys will try to prevent it. Now, put away the cold water. Remove one monkey from the cage and replace it with a new one. The new monkey sees the banana and wants to climb the stairs. To his surprise and horror, all of the other monkeys attack him.

After another attempt and attack, he knows that if he tries to climb the stairs, he will be assaulted. Next, remove another of the original five monkeys and replace it with a new one. The newcomer goes to the stairs and is attacked. The previous newcomer takes part in the punishment with enthusiasm! Likewise, replace a third original monkey with a new one, then a fourth, then the fifth. Every time the newest monkey takes to the stairs, he is attacked. Most of the monkeys that are beating him have no idea why they were not permitted to climb the stairs or why they are participating in the beating of the newest monkey. After replacing all the original monkeys, none of the remaining monkeys have ever been sprayed with cold water. Nevertheless, no monkey ever again approaches the stairs to try for the banana. Why not? Because as far as they know that's the way it's always been done around here. And that's how company policy begins...

Do you believe that story? Would you tell it to someone else as true? I asked my source if the experiment had been ever done, and he did not know. So far as he knew, it was just a story that makes a lot of sense. If repeated enough times, soon "everybody" will believe it, and it will become part of the culture. Is that the way popular acceptance of the litany came about?

If you had lived in Caesar's time (d. 44 BCE), would you have believed in Roman gods because "everybody" did? (Actually, not everybody did).
If you had lived in France in 1572 (Bartholomew Massacre), would you have believed that everyone had to adhere to the same religion, or the nation would fall apart?
If you had lived in Italy in Galileo's time (1564-1642), would you have believed the sun moves around the earth?
If you had lived in Salem, MA, in 1692, would you have believed in witchcraft?
So, what's different about 2001?

Lomborg carefully examines the sources of information that "support" the litany. He does not minimize problems of the environment. He cites studies showing that pollution and other negative effects are occurring. But he finds them vastly overblown in the public mind, and he puts them into perspective. It is a book that everyone concerned with the environment (and who isn't?) ought to read.

The Skeptical Environmentalist may be obtained (paperback) from amazon.com for $19.56 plus shipping. This is not a commercial.

In the next Letter, I will take up global warming, citing Lomborg and other sources as well.

> Yours in Peace,
>> Jack Powelson

READER RESPONES TO LETTER NO. 29 ON ENVIRONMENT

Thank you for your witness through the *Classic Liberal Quaker* messages. It is good to read a point of view that departs from much of what passes for conventional wisdom among unprogrammed Friends.

In diversity, strength..and that also is vital if we are to glean truth in our threshing.

Keep on keeping on.

> In His Light, John Rich, Bethesda (MD) Friends Meeting

I believe that abundance is the natural state that God intends for us. For those who believe that scarcity is the natural state, since the Fall, then there is guilt wherever the possibility of abundance is to some extent realized.

> J.D. von Pischke, Friend from Reston, VA

I have some qualms also about your quotation of reviews, since I don't know from your email what the qualification of the reviewer is. For example somebody who reviewed the book [Bjorn Lomborg, *The Skeptical Environment*] for the *Washington Post* (with what qualifications?) is very [overly] impressed by the number of footnotes, and states, "neither need we fear anything from the genetic modification of organisms." This seems like a remarkably bold statement! I am not one of those who is paranoid about genetic modification, but a statement as bold as this reminds me of the optimism behind the "too cheap to meter" nuclear reactor optimists. I think that a statement like that tends to make me somewhat discount the entire review.

Roger Conant, Mt. Toby Meeting, Leverett (MA)

You didn't mention one very important measure of the human environment, that is some measure of the overall quality of life. We can talk about whether people are fed and housed, but sheer numbers do matter and seriously affect quality of life. I highly value uncrowded places and open space, I highly value other species, and commonly wonder whether humans really are the top life form, as we commonly proclaim. Sheer numbers of humans and constant growth require a constant battle to stay ahead of environmental degradation brought on by that continuing growth in human population. Unfettered population growth of the human species is the single biggest problem we face worldwide. It feeds and exacerbates the other matters we so commonly concern ourselves with: conflict, war, social and economic injustice.

Richard Andrews, Boulder (CO) Meeting of Friends

At the November Friends Committee on National Legislation discussion of the new environmental policy, the most frequent question was, "What makes this a religious policy?" Many complained that Friends have not yet begun meaningful discernment on what are the issues in environmental policy, or of our individual and corporate niches in the answer.

Jack's letter did not effectively address these questions: Where do we get our information? What do we believe? What is important and what is not worrisome? Where do our responsibilities lie?

Karen Street, Berkeley (CA) Friends Meeting

NOTE by Jack: Karen wrote a much longer piece, longer than we customarily publish in Readers' Responses. I have encouraged her to submit it to one of the more widely-distributed Friends' journals.

THE QUAKER ECONOMIST

December 9, 2001

Letter No. 30

Dear friends:

Global Warming

Of all the topics in the CLQ letters, global warming has confounded me most. The subject is so technical (and I am not a techie) and the experts disagree, so that I feel like the selection committee for the Little Minister in J.M. Barrie's book of the same name. One member was so impressed by whoever was called for a visiting sermon that he voted for the one selected only because he was the latest to speak. I find myself agreeing with whoever last argued global warming, pro or con.

I believe that in a subject as important as this one, a scientist should be able to explain his or her position to a lay audience in nontechnical terms. I have been reading all the scientific articles I could find and understand; most I could not find or understand. I have consulted as many scientists as I could. I had luncheon with Kevin Tremberth, one of the top scientists at the National Center for Atmospheric Research (NCAR, fortunately located in Boulder), and have spoken at length with Jack Herring of Boulder Meeting, another NCAR scientist, and Roger Conant, a scientist member of my board. All helped me immensely with this Letter, but I am solely responsible for it.

From all of that, here is what I think: (1) The earth is warming, but how much is anthropogenic (caused by human activity) and how much is natural cycle I do not know. Neither do the scientists. (2) Most of the evidence of anthropogenic warming resides in mathematical models. As an economist, I am familiar with mathematical models, and I know how wrong they can be. (3) Scientists have measured warming at different times, at different parts of the earth, at different heights above the surface, and at different depths of the ocean. The measurements do not all agree. (4) Those scientists who argue that global warming will be small say that the models used to prove its occurrence were fine-tuned: if they did not come out the way the model-maker expected, some of the inputs would be adjusted to conform.

195

(5) The majority of scientists around the world, including many at NCAR, believe anthropogenic is a principal force. (6) I never accept a position just because the majority believes it. (At one time the majority of scientists thought the sun revolved around the earth.) (7) The media have given much more exposure to scientists who tout anthropogenic warming than to those not believing in it. Why? I think because it makes better copy. (8) I'm strongly influenced by Walter Roberts (died 1990), founder of NCAR and a personal friend, who told me that global warming is occurring and we cannot stop it. We should be more concerned about what to do about it than to avert it, he said.

Richard Lindzen, the Alfred Sloan Professor of Meteorology at MIT and the principal proponent that global warming will be small, is a friend of a friend of mine. He reports (through my friend) that his principal evidence is that the temperature in the stratosphere has not changed. While scientists who emphasize anthropogenic warming say it is caused by increased carbon dioxide (the principal greenhouse gas outside of water), Lindzen argues that the increased warming causes ocean evaporation, and the eventual effect of the increased water vapor is a cooling that offsets the warming. He has switched positions on this, and then switched back again, each time with new evidence.

Lindzen, a member of the Inter-Governmental Panel on Climate Change, wrote the following about press reports (*Wall Street Journal,* 6/1/01):

"Last week the National Academy of Sciences released a report on climate change, prepared in response to a request from the White House, that was depicted in the press as an implicit endorsement of the Kyoto Protocol. CNN's Michelle Mitchell was typical of the coverage when she declared that the report represented "a unanimous decision that global warming is real, is getting worse, and is due to man. There is no wiggle room." As one of 11 scientists who prepared the report, I can state that this is simply untrue...

"Our primary conclusion was that despite some knowledge and agreement, the science is by no means settled. We are quite confident (1) that global mean temperature is about 0.5 degrees Celsius higher than it was a century ago; (2) that atmospheric levels of carbon dioxide have risen over the past two centuries; and (3) that carbon dioxide is a greenhouse gas whose increase is likely to warm the earth (one of many, the most important being water vapor and clouds). One reason for uncertainty is that, as the report states, the climate is always changing; change is the norm. Two centuries ago, much of the Northern Hemisphere was emerging from a little ice age. A millennium ago, during the Middle Ages, the same region was in a warm period. Thirty years ago, we were concerned with global cooling. Distinguishing the small recent changes in global mean temperature from the natural variability, which is unknown, is not a trivial task. . .

"We simply do not know what relation, if any, exists between global climate changes and water vapor, clouds, storms, hurricanes, and other factors, including regional climate changes, which are generally much larger than global changes and not correlated with them. Nor do we know how to predict changes in greenhouse gases. This is because we cannot forecast economic and technological change over the next century, and also because there are many man-made substances whose properties and levels are not well known, but which could be comparable in importance to carbon dioxide. What we do know is that a doubling of carbon dioxide by itself would produce only a modest temperature increase of one degree Celsius. Larger projected increases depend on "amplification" of the carbon dioxide by more important, but poorly modeled, greenhouse gases, clouds and water vapor.

"My own view, consistent with the panel's work, is that the Kyoto Protocol would not result in a substantial reduction in global warming. Given the difficulties in significantly limiting levels of atmospheric carbon dioxide, a more effective policy might well focus on other greenhouse substances whose potential for reducing global warming in a short time may be greater." (END OF LINDZEN QUOTATION).

Lindzen is but one of many scientists who have criticized the mathematical models. In "The Human Impact on Climate," *Scientific American* 281(6):100-5, Karl and Tremberth open with "How much of a disruption do we cause? The much-awaited answer could be ours by 2050, but only if nations of the world commit to long-term climate monitoring now."

As Lindzen says, all scientists agree that the earth has gone through natural warming and cooling cycles. Kevin Keigwin, an oceanographer at Woods Hole (MA) observatory, prepared a 3,000 year record of the temperatures of the Sargasso Sea "through analyzing thermally dependent oxygen isotopes in fossils on the ocean floor. He discovered that temperatures a thousand years ago . . . were two degrees Celsius warmer than today's. Roughly confirming this result are historical records - the verdancy of Greenland at the time of the Vikings, . . ." (from *The American Spectator,* May 2001). During the last few centuries preceding the birth of Christ annual temperatures began to decline. The two succeeding millennia in the AD period have seen temperatures substantially lower than the two preceding millennia, again with considerable variation. During this latter period the decline bottomed out roughly between AD 500 and 700. They then rose again reaching a high between 900 and 1200 AD. At the end of the 14th Century temperatures again began to decline. By the beginning of the 16th Century this change started to be noted in writings of the time. The period of this 'Little Ice Age' lasted well into the 18th Century. By the 19th Century, things started to warm again, and have been doing so ever since, with considerable short term variation, of course, but have never approached the temperatures prevalent in ancient times. The causes of these changes have nothing to do with the burning of fossil fuels. (This information was compiled by my brother-in-law, Tom Todd.)

The Harvard-Smithsonian Center for Astrophysics has asserted that the increase in greenhouse gases has been spread over the last century and most of the small earth temperature rises since 1880 occurred before gases from human activity were being emitted. 'The eco-system itself dwarfs human activity in generating or absorbing carbon dioxide.' The eleven-year sunspot cycle has been blamed by some scientists. Sallie Balliunas, an astrophysicist with the Harvard-Smithsonian Center, and her co-workers studied records of the past 120 years and found the Sun responsible for much of the Earth's temperature shifts. Charles Harper, planetary scientist at Harvard, criticized the inter-governmental report for being based more on deficient computer models than on ground-based temperatures during the period in which greenhouse gases were mainly omitted (Quoted from my book, *The Moral Economy,* p. 63.)

In *The Skeptical Environmentalist* (see CLQ 29), Bjorn Lomborg reports that "a recent Atmosphere-Ocean General Circulation Model showed that the increase in direct solar irradiation over the past 30 years is responsible for about 40 percent of the observed global warming" (p. 276), but he also notes that "the connection between temperature and the sunspot cycle seems to have deteriorated during the last 10-30 years . . . Most likely, we are instead seeing an increasing signal, probably from greenhouse gases like

CO-2. Such a find exactly underscores that neither solar variation nor greenhouse gases can alone explain the entire temperature record" (p. 278).

Also, Lean & Rind (*Journal of Climate,*11,1998,3069) show that while "solar radiation changes may have been the predominant climate forcing during the seventeenth and eighteenth centuries, . . . according to simple linear parameterization of surface temperature anomalies and solar irradiance based on this preindustrial relationship, less than one third of the earth's's surface warming since 1970 is attributable to changes in solar radiation."

In "The Coming Climate," in *Scientific American* (May 1997), Karl, Nevills, and Gregory spend many pages on the inadequacies of mathematical models predicting that climate change is caused by global emissions of greenhouse gases, aerosols, and other relevant agents. Yet they conclude that these must be watched as probable causes.

In his book, *The Skeptical Enviromentalist* (see Letter 29), Bjorn Lomborg writes (p. 317): "Temperatures have increased over 0.6C over the past century, and it is unlikely that this is not in part due to an anthropogenic greenhouse effect, although the impression of a dramatic divergence from previous centuries is surely misleading." He argues that fighting the warming earth would be enormously expensive, and we would better spend those trillions of dollars in adjusting to the change, as generations in the past have always had to do, but in a less technological world.

The chief difference between scientists and economists seems to be that scientists do not calculate the costs of whatever action they propose, while economists (like me) often do not understand the science. So, where does this leave us?

We must indeed be concerned about anthropogenic global warming, but we should calculate the costs and benefits of trying to stop it and compare them with the costs and benefits of not doing so. A benefit of trying to stop it would be, "if we are totally successful the climate will warm only to the extent that nature determines." The cost of doing that would be "what all the people of the earth must suffer to make it happen." That could include a much lesser life style than we are accustomed, as well as slowing the growth of the poorest of the world. There are also costs and benefits of not stopping the global warming, which I leave to your imagination.

In each calculation, we must take account of the probability that whatever we propose or think would indeed occur. (We should not pay a high cost to prevent something that is very unlikely, say billions of dollars to ward off a meteor.)

We should also consider the costs versus benefits of doing it part way. While most governments have agreed to the Kyoto protocol (except the United States), they have not put it into effect, and I am dubious that anyone will. A benefit would not be that it would stop global warming, but that it would delay it by a short period (some scientists say no more than seven years). We may also consider that the costs would be so high that, for political reasons, they would never realistically be paid. Should we devote our efforts to fighting this recalcitrance, or to adapting to the circumstance, or part one and part the other? I do not have the answer, only the question. Unfortunately, not enough of us have been asking the question.

How would we adjust? I do not trust the government to take the initiative. Any government or inter-governmental body, with its defense of power bases, its "all-must-be-alike" thinking, its attempt to please everybody (or at least the majority of voters, who also don't count costs), and with its bureaucratic squabbles, would never be able to coordinate the effort of adjustment.

Instead, millions upon millions of individuals would do the adjusting, calculating their own private costs and benefits. Some would insulate their houses, some would sell their farms and move father north; some would inoculate against new diseases; some would give up farming and take other jobs, some would install air conditioning, some would irrigate, some would move farther from the seashore. And so on. Fortunately, the warming will be so gradual that each generation would bear only a small part of the long-run cost.

On a few points we should all be agreed. Global warming or no, we should decrease automobile and factory emissions, fouling of rivers, and other kinds of pollution. The benefit might not be to stop global warming but merely to make our Earth a more pleasant place to live. How much cost are we willing to pay for that?

In Peace, from your friend,
Jack Powelson

READERS' RESPONSES TO LETTER NO. 30

Why do people in the present era in the US almost instinctively side with the pessimists, the panic-button-pushers? Why do advocates arise on the side that tends to increase costs rather than on the side that tends to compare costs and benefits? There have been a few books lately about public perceptions of risk as opposed to statistical probabilities, and these may offer clues. It might also be a matter of where confidence and trust are placed, but this would have deeper roots. Possibly stuff for contemplation in a future Letter.

J.D. von Pischke, a Friend from Reston (VA)

Apparently, Mars may be warming, too. It is unlikely that the change in Mars' climate is entirely due to the presence of human probes in that region of space. Here is a quotation from the report, from the *New York Times,* 12/7/01:

Photographs of the south polar ice cap of Mars, taken by a spacecraft in 1999 and again this year, have revealed a marked erosion of the year-round reservoir of solid carbon dioxide there, scientists reported in an article being published today in the journal Science.

Gusten Lutter, Mountain View Meeting, Denver (CO)

Jack's letter credits Lomborg's analysis of the high cost of trying to stop global warming. Lomborg, in turn, quotes Nordhaus extensively on the high costs of mitigation policies. Nordhaus has been criticized for ignoring the economic gains from new technologies which would replace carbon based generation of power. For example, Nordhaus's 1990 analysis estimates a cost of 200 billion/year. Von Weizsacker and Lovin (Factor Four, 1997, p. 150) argue the magnitude of this number is about right, but the sign is wrong, if one brings into the calculation conservation, efficiencies and new technologies, which Nordhaus neglected. There is a report from the World Resource Institute by Repetto and Austin (The Cost of Climate Protection: A guide for the perplexed (1997)) which points out how drastically economic models of the cost of climate protection depend on such often hidden assumptions. One conclusion of theirs: "Under the best—case assumptions, a reduction in CO_2 emission by 2020 would result in a substantial improvement in GDP relative to its business—as—usual path".

Jack Herring, Boulder (CO) Meeting of Friends

When it comes to taking care of our bodies, we don't simply wait for absolute proof or insist on absolute perfection. Nor do we set our health targets based on simple cost benefit analysis. We pragmatically accumulate a regime of practices that contribute to the longevity *and* happiness of our lives. Of course, we are careful not to accumulate bad habits also. This is in some way a pragmatic expression of thankfulness to God for our bodies. We would do well to apply the same thankfulness and pragmatisim to our care of the planet as well.

Patrick Koppula, Golden Gate Lutheran Church, San Francisco (CA)

"Fortunately, the warming will be so gradual that each generation would bear only a small part of the long-run cost."

Not necessarily true. If (or when, if warming continues) the Antarctic ice cap falls into the sea, that generation will pay heavily. Coastal areas under water and untold millions drowned would be only the immediate effects.

Jim Caughran, Toronto (Ontario) Monthly Meeting

I think your paragraph starting, "How would we adjust?" is vulnerable. To the extent that the optimal measures are ones that people have incentives to take, of course there is no problem. But to the extent that the optimal measures are ones for which there is no incentive in ordinary market conditions, e.g., to cut back on activities that generate greenhouse emissions, your apparent approach will lead to underuse of those measures. Of course one can argue that the bureaucracy, etc., associated with creating incentives of this sort will be costly and itself generate errors, but it isn't clear that—if anthropogenic global warming is serious—avoidance of those errors justifies foregoing the potential advantages.

Steve Williams, Bethesda (MD) Meeting

My rather simplistic view has long been that, even if the chances of significant human-made effect are small, the costs of global warming, even though spread over a century and more, would be sufficiently high to warrant doing what we reasonably can to reduce that effect, especially considering there are other probable benefits to "doing what we reasonably can," e.g., more efficient use of hydrocarbons for fuel, e.g., driving an SUV a mile or more to buy a quart of milk.

  Don Marsh, Seattle (WA)

Your thoughtful letters are, as usual, thought-provoking and a joy to receive.

  Tom Selldorff, Weston (MA)

You are right to be suspicious, or at least wary, of computer models, but computer models are all we have to go on. The only alternative is just intuition, for example unscientific generalizations from facts such as that the last few years have been the hottest in the last millenium. Yes, computer models can be wrong, but they can be right too, and if you believe in the process of science in which good science expels bad science (under peer review, testing, etc) then there is reason to believe that the models of climate change are evolving to become more and more accurate. There is no alternative to computer models, is there?

  Roger Conant, Mt. Toby (MA) Meeting

THE QUAKER ECONOMIST
December 19, 2001

Letter No. 31

Dear friends:

Will the United States follow Argentina?

The Government of Argentina will likely default on its government bonds, abandon the peso, and adopt the U.S. dollar as its national currency, all of this in 2002. For two main reasons: First, for many, many years the Argentines have wanted to take out of the government pot far more than they are willing to put in (in taxes). Second, each sector is so adamant about its "rights" that it will not compromise by reducing its take. Each sector is willing to destroy the social fabric, shutting down the entire economy, by striking, until it gets its way. How did this come about? Will the United States ultimately do the same?

If you were an impartial observer in, say, 1890, you would not easily guess which country - the United States or Argentina - would be the dominant economic power in the Western Hemisphere a century later. Both were developing their manufactures and their agriculture. Both had good school systems, educated labor, and among the highest living standards in the world. But there were already subtle differences that most eyes could not see. In my book, *Centuries of Economic Endeavor* (Michigan 1994:270) I wrote of three historic properties that have seemed to permeate Argentine society from colonial days to the present:

- Power for its own sake - not just for the economic advantage it brings - is demanded by competing sectors.
- Regardless of statements affirming democracy, every group in power has both favored and sustained an interventionist state. All sectors of society endorse this precept, and all solutions or *modus vivendi* are designed accordingly.
- Confrontation characterizes the political process. There is no longer an "elite," for those who govern include persons of all classes, from descendants of immigrant laborers to the traditional landowning aristocracy. But these groups do not trust each other, they communicate imperfectly, and they make impossible demands upon one another.

Argentines believe increasingly in the government to super-manage the day-to-day affairs of the economy - what prices will be charged, what wages paid, who will control capital, and so on. The government, in effect, tells business how much it must/may pay in wages. Unions are mainly political, making their demands through government. For decades the government has printed money to "satisfy" demands that collectively exceeded the possibilities. Horrendous inflations ensued, and three zeros have been lopped off the currency more than once. In one visit to Argentina, I thought I would collect one-peso coins for my children to use as play money. But none were to be found. When I told a friend in the central bank about this, he brought me three bags full, which I took home. For years, Argentine pesos kept appearing in various corners of the house.

In the United States, on the other hand, individuals have far more freedom to innovate, put new products on the market, and determine their prices, styles, and quantities. Our inflations have been mild, compared to Argentina. For the most part, wages are determined by bargaining between employers and unions.

As I was lecturing in a university in Córdoba, Argentina, a few years ago, the students told me they were about to go on strike. Why, I asked? Two reasons, they said: (1) Out of sympathy for civil servants who had not been paid for months because the government did not have the money, and (2) to counter the proposal that students pay tuitions for education that had heretofore been free. They thought the government should both pay the civil servants and provide free education, with no increase in taxes.

As the year 2002 dawns, the Argentine government is at an impasse. It cannot pay its debts. If it defaults, the country's credit rating will be ruined, and it will not be possible to obtain foreign investment capital. If capital is not available, companies will close down, workers will be thrown out of work, and chaos and riots will result. The next option is to increase taxes. Without getting out the military and invading people's houses and businesses, however, it cannot force them to pay. Judges will not hand down decisions against their friends. The third option is to decrease expenditures. These, however, have built up over the decades as the government has favored one sector after another. (The government also finances the provinces by annual grants). But no sector will make the sacrifice, and all can hold the government in thrall one way or another. Social services, education, and health are underfunded. Pension funds are not secure, because the government has forced businesses to invest them in the about-to-be-defaulted government bonds.

"Tens of thousands of unemployed workers, public employees and students blocked scores of major highways and city streets across Argentina today to protest new government spending cuts aimed at diverting a default on the foreign debt" (*New York Times*, 8/1/01). "Several major unions staged a 24-hour nationwide strike today, crippling businesses and government functions" (*New York Times*, 12/14/01). In my writings, I have referred to these actions as "break-the-system." In some cultures, a sector will be powerful enough, and willing, to bring down the social system or the economy just to get its way on a particular point. "Break-the-system" mentality is widespread in Argentina.

The Dirty War

To preserve the political power of the government against protesting students, during the 1970's the military conducted a "dirty war." They kidnapped dissidents, tortured them, drugged them, and dropped them from airplanes over the ocean. The mothers of missing students still march in front of the presidential palace every Thursday, demanding information the government would not give them. My last visit to Buenos Aires did not occur on a Thursday, but I walked around the Plaza in my own show of support for those mothers.

Until only a few years ago, the military had great power and would even overthrow governments. They believed that their society would collapse into chaos if they did not defend "law and order." More recently, civilian governments have replaced them, yet the military stand ready "if needed." In the United States, our military has never had the power over government, but we occupy the position with respect to the world that the Argentine military does for their country. "For more than fifty years American foreign policy has sought to prevent the emergence of other great powers - a strategy that has proved burdensome, futile, and increasingly risky," say Schwartz and Layne in the January 2002 *Atlantic*. Is this not the Argentine military writ large?

Other Confrontation

In Argentina, "I was ordered to do it" has been a valid defense for torture and even murder. When repeal of this law was proposed, "the session ended in a free-for-all screaming match, with human-rights activists rushing on to the floor of Congress and two members trading blows" (*New York Times,* 2/14/98). One cabinet minister has publicly denounced other cabinet ministers, congressmen, and businessmen as thieves, liars, and mafiosos (*New York Times,* 11/23/96). In 1983, the President of the Central Bank was indicted for treason because he had negotiated an agreement with the International Monetary Fund.

We do not go to these extremes in the United States. Quakers, in particular, insist on nonviolent protests. Yet some Friends join, even support, those who smash windows to protest the World Trade Organization, the International Monetary Fund, and the World Bank. Each time this happens, I wonder again if we are on the road to Argentina.

Corruption

Argentine society is permeated by corruption: in the government, court system, military, businesses, everywhere. Often it is impossible to complain because the system is so inter-linked that any remedy would affect dozens of people, some of whom could obstruct the complaint. How do I know? Mainly from talking to Argentines during my visits there, but also from the abundant newspaper clippings I have been collecting for over a quarter of a century. Here are just a few snippets:

"Private talks with executives, both foreign and local, yield accounts of how provincial and Federal officials have to be paid 'commissions' to get jobs done. Very few can take their complaints to court because most who might complain have themselves paid bribes and know they would be exposed if they tried to expose others" *(New York Times,* 7/17/94.) "Both foreigners and residents say corruption is endemic in Argentina. In a study in the late 1980s, Graciela Roemer, a political consultant, found that most Argentines thought that tax evasion was smart and paying up was stupid" (*Economist,* 10/18/97).

I believe there is far less corruption in the United States, for (1) we have better auditing, and (2) better systems of internal control. Internal control means that if someone embezzles, the accounting system is such that others are bound to find out. But when, as in Argentina, embezzling and bribery are everywhere, it hardly matters if one is found out. For the auditing systems to work, I speculate that we have developed - over centuries - a sense of individual responsibility, taught in our families, schools, and churches, that the Argentines do not have. I have no way of knowing this for sure, but it seems to me so. I am also leery of whether this sense of responsibility will continue as government increasingly takes charge of personal behavior (health, retirement, etc.) that was once the province of the individual.

Corruption increases as powers of government increase. In the United States, about one-third of the national product is consumed by the federal government; if we add the state and local governments, this fraction advances to slightly less than one-half. As the amount of money captured by governments keeps increasing, will not corruption increase as well?

Distribution of Income and Wealth

In the United States, the wealthy have become wealthier in recent years, but the poor have - probably - not become poorer absolutely. I say "probably" because the point is disputed, but after studying the data and reports, it is my impression that this is so. The disparity is caused mainly by the innovations of techies and the stock market depending on them. All this may change, as the technological revolution flattens out, and the stock market has already gone down.

In Argentina also, the rich-poor gap is greater than ever before. But the rich have not become rich because they and their companies are technologically efficient. They have done so mainly because they have the connections and the political savvy to effect distributions in their favor. The poor have become poorer absolutely (as well as relatively) because they are less able to withstand the collapse of the economy than are the rich.

Argentina is one of my favorite countries in Latin America: the people are friendly, and Buenos Aires is a garden city, reminding me of Paris. And the Andes are as spectacular as the Alps. But ringing BA are the *villas de miseria,* or slums, with houses of makeshift materials and mud in the streets. There I have spent many hours making friends with the poorest of the poor. In the center of BA is the cemetery *Recoleta,* full of marble mausoleums with gold door knobs. Yes, in Argentina the rich dead live much better than the living poor. But it is a beautiful country nonetheless.

Money and the Government Debt

To prevent the government from indefinitely printing money, Parliament ended the central bank and established a currency board in 1991, which was legally allowed to print pesos only to the extent that it held U.S. dollars in reserve. Any Argentine could trade in pesos for dollars at any time. This law stopped inflation in its tracks.

However, the government continued to issue bonds denominated in pesos. Presumably a bondholder could cash in his bonds at maturity and exchange the pesos for dollars. But the government issued these bonds in amounts way beyond its capacity to redeem without violating the peso-backed-by-dollar requirement. As this situation became evident in financial circles, Argentines began withdrawing their money from banks, to convert them into dollars. This month, the economy minister limited the amount they could withdraw, an event that further diminished Argentine financial credibility. He has also "persuaded" current bondholders to accept less than their contractual interest. Since their alternative is default, they had to go along.

Who will invest now, if the peso is about to become worthless? So the proposal is that all outstanding pesos be redeemed for the dollars in the currency board, and hereafter only the U.S. dollar will be legal tender. Ecuador and El Salvador have earlier made this exchange. Doing so means surrendering control over the currency to the U.S. Federal Reserve, since the Argentine (Ecuadorian, Salvadoran) government cannot be trusted.

Argentina and the United States

Do you see any parallels between Argentina and the United States? Surely our economy is much better organized and better run; we trust each other more. But as the Argentine government maintained control over social welfare (education, pensions, health), did it not begin to feel very powerful, maybe like God? So maybe the time had come to take back the Falkland Islands, starting a bloody war with Britain? As the American President finds he is looked to for social security, health care for the elderly, and education, does he not also begin to feel like God? A little problem in

Kosovo? "I can take care of that! Send over the bombers." "Afghanistan? A minor problem; we'll get them"

When you give government the power to manage the lives of the people for their own good, you create a culture in which government is looked to as the solver of many other problems as well. Such cultures allow their governments to wage war. On the home front, the government tries to answer all calls. When it oversteps itself - as in Argentina - the economy will fall apart. Have you felt that government bonds are the safest possible investment? So did the Argentines, one hundred years ago.

Is the United States on the road to Argentina? Not yet, I think. We don't suffer from the same historic properties: we want power for its economic advantages and not for the sole reason of commanding. We have more economic freedom, and we don't confront as much. But in many ways, the path is similar. We're just not so far along. How do Friends feel about entrusting more and more powers to your government to do "good?"

> Yours for peace and freedom,
> Jack

READERS' RESPONSES TO LETTER NO. 31 ON ARGENTINA

Forgive me if I seem obtuse. I have never had any courses in economic theory. What advantages does Argentina have in switching to the dollar. I can understand that Argentina is helped automatically because the dollar is strong relative to the peso. If Argentina doesn't have the infrastucture we have, how can their adopting the dollar help them?

> Dennis Bentley, Freethinker, Morganton, North Carolina

ANSWER by Jack. You are not at all obtuse; that is a reasonable question. There is no advantage whatsoever, unless the enormity of the move shocks them into living within their means. It is hoped that the psychology of a sound currency, instead of the discredited peso, will cause this to happen. In Ecuador and El Salvador, that has worked (so far).

Your letter is most thought provoking and I share many of your observations. Governments of, by and for the people inherently encourage citizens to ask for things from their government. After all it is the peoples' government. This is why strong limitations are needed on government power. Our constitution in theory does this but its   authority, I am afraid, has been eroding over many years. Also we are   more exposed to the corrupting influence of money with ever rising special interest contributions to legislators. Not necessarily the same corrupting influences as in Argentina, but there may be parallels.   Increases in government power in general ultimately seem to benefit the more affluent sectors of our society.

Joseph Mills

Hi Jack! I have just a simple question: in your letter, you imply that government expansion in a country's internal affairs is linked to expansion or aggression abroad. I guess the converse would be that a libertarian state would tend to be pacifist also. But I don't see why this should be true. What is the connection you find between our "war against terror" in Afghanistan and federal management of our own economy?

Nicholas Williams, Bethesda (MD) Friends Meeting

ANSWER by Jack: Well, Nick, this is a matter of opinion, and yours is as good as mine. Mine is that the more power we give to a President to do "good" things (or anything), the more likely he or she is to think he or she is God and the more likely to go to war. A libertarian government, with virtually no power, might not think that. (Don't presume from this that I am libertarian, just classic liberal).

Chuck Rostkowski, Salt Lake (UT) Meeting, writes:
"For the past few years I have been giving serious thought to leaving Quakerism because, although I love silent worship, I cannot stand the left wing politics, the lack of any knowledge of how capitalism really works, the unwillingness to view anything on the political left, especially Stalinism, as truly evil, and the automatic default position that the United States is wrong in just about everything it does."

Friend speaks my mind! I'm not quite ready to leave Quakerism, but the only way I can stay is to ignore all of this stuff. I often feel like a misfit among misfits!

Dick Bellin, Friends Meeting of Washington (DC)

"Corruption increases as powers of government increase. In the United States, about one-third of the national product is consumed by the federal government; if we add the state and local governments, this fraction advances to slightly less than one-half. As the amount of money captured by governments keeps increasing, will not corruption increase as well?"

What makes you think so? Is the UK more corrupt than the US? Isn't corruption, in society in general, more prevalent in authoritarian states where the government does little for the people, and business is less regulated?

Jim Caughran, Toronto (Ontario), Canada, Friends Meeting

ANSWER, by Jack: Because it is always secretive, no one can truly investigate how much corruption there is. Our inferences come from interviews with business people and others, to ask what bribes they have to pay, and we do not know if they give the true answers. Add to that my own conversations with officials and students in the thirty-five less developed countries where I have had professional assignments.

Hernando de Soto of Peru assigned his students to set up a textile business without paying bribes unless they had to. It took them several years to complete all the regulatory requirements, and they did have to pay a few bribes. My guess is that the more regulation the government can do - i.e., the more permissions required and therefore the more discretion officials have - the more corruption money can be demanded.

I don't know anything about the U.K. compared to the U.S. But I do guess that there is far more corruption in Asia, Africa, and Latin America than in the more developed regions. Virtually all professionals I have met, who have served abroad, tell me that is so.

THE QUAKER ECONOMIST

January 4, 2002

Letter No. 32

Dear friends:

Skeptical of the Skeptical Environmentalist

In CLQ 29, I quoted favorable reviews in *The Economist* and the *Washington Post* of Bjorn Lomborg, *The Skeptical Environmentalist.* Lomborg is a Danish professor of statistics who examined the claims of environmentalists that the world is getting worse, and found them to be mainly wrong.

Now come the negative reviews, primarily in *Scientific American,* January 2002; the web pages of the Union of Concerned Scientists and the World Resources Institute; and the December 12 issue of an online journal, *Daily Grist.* There are many more, but these cover the ground very well.

The statement by the Union of Concerned Scientists is representative of the whole: "The heavily promoted book, published in September by Cambridge University Press, has received significant attention from the media and praise from commentators writing in *The Economist, The New York Times,* and *Washington Post. . .* Does this book merit such positive attention? Does Lomborg provide new insights? Are his claims supported by the data? . . .

"To answer these questions, UCS invited several of the world's leading experts on water resources, biodiversity, and climate change to carefully review the sections in Lomborg's book that address their areas of expertise. We asked them to evaluate whether Lomborg's skepticism is coupled with the other hallmarks of good science – namely, objectivity, understanding of the underlying concepts, appropriate statistical methods and careful peer review. . .

"These separately written expert reviews unequivocally demonstrate that on closer inspection, Lomborg's book is seriously flawed and fails to meet basic standards of credible scientific analysis. The authors note how Lomborg consistently misuses, misrepresents or misinterprets data to greatly underestimate rates of species extinction, ignore evidence that billions of people lack access to clean water and sanitation, and minimize the extent and impacts of global warming due to the burning of fossil fuels and other human-caused emissions of heat-trapping gases. . ."

So, was I "taken in" by Lomborg when I wrote CLQ 29? Possibly, and I will eat humble pie if I deserve it. Before doing so, however, a few points disturb me. First, while I respect these scientists and am influenced by them, I also know of other scientists who disagree with them. For example, Richard Lindzen, the Alfred P. Sloan Professor of Meteorology, Department of Earth, Atmospheric and Planetary Sciences at M.I.T., finds that the earth has ways of offsetting temperature changes. While he believes that global warming is occurring, he finds it to be a natural phenomenon, since the earth has warmed and cooled many times over the centuries (see CLQ 29). A quote from CLQ 30: "Sallie Balliunas, an astrophysicist with the Harvard-Smithsonian Center, and her co-workers studied records of the past 120 years and found the Sun responsible for much of the Earth's temperature shifts.

"The scientist critics reply that most students of this subject believe the sun cannot be responsible for the warming of 1970-2000. (Some say it is responsible for 30%, Lomborg says 40%).

"Charles Harper, planetary scientist at Harvard, criticized the inter-governmental report for being based more on deficient computer models than on ground-based temperatures during the period in which greenhouse gases were mainly omitted."

The scientist critics reply that because ground-based temperatures are inconsistent with each other, the computer models are all we have, deficient though they may be.

Second, some of these same scientists made predictions about running out of resources by the year 2000, which turned out not to be true. Lomborg cites these predictions.

Third, from United Nations data, as interpreted by Nicholas Eberstadt, demographer with Brookings Institution, and William Nordhaus, economist at Yale, I am persuaded that population in the more developed areas is already decreasing, and in the less developed countries the growth rate is declining, so much so that world population growth will probably level off to zero by 2050. The world's agricultural capacity to feed such a population will be more than sufficient. (See CLQ 6). However, the scientists criticize Lomborg for saying just that.

Fourth, scientists and environmentalists frequently do not take costs into account. It is here that economists would be of help, but they are generally ignored. Scientists would explain the environmental facts as best they know them, and together with economists (and other social scientists) they would propose policies, of which the economists would calculate the costs. This would be a cooperative enterprise.

I wish scientists and economists jointly would write a book as easily read by lay people as Lomborg's is, to explain all environmental problems in lay language, covering the disagreements among them and the uncertainties. The anti-Lomborg reviewers write of a "consensus" among scientists (theirs), when in fact there is no consensus. Yet they appear to be on more solid ground than Lomborg. If any of you know of such a book, I would appreciate your telling me.

Nevertheless, we seek the truth. So, I must make up my own mind - inexpert as I am - since I believe anyone living on this earth should have an opinion and a policy. I do not have the qualifications to perform the studies myself, so I am at the mercy of those who do. Combining Lomborg with the scientists' reviews, I come to the following inexpert opinions - subject to change with new evidence.

1. Environmentalists have been guilty of exaggerating the ill effects of environmental change. Lomborg pinpoints these exaggerations. The scientist reviewers say that no responsible scientist holds them anyway, yet among the reviewers are the guilty ones. These exaggerations should be resisted and reasonable estimates publicized, along with their probabilities.
2. Global warming is indeed occurring, but no one knows how much is anthropogenic (human induced) and how much is the natural cycle in which the earth warms and cools. The vast majority of scientists believe that anthropogenic warming is serious (more than Lomborg does), and they have persuaded me. But they do not agree on how much so.
3. We should already be thinking more about how to adjust to the effects of global warming than how to prevent it. To the extent that global warming is part of the natural cycle, it cannot be prevented.

To the extent that it is anthropogenic, prevention will be politically difficult (or impossible) because peoples not directly affected will refuse to pay the cost.

4. Given that world population is now as large as it is (and we do not want to take lives through war or starvation), biotechnical seed breeding probably saves many lives, as Lomborg points out. Potential ill effects - such as the spreading of "monster seeds" - should be controlled as best we can.

5. While Lomborg points to only a small decrease in the land devoted to forests, he does not distinguish between primeval forests and tree plantations. The primeval forest is needed to promote a desirable diversity of species. I am persuaded by the scientists that Lomborg has underestimated the extinction of species.

6. Policies should be formed to conserve water and energy and to inhibit the pollution of air and water if only because doing so creates a more desirable world, regardless of whether it prevents global warming. These policies should be implemented as far as is politically possible, but we should not attempt the impossible. Scientists have not adequately addressed the political and cost aspects. That is not their field, but they have not sufficiently cooperated with those whose field it is.

7. Governments are not satisfactory agencies for implementing these policies, since governments represent polluters as well as environmentalists. Instead, we should seek market-type instruments for controlling pollution. The tricky point is that governments may be necessary to develop the market-type instruments. Political activists, get to work!

8. Following the Clean Air Acts in the United States, among the market-type instruments are pollution permits. Determine a maximum permissible amount of any type of pollution, and issue permits for that amount, according to some political process. The permits would be salable. Those who can reduce pollution more cheaply than the market value of the permits would sell their allotments to others for whom pollution reduction would be more expensive. Thus pollution would be limited to the permissible amount at least cost.

9. Martin Feldstein, professor of economics at Harvard, has offered a similar plan to reduce dependence on foreign oil. Determine the maximum amount of gasoline that should be permitted, and issue

permits for it. Those who buy gasoline would pay the pump price, plus the cost of a permit. Having to pay for both would constitute an increase in price.

10. But energy prices should be allowed to rise anyway, because only then will renewable energy sources, such as windmills, fuel cells, and photo-voltaic cells become cost-effective.

11. If we wish to protect the poor against increases in energy prices, we should give them money. If they decide to spend it on other things than energy, so much more energy will be conserved.

One of my editorial board members commented that it would be difficult for me, having backed Lomborg so enthusiastically, now to backtrack. Why? Don't we seek the truth? And doesn't the truth come in small morsels?

I do not expect all readers to agree with my opinions, and I certainly do not aim to persuade you. Rather, I like to hear what you think. Remember, this is an interchange, and I learn from you.

> Peace, and a Clean World,
> Jack

P.S. I am indebted to CLQ readers Jack Herring, Merlyn Holmes, and Karen Street for bringing these reviews to my attention.

READERS' RESPONSES ON LETTER 32

Hello Jack. This is simply to let you know that, insofar as my limited time and energy allow, I read and try to understand what you are saying to us Friends — and will continue to do so. Please don't interpret my lack of substantive response to your series of essays as lack of appreciation for your considerable effort and knowledge.

> Wilmer Tjossem, Des Moines Valley (IA) Friends Meeting

I sent out my own condensation of *The Economist* article on Bjorn Lomborg's book to a Quaker Feminist e-mail list and received back two responses from women who work for environmental organizations — both of whom wish to remain anonymous. They each had checked the info in *The Econo-*

mist article with their higher-ups and found that the scaled back evaluations that Lomborg gave were known to their organizations. They were both told, however, that the higher numbers and shorter time periods Lomborg cited as exaggerations would continue to be used for fundraising purposes.

One of the women commented that there were a couple of scientists who had literally made their reputations on "scare stories" about the environment who had indicated that they weren't about to reverse themselves now. One stated that he thought Lomborg could be discredited, and he intended to work on that.

Janet Minshall, Anneewakee Creek Friends Worship Group, Douglasville (GA)

You cite costs as something an economist can help with, but do you take into account all of the costs?
a) One that has been evident has been freaky weather, more than usual. The reinsurance companies, who are the ones who will have to pay for it, have been worried.
b) If the tundra warms up, it won't help a lot with food because there's little topsoil. If the growing areas of the world heat up, who knows what will happen? It might become too dry for many crops, or it might require different crops with less yield, or unknown things may happen.
 c) Tropical diseases may spread north.

In all, the uncertainties are huge, and potentially devastating. Cleaning up is something we SHOULD do, and if it makes life better (or possible), that's a great side effect. Much of the opposition to cleaning up seems to come from companies who seem to think that cleaning up their act will cost them money. Not cleaning up their act may cost all of us much more, perhaps even our civilization.

Given uncertainty with a huge amount at risk and a finite cost, I think the conservative thing to do is to radically change society to prevent further damage.

Jim Caughran, Toronto (Ontario, Canada) Friends Meeting

Although I am not a scientist, I have followed environmental disputes with great interest for years. It seems to me that many environmentalists, even scientists, treat their beliefs like a religion. They are quite emotional about it and often have the attitude that they *can't* be wrong. Also, they act as if people who disagree with them are immoral rather than mistaken. But over the years they have been proved wrong time after time. So my gut instinct is to take these debunkers of Bjorn Lomborg with many grains of salt. Lomborg, don't forget, started out very hostile to Julian Simon, whom he set out to disprove. But he is that rare man: an honest environmentalist, and he went where the data led him, by all accounts.

Judy Warner, Lutheran, Rohrersville, Maryland

THE QUAKER ECONOMIST
January 15, 2002

Letter No. 33

Dear friends:

What is a Classic Liberal?

Classic liberalism is the liberalism of the seventeenth century, the period in which Quakerism was born. Being free of the king's commands was a central focus of early Quakers. Over the three centuries that followed, the term "liberalism" became associated with progressive ideas, such as a public school system, antitrust laws, social security, and regulations to make corporations behave like "good" citizens. As these rules were effected by government, "liberalism" became interventionism, the exact opposite of its classic meaning.

A classic liberal is one who would leave the people free to choose the goods and services they buy, at prices agreed between buyer and seller, and who does not want the government to choose for them or set the prices. Nevertheless, a classic liberal society has rules (for trading, paying debts, etc.) "Liberal" does not mean "license." The rules are made primarily by those who must abide by them rather than imposed by a ruler.

This definition is the basis for classical economics, as developed and taught by the great economists, beginning with Adam Smith in 1776, continuing through John Stuart Mill, David Ricardo, and Léon Walras in the nineteenth century, and culminating in Alfred Marshall in 1890. Joseph Schumpeter (in whose classes I studied) elaborated on it in the twentieth century. It is *mainstream* micro-economic thinking today.

The classical economists were pragmatic, but (except for Mill) not particularly compassionate. Three amendments are necessary to make for a compassionate, classic liberal society. I suggest the following:

First, if the poor cannot afford a minimum standard of living, the government should subsidize them, either with cash or housing vouchers, health vouchers, and the like. For those whom we believe incapable of making appropriate decisions, we should offer counsel or - in extreme cases - caregivers.

Second, power must be dispersed as much as possible. Although the classical economists did not make a point of this, I showed, in *Centuries of Economic Endeavor* (University of Michigan Press, 1994) that the emergence of classic liberalism required a certain power diffusion. The king had to lose power, and the peasants and merchants had to gain it.

Before turning to the third amendment, we must define efficiency and cost.

A cost is any resource consumed, such as labor and materials in production. Costs include the degradation of resources, for example pollution of air, which diminishes in value. If a producer does not pay for sewage dumped into a river, he or she effects a social cost but not a private cost. Social costs include those suffered by anyone or everyone, while a private cost is a resource consumed and paid for privately. (Private costs are a subset of social costs).

The efficient producer is one that produces any given output at the least private cost. ("Given" includes quality as well as quantity). The most efficient society is one where private costs and social costs are identical - that is, the producer pays for all of his or her pollution and other social costs.

My third amendment is that rules must be made so that the producer pays all costs of production, including social costs. Douglass North, a Nobel laureate in economics, found that the greatest economic development had occurred in the Western world where producers tended, more than in other places, to pay their social costs. Obviously, they do not do so completely, since air and water are often polluted at no cost to the polluter.

As economic historian, I look for slow changes over centuries. To those who cannot see the hands of the clock turn, the following outcomes of classic liberalism will appear impossible. But I do believe that I see, in our society today, tiny changes that will accumulate. This - or something like it - is how I see world society 100 to 500 years from now:

1. Whoever creates a social cost will pay for it. For example, instead of regulations mandating that automobiles achieve a certain mileage per gallon, drivers will be required (by law) to pay for their pollution. They might pay in taxes or by buying limited-issue pollution permits or in other ways. Thus the market will encourage them to demand fuel-efficient cars.

2. Private persons will also pay their own costs, including health care, education, social security, housing, and other benefits now provided by government or employer. Doing so creates a society of personal responsibility, not one of dependence.

3. Since these benefits should be available to everyone, those unable to pay may receive cash (as in a negative income tax, where the government pays you rather than vice-versa). If we believe they will not use the cash well but spend it on drink or drugs, we may give them vouchers instead, usable only for specified purposes. For example, a housing voucher, a health-insurance voucher, or an education voucher. Gradually, these social benefits will be transferred to the private sector, but no one will be denied them for want of resources.

4. Private advisory organizations may be set up to advise less knowledgeable persons on how best to spend their incomes. This would be an appropriate activity for Quakers and other religious groups.

5. Insurance will be sold by private companies to those who pay premiums. With one exception, the government will provide no insurance, not even for floods. People who build in the Mississippi Valley will pay for flood damage to their properties, or else they will buy private insurance at high premiums. Thus they will be discouraged from building there. The one exception might be non-recurring, major disasters, such as victims of the Twin Towers tragedy, whom Government might help.

6. Unemployment insurance will be bought privately, in amounts necessary to sustain a family through a long period of depression. If everyone had sufficient insurance, there would be no depressions. Re-insurance will be required (in which insurance companies spread their risks to other companies). For those who cannot afford the insurance, vouchers will be provided.

7. But there is no such thing as absolute security. Even governments have refused to pay their obligations, as Spain has done several times, Germany right after World War I, the United States in 1933 (by not redeeming dollars in gold), and Argentina this month, by defaulting on government bonds.

8. Certain purchases will be required by law, such as adequate health and unemployment insurance, to prevent free riding. A free rider is one who takes advantage of society's compassion by not paying for insurance or other private costs. For example, our society is too compassionate (I think) to let a person die in the street because he or she does not have health insurance.

9. A productive unit (e.g., corporation) will be induced by the market to be the right size. Following a rule of microeconomics, a corporation tends to combine productive units (sales, materials procurement, engineering, etc.) into one company only if doing so saves the costs of buying from independent producers (outsourcing). Only bad management or limited future vision would keep it from doing so.

10. Government will need less money because so many programs will have been transferred to the private sector. Taxes may be decreased accordingly.

11. No producer will be subsidized, not even farmers. Farmers will learn to save in good times to tide themselves over in bad. Poor people will not have to pay more for food or taxes, as they do in the present system.

12. Many similar prescriptions will be provided; these are just examples.

Why is this a better society? Because in our present society, over the past 150 years we have tended to transfer power from people to government, and the classic liberal society would transfer it back again. Power and responsibility go together.

Did you ask yourself how all this might this happen? Sorry, the devil in the details requires books on economic history, for which I do not have space here. I did spell out the details of these ideas in my two books, *Centuries of Economic Endeavor* and *The Moral Economy,* but I don't expect you to read them, any more than I read what I don't have time for. Nor do I expect you necessarily to agree. Please just know that I have given careful thought, and this is the scenario I come to.

Can't wait 500 years? Every one of these conditions could be brought about immediately, if concentrated power and interventions did not prevent them.

Classic liberals are incorrectly called "conservative." We are not. A conservative typically wants to conserve society as it "always has been," whereas a classic liberal welcomes innovation and change. The government may make a few innovations, but generally it did not invent, finance, or market the products that bring prosperity and happiness.

This twelve-step program constitutes the direction in which the world is now heading. Vast majorities in less developed countries want the economic freedom that has been denied them by their rulers and by trade restrictions in the more developed world. Interventionists are fighting a rearguard battle against the tidal force of freedom.

Most unprogrammed Quakers are interventionist. They sincerely want to help the disadvantaged, but they have unwittingly joined other interventionists in creating a society in which individual responsibility has eroded, and in which taxpayers want to take more out of the common pot than they willingly put in. There is never enough money for health care, affordable housing, unemployment insurance, and other social benefits for the poor. In the long run, the result is societies like Argentina, Mexico, India, and China, where individual creativity is hampered, would-be producers are suppressed, and poverty is the lot of many. Another result of the interventionist society is that government can - during an "emergency" - take funds out of the social-benefit pot to pay for war.

But history will slowly dilute the scenario of the interventionists. It will gradually be discovered that unhindered voluntary transactions add up to the most prosperous world with the most fair distributions of income and wealth (as witness Hong Kong, Singapore, and Taiwan). Throw in some redistribution of incomes (say, a negative income tax), and no one is poor.

That, or something like it, is the classic liberal world that I consider inevitable, long after I am gone. If we intervene because we can't wait, we only postpone it. I started CLQ in order to bring to Quakers a new insight, since most of the current Quaker press and Quaker organizations are primarily interventionist. Perhaps you would like to review earlier Letters (at http://clq.quaker.org) to see if that is what I have done.

To what world do you aspire?

Your friend indeed,
Jack Powelson

READERS' RESPONSES TO LETTER NO. 33

Having read the report], I was (mildly) more impressed by the World Bank's recommendations than Jack was. They do emphasize the state suddenly becoming kinder and gentler, which seems quixotic at best. But they also make quite a point of the fact that NGO's rarely try to support local poor in either developing social capital, or local capacity, or really in anything other than handing off materials (although there are some distinct exceptions). They urge NGO's to pay a lot more attention to helping to train and organize the poor, and to work with and develop local capacity, and less attention to worrying about purely material issues. They repeatedly point to the fact that almost nobody ever bothers with developing that social capacity among the poor.

Geoffrey Williams, Bethesda (MD) Friends Meeting

Waiting forever for the poor to gain power by themselves may or may not necessarily be effective. Historically, that has only worked part of the time — even then if you look at some of the "model" countries that history points us to, they (and we) have a pretty poor track record and still have large numbers of poor and dispossessed. I feel that we have to continue to try other routes, that we have to try to consciously evolve beyond the unacceptably slow and largely ineffective historical models, and that the World Bank summary's emphasis on increasing communication is an excellent direction to go in. If the "willingness or interest on the part of the state" is, as you say, missing, then that is the strongest indication that communication needs to be improved right there.

Merlyn Holmes, Unitarian, Boulder (CO)

I see [the World Bank report on poverty] as true in Anacostia DC also. There is the addition of inflated expectations, from TV and successful criminals and entertainment and sport figures. There is generally a lack of respect for booklearning and knowledge.

Faith Williams, Bethesda (MD) Friends Meeting

NOTE: Faith is librarian in an inner city school in Anacostia, DC.

Thanks for your wonderful, thought-provoking letter, as usual. A comment on the poor in Europe gaining power: The Black Plague killed so many people that labor was in very short supply. Thus the serfs gained a great deal of bargaining power; they could leave their lords and travel around to find higher wages. This led to a huge shift in the economies of the European countries.

Judy Warner, Lutheran, Rohrersville, Maryland

How sad that the World Bank offers such an unpromising approach. Does the book address or consider the extent to which the poor's current coping mechanisms include the germs of a capacity to challenge the state and others depriving them of basic liberties?

Stephen Williams, Bethesda (MD) Friends Meeting

There is something that the developed countries can do. They can get our governments to remove the import quotas and tariffs on the goods poor countries produce - usually agricultural. Sugar in the States is twice the price on the world market for instance. I totally agree, trade not aid - people want a job, not a handout, and our wealthy countries are trying to keep all the wealth to ourselves by using any unfair law, backed by our military (the Monroe Doctrine - Latin America is ours for US companies to exploit, backed by the "big stick" of our military supporting dictatorships that allow US companies to exploit workers in their country). Opposition to NAFTA in the US was overcome only by making it so Mexico had to open its markets years before the US did - Mexicans rushed to the stores to buy US goods and impoverished their own country and destroyed their own industries. We are scandalized that Japan trades unfairly by keeping its economy closed, but how about the US (and EU) giving big farm subsidies and having protectionist quotas and tariffs on farm products?

Doug Fenner, Queensland, Australia

THE QUAKER ECONOMIST
January 25, 2002

Letter No. 34

Dear friends:

Enron and Corporate Culture

Clearly, Enron defrauded its employees, stockholders, and creditors. It exaggerated its profits by transferring debts and losses to allied companies. The management encouraged employees to buy Enron stock which they knew would soon be worthless. The proceeds helped finance millions of dollars in bonuses they paid to themselves just before the collapse. They laid off 4,000 workers and filed for bankruptcy in December, and in January they shredded company papers.

Having invested the bulk of their pension plans in Enron stock, many employees faced retirement without the reserves they had counted on. Enron froze the assets of the pension fund, so employees could not sell their stock as they watched it plummet in value.

Instead of acting as the watchdogs that they were purported to be, Enron's auditors, Andersen CPAs, were complicit in this trickery. Shortly after the bankruptcy, Andersen shredded records of its audits. The accepted practice would have been to save them until after the statute of limitations had passed.

What happened to the famous checks and balances in the American economy, which were supposed to see that such a tragedy could not occur?

Me, CPA

Fifty years ago I passed my CPA exams in the State of New York. My first two jobs were with the then two largest accounting firms in the world: Haskins & Sells (now absorbed into Deloitte Touche) and Price Waterhouse. With H&S, I audited the books of the Hearst Corporation for nine months every year. We published a consolidated statement, showing the assets, liabilities, income, and expenses of the Hearst organization as a whole: all the newspapers, all the magazines, all the art works, even a castle. It would have been unthinkable to deceive investors, bankers, and others by hiding liabilities or losses. Using principles established by the Financial Accounting Standards Board and the American Institute of Certified Public Accountants (both private organizations), we certified the statements as correct "according to generally accepted accounting principles." We were the watchdog of transparency.

What has happened in the meantime? CPA firms have discovered that consulting services are more profitable than auditing, so they have advised the very firms whose books they audit. Fifty years ago, the total independence of the CPA firm from the client was a mark of our integrity. (We could advise on improving the accounting system but not on financial management.) Now there is a conflict of interest. How can a CPA firm certify the statements of a company to which it has given financial advice? Andersen even kept some records for Enron, so it was auditing its own accounting. That would have been a total "No-No" in my day.

(NOTE: At age 30, I took a PhD in economics and changed my profession).

Profit of the Manager or Profit of the Company?

Economists have long known that corporations do not necessarily seek the greatest profit. Instead, each officer within the company wishes to acquire the greatest power and wealth that he or she can, within the constraints of possibility and cost. Doing so may or may not coincide with the greatest good for the company or the stockholder. For this reason, checks and balances are set up within the company. A "system of internal control" makes sure that no official can embezzle funds without some other official knowing. But no system of internal control is 100% foolproof if the managers collude. The job of the auditor is to uncover such deceit. If, however, the auditor is himself or herself part of the deceit (again, unthinkable in my day), no system will work.

Was Enron Politically Connected?

Enron lavished millions of dollars upon Congressional campaigns for both parties, and it contributed significantly to the Bush campaign. In return, it had the ear of prominent politicians, whose policies it influenced. As a result of lobbying, in 1997 Enron received an exemption from the Investment Company Act of 1940, which enabled it "to structure financial operations [in South America and Europe] to both conceal them from investors and shift debt off their books" (*New York Times,* 1/23/02). To avert bankruptcy, it called on its political supporters, including the President, for help in securing more bank loans. So far as we know, no help was given - nothing can be proved.

What to do about it? Two paths

Historically, Europeans and their American descendents held themselves accountable through checks and balances, privately agreed upon but legally enforceable. Thus unions would negotiate (privately) with employers and make contracts (legally enforceable). Only after private organizations had determined the rules of trade (such as debt settlement, quality of goods, safety in factories, and bankruptcy procedures) were they written into law. Late in the nineteenth century, however, government (Congress and President) began taking over these negotiations on behalf of the citizens to be "protected." The Act to Regulate Interstate Commerce (1887) and the Sherman Anti-Trust Law (1890) were among the first of the new genre.

When Alexis de Tocqueville visited the United States in the mid-19th Century, he was impressed by Americans as joiners. Civic associations sprang up everywhere - social, intellectual, political, and recreational. Knowing one another through these associations was a major force in developing the trust that Americans have felt for each other.

In 2000, Robert Putnam published *Bowling Alone,* decrying the sharp decrease in these associations. Americans now sit in front of TVs, he says, and sign checks for organizations in which they do not participate personally. This decrease, Putnam feels, has led to a decline in social trust. On top of this great loss, I add that we have relinquished many of our cherished checks and balances to government regulators. Unions did not protest that Enron was mismanaging employee funds; no stockholder association observed that their members were about to be gypped; bankers did not pay attention that the CPAs were derelict.

Government regulation is often desirable, even necessary. But regulators do not know how to run Enron, or any other business. We have seen how governments in less developed countries have not only been incapable of managing businesses properly, but how they too - like Andersen - have misused their power. In Argentina (see Letter 31), China (Letter 1), and Russia (Letter 4), political managers have milked state-owned enterprises.

Most politicians are far more concerned for their own power than they are in "protecting" their charges. "Protection" then becomes a path to power rather than power a way to protect. Are we sure this will not happen (or is not happening) in the United States?

So, how can we see that the Enron scandal will not be repeated? The main outcry is to give government more power to regulate companies, stockholders, and CPAs. The way I would prefer would be to renew our sense of civic obligation, to strengthen our associations and checks and balances, so that our society works from a balance of power rather than a central focus of power that we "trust" to be benign.

In this way we would return to individual responsibility, checks and balances in the culture (not only the law), and bargaining through civic associations. Instead of controlling campaign contributions, we would take away the powers of government that special interests "buy." Unions would once again be the watchdogs for employees, bankers would not lend to companies that did not live up to accepted practices, employees would organize and manage their own health care and pensions. Advisory organizations would be set up to help them. Some income redistribution (such as a negative income tax) might be necessary so poor people could pay for their necessities.

Is this a Quakerly way to live, or have I misjudged?

> Yours in friendship,
> Jack Powelson

READERS' RESPONSES TO LETTER NO. 34

Your letter is very timely, and useful and your experience as a CPA is enlightening. I agree it would be preferable to encourage civic mindedness again, but how do we do that? Maybe World War II engendered a feeling of community that has not been repeated since, and would be difficult to foster.

Virginia Flagg, San Diego (CA) Friends Meeting

The reason lobbyists and political contributors are powerful is that politicians have put themselves in the position of controlling so much of the economy through laws and regulations. It is a conflict of interest, of course, but it feathers their nests. Until the public understands this and realizes that the "protection" that the current regulatory system provides is chimerical in all too many cases, nothing will change—no matter which political party is in control.

Ken Allison, Episcopalian, Paradise Valley, AZ

How many times in recent years have we heard, "I didn't do anything illegal?" Reading your comments on Enron, etc., I realized how disingenuous this was, especially when made (as it usually is) by people involved in the making of the laws in the first place. This is the new process: if you want to do something unethical, write a law that allows or ignores it, then say that you didn't do anything illegal. If it is mentioned in the law, change it or get an exception. "It was perfectly legal . . ." In any case, get permission from someone else to do something you know is wrong. Then it's okay - you can ignore your own conscience.

Gusten Lutter, Mountain View Friends Meeting, Denver (CO)

"*Timeo Danaos, et dona ferentes.*" Translated here, I would never trust the New York Times. It may be right, but government is now in the incessant business of granting and denying exemptions, and whether lobbying (as opposed to perfectly proper presentations to the deciding agency on the merits) were determinative is likely to be tricky. The NYT's resolution of the issue can be somewhat discounted: even though the officials must have belonged to the Clinton administration, the episode relates to campaign finance, and the NYT, like the Washington Post, is very eager for more restrictions (on everyone except the media).

Two related issues: (1) Right now, in our society, the victims of the fraud can sue the perpetrators and recover—up to the extent of the perpetrators' assets. (2) Surely the "liberal society" cannot be free of fraud. Men will not become angels in the liberal society.

As I was noting over the weekend, it is not clear to me that any buying of government influence, no matter how defined or how much may go on, has actually been relevant to this case.

Stephen Williams, Bethesda (MD) Friends Meeting

I thought I'd never see another classical liberal Quaker after Hoover died. They get in shorter supply the closer one gets to Lake Michigan.

William Urban, Peoria-Galesburg Monthly Meeting

The "cult of quarterly income statements" to drive up stock prices led directly to Enron hiding debt off their balance sheet and the debacle that has followed. Enron ignored Parkinson's Law for Company Presidents, "If things are so bad you have to lie about them, they will be even worse when you are found out."

Gordon Johnson, Episcopalian, Arlington VA

I am a member of Sweden YM, although I feel more united with the original Quaker message as today is expressed more clearly by New Foundation Fellowship. Trained as an economist, I used to be politically active as a classical liberal (libertarian), or anarcho capitalist in Sweden, which, to me, ought to be the political agenda of Friends. It is the only agenda I feel is compatible with Friends rather individualistic view on religion, the only agenda that values individual freedom enough. I am somewhat surprised by how modern Friends can unite in favor of semisocialistic views, when respect for the individual ought to follow from their religious views.

Peter Brolin, Sweden Yearly Meeting

I really enjoyed reading your perspective, as usual. But I think you made a stronger argument for the regulation of CPAs, disallowing conflict of interest practices, than for the conclusion you presented. I may have just missed their subtlety, but for me, the beginning and middle of your letter did not present the steps that would lead to the conclusion.

Ann Dixon, Boulder (CO) Meeting of Friends

What is a negative income tax? I commend you on your timely selection of essay material. Being an advocate of the poor makes you a man after mine own heart. I shouldn't have to ask this question if I had been observant, but how do I access your previous articles?

Dennis Bentley, Morganton, NC (no Friends Meeting in my town)

ANSWERS: (1) A negative income tax is one where low-income people receive money from the government instead of paying it. The tax progresses as one's income rises, first to zero and then to positive amounts. (2) To access previous letters, visit http://clq.quaker.org.

I definitely enjoyed CLQ 34. I agree with you about culture. I've noticed that some Wall Street Journal editorialists take the position that it's silly to expect auditors to be honest watchdogs, which I find very disturbing. The one thing the WSJ tends to come through on (in my opinion) is the old JP Morgan values of character and probity - that they are so ready to toss them aside now seems like a very bad sign.

Geoffrey Williams, Bethesda (MD) Friends Meeting

I, too, am a CPA and not practicing auditing. I have taught accounting and auditing at the college level. The more I learned my craft, the more I realized that creative accounting" (It's an art, not a science!) was what the businesses of the world wanted, not the best picture of what was actually happening to a business's numbers. I ended up resigning from the American Institute of CPA's in 1978, after I discovered how badly the numbers were being "crunched" to create the image that management wanted.

Free Polazzo, President, Friendly Systems, Inc. Anneewakee Creek Friends Worship Group (Douglasville, GA)

In a First-Day school class I was trying to counter the contention in the book I was given that hungry countries should grow food rather than more valuable exports. I had them suppose that people in a hungry country discover that they can make a hat that is popular in Europe and America and that the market value of the hats exceeds the market value of the food they could have produced with the same labor. At that point, one of the young ladies said, "As soon as they showed a profit, a greedy American company would swoop in and take over their business."

We discussed her point, and I made many of the comments that I think you would in that situation. But what got my attention is that a high-school sophomore raised in a nearby meeting had been conditioned so thoroughly that I could elicit such a knee-jerk reaction to my simple example. I shouldn't be surprised. Over the last few years I have met many adult Friends around here who believe that all corporations are evil and that multinationals are even worse. It is natural that they would inculcate this in their children. I suspect that this view of the world economy has become a feature of the First-Day school curriculum wherever I am not teaching.

> Asa Janney, Herndon (VA) Friends Meeting

Let me make some specific recommendations along the lines that Jack suggests. Convict the nogoodniks. White collar crime, is a crime. I think it might be wise to forbid Arthur Andersen from doing any more audits of public companies. I think that the SEC might already have that power. We need to be doing a better job of recognizing outstanding ethical behavior in business. There is a lot of it out there. We need to encourage it. I am Executive in Residence at Bellarmine University here in Louisville. Ethics are an important component of every course.

> Lee B. Thomas, Jr., Friends Meeting of Louisville (KY)

THE QUAKER ECONOMIST

January 31, 2002

Letter No. 35

Dear friends:

Enron again

Why do we need a massive Congressional investigation of Enron? If Enron, or Andersen CPA, has broken the law - and I believe they both have - should that not be cause for a trial in the normal court system? The alleged reason for the Congressional investigation is to determine whether any new laws should be passed, to keep the situation from being repeated. However, the "court" (Congress) that is trying Enron is the very body that was bought by Enron with its contributions. Now we have the fox guarding the chicken coop.

In a classic liberal society, those harmed by Enron would take Enron to court. Such a society would require a new national outlook, in which individuals and groups take care of themselves instead of entrusting their "protection" to government. It would beef up labor unions, so they would keep watch over how their members may be bilked by management. It would teach banks to examine how well their loan clients are audited and to refuse loans to companies that do not hire external auditors with integrity. It would teach stockholders (or mutual funds) that they can't rely on improperly audited companies, and if they do, they take the consequences.

All this boils down to: we have entrusted to the government to look after our interests in multiple ways, and then we have allowed a major company to "buy" the government. Now we are looking to the government to regulate that company.

Many look on Enron and Andersen as deficiencies in our capitalist system. I look upon them as a case study in how capitalism evolves. Many firms are now looking at themselves, to make sure they do not become another Enron. So are the CPA firms.

The alternative society that we seek will evolve out of the present society.

The Exclusion of the Poor

In CLQ #33 I wrote of how the poor are excluded from modern institutions. "In most of the world, the poor live in a society distinct from the affluent - different institutions, organizations, and customs, and little communication between the two. The poor are looked down on and denied the courtesies available to others." How and where has this happened? Mainly in less developed countries (LDCs), not so much in more developed countries (MDCs).

The poor have far more access to modern institutions in MDCs than they do in LDCs. MDCs are the very ones in which power has become diffuse (though still more diffusion is desirable) and trade has been mostly free. In Hong Kong, Singapore, Taiwan, and South Korea - where enterprise and trade have also been free - in only one generation, the poor have raised themselves from Third-World poverty to wages and respect on a par with Europe.

If the United States and Europe were to open their markets to the textile, clothing, shoe, and other basic industries in the LDCs; if the elitist governments of LDCs would open the economy to the initiatives and inventiveness of all people; and if the poor were to gain property rights to the land they till (which is now owned mostly by governments), they would find jobs, borrow by mortgage, and start their own enterprises. It would take some doing, but all this would gradually lift them out of their poverty.

It is by concentration of power in LDCs (in overwhelming regulations, state enterprises, property ownership by government, and other restrictions) and in protective tariffs of MDCs that the world's poorest are kept in their poverty.

Again, let us evolve toward an alternative society. I propose classic liberalism.

What is a Classic Liberal?

Classic liberalism is the liberalism of the seventeenth century, the period in which Quakerism was born. Being free of the king's commands was a central focus of early Quakers. Over the three centuries that followed, the term "liberalism" became associated with progressive ideas, such as a public school system, antitrust laws, social security, and regulations to make corporations behave like "good" citizens. As these rules were made by government, "liberalism" became interventionism, the exact opposite of its classical meaning.

If our society today were classic liberal, the Enron scandal could not have occurred. There would have been no favors for government to sell, so Enron could not have bought any. Consumers, bankers, stockholders, creditors, and employees would all have formed private agencies to look after their interests and bring to court any person or company that violated them. Environmentalists are doing this already. But over the last 150 years we have eroded most of these pressure groups by entrusting our protection to a government that can be bribed to betray us.

A classic liberal is one who would leave the people free to decide which goods and services they will produce and how they will produce them, with sales at prices voluntarily agreed between buyer and seller. The classic liberal does not want the government to choose or regulate or set prices.

How then does a classic liberal society prevent scandals, environmental orgies, and deception? First, it has rules (for trading, paying debts, property ownership, violations of the environment, etc.) that are enforced in courts of law. "Liberal" does not mean "license." The rules are made primarily by those who must abide by them rather than imposed by a ruler. Second, class action suits are undertaken by those who suffer from violations of the rules. In these ways, the plethora of government regulations is supplanted by private actions of those who suffer from abuses.

A classic liberal society is one of *balance of power.* Consider the world as a giant jigsaw puzzle, solved and sitting on a table. Each piece represents an individual or organization (unions, employers' associations, consumers, bankers, etc.). The power of each piece is represented by its size. Each is trying to increase its power by pushing against other pieces, which push back if they can. "Power expands until other power stops it." The various groups and organizations, by holding each other in place, keep each other from exerting too much power. The bankers' associations, creditors' associations, employee unions, and similar groups that would have sued Enron are pieces in the puzzle. So are Quakers, wanting to empower themselves; better to protect the underclass.

For example, the classic liberal society would not depend on government to bail out banks that make bad loans. This would encourage banks to put pressure on external auditors to give correct opinions. It would encourage stockholders to invest in properly audited companies, to avoid taking losses. Stockholders are better placed than government, and have more incentive, to perform this regulatory function.

Tragically, the greatest classic liberal of our day, Professor Robert Nozick of Harvard, has just died of stomach cancer at age 63 (the same disease that took Robin's and my beloved daughter, Cindy, at age 37). In his obituary (1/24/02), the *New York Times* states: "In his first book, "Anarchy, State, and Utopia,". . . Professor Nozick starkly and vigorously attacked the forms of paternalistic government that 'forbid capitalistic acts between consenting adults.'"

Classic liberalism is the basis for classical economics, as developed and taught by the great economists, beginning with Adam Smith in 1776, continuing through John Stuart Mill, David Ricardo, and Léon Walras in the nineteenth century, and culminating in Alfred Marshall in 1890. Joseph Schumpeter (in whose classes I studied) elaborated on it in the twentieth century. It is *mainstream* micro-economic thinking today.

The classical economists were pragmatic, but (except for Mill) not particularly compassionate. Although not all classic liberals agree, I believe some amendments are necessary to make for a compassionate, classic liberal society. I will write about these in CLQ 36.

I repeat (from a previous CLQ) what my interpreter told me after I had given a talk in Ukraine: "All our lives the government has taken care of us. Now that the government has failed us, we do not know how to take care of ourselves."

But a classic liberal society alone won't do it

Historically, classic liberalism has correlated with the freedom of "lower" social classes to innovate. This freedom has propelled economic development and more egalitarian distributions of income and wealth in northwestern Europe, North America, Oceania, and Japan than anywhere else in the world.

But classic liberalism merely opens the way. Institutions (education, banking, production, collective bargaining, and others) are more likely to embrace the poor in classic liberal societies than they are in societies where the elite wield power, as they do in LDCs today. The process will be gradual.

In MDCs, the resumption of responsibility by organizations of consumers, stockholders, bankers, employees and others will be gradual in a society where we have become accustomed to leave our protection to the government. More fiascos like Enron will be suffered before the idea of group responsibility at the lower levels sinks in.

In the next CLQ Letter (#36), I will outline my suggestions to make a classic liberal society more compassionate, and how a classic liberal society might prevent environmental degradation and help those unable to fend for themselves.

Sincerely your friend,
Jack Powelson

READERS' RESPONSES TO LETTER NO. 35

I do not mean to flatter you, but I must say that in reading about your work, and in reading your work, I have found many chords that ring with my own beliefs. As I am only 26 my beliefs are still in their formative stages. As such when I come across ideas that articulate what are my nascent urgings I get excited. This is the sentiment I had in coming across your web site. I am just now exploring the Society of Friends and have been a free-marketer/libertarian since my college days. To see that you attended both Wharton and Harvard was very interesting, as I will be applying to both MBA programs next year.

Adam Jones, who is considering attending Palo Alto or San Jose Meeting, Sunnyvale CA

There has been so much government intervention in the economy that most alternatives have been forced out of the market. So people see government as the only source of solutions, only because government action has caused other solutions to fail.

For example, the Long Island Motor Parkway was a private road. It was the first concrete limited-access highway. It charged tolls, and stayed in operation until 1938. Why did it go out of business? Because the government out-competed it! The Northern State Parkway, which travelled over much the same route, was "free" (translation: paid for by tax dollars). How can private parties compete with solutions given away by government?? It can't — dumping is illegal when a private company does it to another, but is not illegal when the government does it!

> Russ Nelson, St. Lawrence Valley (NY) Friends Meeting

A fair bargain requires that both sides have comparable access to information and power (options).

> Vici Oshiro, Minneapolis (MN) Meeting

I have a problem with your concept: " .in a classic liberal society, those harmed by Enron would take Enron to court .", because such a court would necessarily pass judgment based on laws, and who would create those laws, if not some kind of representative government .which is what we have now. Fixing the problem of government corruption will not be easy, but taking money out of the election process would be an important first step. This is, in priciple, the aim of the campaign finance bills. However, these run so much counter to the self-interest of the incumbent politicians, that it is hard to see how these will pass .unless there is an enormous popular movement to " .throw the rascals out ." and replace them with a set of less self-serving individuals. Let's hope that the Enron affair, and others like it, will be the seed for such a development.

> Tom Selldorff, Weston (MA)

About 10 years ago my friend, the late Phil Stern wrote a book, "Still the Best Congress that Money Can Buy. I recommend it to you.

> Lee B. Thomas, Jr., Friends Meeting of Louisville (KY)

I'd be interested in hearing more about regulation, and why you are against it. Do we want rancid meat, unbreathable air, dangerous cars and water with E-Coli? Take your pick.

The air pollution position seems to be a classical "commons" situation, where a company can simply make more money by not cleaning their effluent. In Fox's day, industry was only able to pollute something directly down wind, at short range.

Jim Caughran, Toronto (Ontario) Meeting

ANSWER (because one is asked for): There are many ways in which these malignancies are overcome. On rancid meat, dangerous cars, and pure water, pass laws to designate the permissible limit on these events, and have consumer organizations file class action suits when the they are violated. On air pollution, sell tradable permits to pollute up to but not exceeding the limit that will be cleaned naturally (by the wind, for example). Actually, we do all these things now.

In a classic liberal society, the prohibition is against the event - cars may not pollute beyond a certain amount. Make your gasoline however you will, but there is a pollution limit. In a regulatory society, the prohibition is usually against the method. Make your gasoline this way, not that. Usually the manufacturer, not the regulator, is the one who knows the least expensive way to achieve the result.

THE QUAKER ECONOMIST

February 12, 2002

Letter No. 36

Dear friends:

What is classic liberalism (continued)?

In CLQ #35, I introduced the classic liberal society. It is the society toward which the Western World has been gravitating for ten centuries, with a few deviations, such as during the twentieth century. But we have always returned from the deviations, and the world is returning right now. In the classic liberal society, power is distributed among "low-level" people and groups. It is not concentrated in king, shogun, emperor, or democratic government.

The classic liberal society seeks balance of power among social groupings, in which socially desirable behavior is imposed sidewise - by group acting upon group - rather than downward, through government regulation. Environmental and other social goals are sought by nongovernment agencies as much removed from politics as possible, while social assistance is administered by private agencies financed in part by cash or voucher grants supplied by government, or by a negative income tax.

This society is described in detail in my book, *The Moral Economy.* In Part 1, seven current major problems are introduced: poverty, population, environment, ethnic bias, welfare, social security, and health care. In the classic liberal society, these problems will be resolved by a new culture, or new ways of behaving, as outlined in part 2. These ways include new accountability for the management of resources, greater interpersonal trust, new property definitions, and new concepts of money, law, taxes, education, religion, morality, and values. Laws may be passed, but basically these modes of behavior are shaped by the interaction of social groupings with relative balance of power, rather than by government mandate.

How do modes of behavior change in all the ways mentioned above? First, by people deciding that a new mode - say, in management accountability - is better for a certain occasion, such as the Enron scandal. Then it is repeated. When it is successful many times, it becomes cultural, or moral. (We wouldn't think of doing otherwise!) At that point, a law may be passed to bring in the stragglers. But a law that is passed before any of the above may breed distrust instead of trust.

A classic liberal is one who thinks first of how the problem may be overcome by ordinary people taking responsibility. An interventionist finds the solution first in government regulation. These are definitions, not stereotypes. You can be classic liberal with respect to one problem and interventionist with respect to another.

The world in 2302

As economic historian, I look for slow changes over centuries. To those who cannot see the hands of the clock turn, the following outcomes of classic liberalism will appear impossible. But if you had lived in George Fox's time, and someone had predicted the world in 2002 exactly as it turned out to be, would you have believed it? The changes I see for 2302 may not be right, but they are no greater than changes since the time of George Fox. Here they are:

Whoever creates a social cost such as pollution will pay for it. Instead of regulations mandating that automobiles achieve a certain mileage per gallon, drivers will be required (by law) to pay for their pollution. They might pay in taxes or by buying limited-issue pollution permits or in other ways. Thus the market will encourage them to demand fuel-efficient vehicles. (I leave it to science fiction writers to design these future vehicles).

Private persons will pay their own costs, including health care, education, social security, housing, and other benefits now provided by government or employer. Doing so creates a society of personal responsibility, not one of dependence. Since these benefits should be available to everyone, those unable to pay may receive cash (as in a negative income tax, where the government pays you rather than vice-versa). Then they buy the services from the providers that they choose.

Insurance will be sold by private companies to those who pay premiums. The government will provide no insurance, not even for major catastrophes like the World Trade Towers. Major catastrophes are not unusual. For all those affected by the Twin Towers tragedy, many more have suffered the same catastrophes, but being dispersed they have not received the same attention. All should be covered by private insurance, which would be required and subsidized for the poor. People who build in the Mississippi Valley will pay for flood damage to their properties, or else they will buy private insurance at high premiums. Thus they will be discouraged from building there.

Unemployment insurance will also be bought privately, in amounts necessary to sustain a family through a long period of depression. Those who do not have adequate funds will be subsidized by government, up to an amount to be democratically decided. Re-insurance will be required (in which insurance companies spread their risks to other companies). For those who cannot afford the insurance, vouchers will be provided.

Since everyone will have sufficient insurance, there will be no depressions. Insurance proceeds will keep incomes high and thus allow consumer demand to continue. The consumer demand will call for investment, which will lead to full employment. (So there! Mr. Keynes).

But there is no such thing as absolute security. Even governments have refused to pay their obligations, as England did in the fourteenth century, Spain several times in more recent years, Germany right after World War I, the United States in 1933 (by not redeeming dollars in gold), and Argentina last month.

Certain purchases will be required by law, such as adequate health and unemployment insurance, to prevent free riding. A free rider is one who takes advantage of society's compassion by not paying for insurance or other private costs. For example, our society is too compassionate (I think) to let a person die in the street because he or she does not have health insurance.

Why is this a better society? Because the poor will have contracts, enforceable by law, for social services. Right now, the government betrays the poor, who are the first to suffer in financial crises. The Administration is cutting back on Medicaid, and Bush's budget for the next ten years is less than adequate to finance Medicare.

Most unprogrammed Quakers are interventionist. They sincerely want to help the disadvantaged, but they have unwittingly helped create a society in which individual responsibility has eroded. Taxpayers want to take more out of the common pot than they willingly put in. There is never enough money for health care, affordable housing, unemployment insurance, and other social benefits for the poor. In the long run, the result will be a society like Argentina, Mexico, India, or China, where individual creativity is hampered, where would-be innovators are suppressed, and where poverty is the lot of many. Another result of the interventionist society is that government can - during an "emergency" - take funds out of the social-benefit pot to pay for war (as the U.S. is doing right now).

But history will slowly dilute the scenario of the interventionists. It will gradually be perceived that unhindered voluntary transactions add up to the most prosperous world with the most fair distributions of income and wealth, as witness Hong Kong, Singapore, South Korea, and Taiwan. Throw in some redistribution of incomes (say, a negative income tax), and no one is poor.

The European Union, the worldwide movement toward deregulation, massive tariff reductions since 1929, alternative schools, and privatization of state enterprises in less developed countries, are all harbingers of the classic liberal society. Just this week, India announced "the privatization of several state-owned companies, an end to restrictions on the stocking of some agricultural commodities and a plan to shed excess government manpower" (*The Economist,* 2/9/02).

How does classic liberalism differ from anarchy?

Classic liberalism has rules, laws, and property rights, as was mentioned in CLQ #36. How does it differ from libertarianism? I believe the classic liberal economy is more compassionate, in three ways:

First, if the poor cannot afford a minimum standard of living, the government (i.e., taxpayers) should subsidize them, either with cash or housing vouchers, health vouchers, and the like. For those whom we believe incapable of making appropriate decisions, we should offer counsel or - for the mentally disabled - caregivers.

Second, power must be dispersed as much as possible. Although the classical economists did not make a point of this, I showed, in *Centuries of Economic Endeavor,* that the emergence of classic liberalism in northwestern Europe and Japan required a certain power diffusion. The king had to lose power, and the peasants and merchants had to gain it.

Third, rules must require the producer to pay all costs of production, including social costs. Private costs include any resource consumed, such as labor and materials in production. Social costs include the degradation of resources, for example pollution of air, which diminishes its value. If a producer does not pay for sewage dumped into a river, he or she incurs a social cost but not a private cost. Social costs include those suffered by anyone or everyone, while a private cost is a resource consumed and paid for privately. Private costs are a subset of social costs.

When the producer pays all costs these are automatically passed on to the consumer. Assuming voluntary exchange, consumers take on these costs because they are the ultimate users of the resources consumed. This completes the circle, and by their independent actions as consumers (to buy or not to buy, to buy this and not that, etc.) they determine resource use. If we wish to tame the appetites of consumers or control the waste of resources, we need to work on people's consciences.

The efficient producer is one who produces any given output at the least private cost. ("Given" includes quality as well as quantity). The most efficient society is one where private costs and social costs are identical - that is, the producer pays for all of his or her pollution and other social costs.

Douglass North, a Nobel laureate in economics, found that the greatest economic development had occurred in the Western world where producers tended, more than in other places, to pay their social costs. Obviously, they do not do so completely, since air and water are often polluted at no cost to the polluter.

I believe the classic liberal path is but a continuation of the road the Western world has been following for ten centuries. If we intervene to speed it up, we only postpone the results. I started CLQ in order to bring to Quakers a new insight, since most of the current Quaker press and Quaker organizations are primarily interventionist. Perhaps you would like to review earlier Letters (at http://clq.quaker.org) to see if that is what I have truly done.

To what world do you aspire?

Your friend indeed,
Jack Powelson

READERS' RESPONSES TO LETTER NO. 36

How is the European Union a harbinger of a classical-liberal society? (I had been thinking of it as the reverse—a wide-reaching standardization and proliferation of government regulations.) I'd be delighted to understand otherwise.

Catherine Cox, Goose Creek (VA) Meeting

ANSWER (I usually comment on Readers' Responses only when requested to do so). The European Union is all that you say, but there are some balancing factors, mainly the free movement of labor and goods across borders and mergers of national corporations for greater efficiency. Much of this is resisted by national governments, mergers for instance, but I believe that on balance it is a step toward globalization and the classic liberal economy of three centuries hence.

The Washington Post reported yesterday that the US Olympic Comm. spent about $20 million more to train athletes for this winter's games than for the Nagano Games. Also, the US won about 20 medals more than at Nagano. Conveniently, this works out to a million bucks per marginal medal. My question to you is this: Do you think that it was a worthwhile investment? Other thoughts on the matter?

Asa Janney, Herdon (VA) Friends Meeting

NOTE: Answers to this question will be welcomed and probably published.

Let me suggest a modification to just one paragraph in CLQ #36, where you say insurance has the potential to do away with depression. (If we are all insured against unemployment, there will be no drop in consumption). You also invoke Mr. Keynes.

Inflation is purely a monetary supply problem. Think of money not as "money", but as a thing you barter goods and services for. Just as you would sometimes want more flour than other times (e.g. Christmastime), you might want more money sometimes than other times. This is called liquidity only by recognition that money has the special characteristic of "that thing which is barterable for nearly everything else".

The problem with bits of green paper (our current money) is that our government can easily adjust the supply of them. It's far too tempting for the government to raise money by printing up new dollars and spending them. Since the supply is now increased, the demand falls, and the "price" of money falls (i.e., other prices go up in terms of money). Every depression or recession has been preceded by a boom, and the boom by an increase in the supply of money. Some people (e.g. Mr. Keynes) believe that the cure is the tail of the dog which bit ye — i.e. more inflation. And indeed, a recession can be staved off by printing up more dollars. But the example of Weimar Germany, and today's Turkey (a Big Mac Meal costs four million Turkish lira), shows that it only pushes a worse problem into the future. Consumer demand has nothing to do with this.

Russ Nelson, St. Lawrence Valley (NY) Friends Meeting

I heard a news announcement that a radical animal rights organization was now being accused of being the leading domestic terrorist organization in the US. I got to thinking and realized that the Klu Klux Klan was a terrorist organization- that's exactly what their purpose was. Terrorize blacks into keeping quiet about any amount of discrimination and unjust treatment the white community wanted to dispense. KKK would still be happy to do this. Ah, and then I thought of another fine group. The right-to-lifers who get just a little carried away and bomb abortion clinics and shoot doctors in the back. And a variety of other tactics designed to intimidate and terrorize doctors and clinics from engaging in a legal practice. I can remember when bombing churches was a favorite tactic against blacks, too.

I wonder if Bush and his friends will move as aggressively on the clinic bombers and doctor shooters as he did in Afghanistan? Not holding my breath. (I've been out of the country for a few years- maybe that sort of thing no longer happens- hope so.)

Doug Fenner, Queensland, Australia

THE QUAKER ECONOMIST

March 4, 2002

Letter No. 37

Dear friends:

Ideological literature

Last month Bill Moyers appeared on television to condemn multinational corporations (MNCs) and NAFTA (the North American Free Trade Agreement). Our local Peace and Justice Center sent a notice urging all peace-loving people to see it, as did other anti-globalization, anti-MNC, and pro-peace groups. So I watched the show, taped it, and invited my students over to my house to see it with me. We then discussed it.

Bill Moyers charged that Canadian MNCs are using Chapter 11 of the NAFTA to demand millions of dollars in redress when an environmental protection law, or other law, is passed that infringes on their right to do business in the United States. The principal case was that of Methanex, whose profits were reduced because California passed a law forbidding its product, MTBE, to be added to gasoline. California had discovered that MTBE leaked out of the tanks and poisoned the water supply.

NAFTA provides for progress toward free trade among Canada, Mexico, and the United States, so that ultimately the goods from any of the three countries will be treated alike in all three. Economically, it would be like a United States of Mexico, US, and Canada. As part of this effort, Chapter 11 was written to protect foreign investment from expropriation. Thus all investment across the "United States" of Mexico, US, and Canada will be treated alike, no matter in which country it originates.

This is set forth in Article 1102 of Chapter 11: "Each Party [i.e., Canada, United States, and Mexico] shall accord to investments of investors of another Party treatment no less favorable than that it accords, in like circumstances, to investments of its own investors with respect to the establishment, acquisition, expansion, management, conduct, operation, and sale or other disposition of investments."

As I read NAFTA, Methanex would lose its case, because California was applying the same rules to U.S. corporations as to Methanex. It would also lose because of Annex III of the NAFTA agreement, which reserves for the home government the "transportation, storage and distribution up to and including first hand sales of the following goods: crude oil; natural and artificial gas; goods covered by Chapter Six (Energy and Basic Petrochemicals) obtained from the refining or processing of crude oil and natural gas; and basic petrochemicals." If not covered by other clauses, it seems to me that California's right to protect gasoline and other oil products is reserved by this clause.

Case open and shut, it seems to me. But *Bill Moyers did not mention that so far, no decision has been reached. He said only that Methanex had filed suit. He also implied that the company could collect millions from the United States government.* In fact, only one of the many cases he cited has reached a NAFTA tribunal decision. Now, if you accidentally push me aside, with no harm to me, I can sue you for a million dollars. But I wouldn't win. Likewise, Methanex is widely expected to lose its case. *Why would not Bill Moyers say so?*

Bill Moyers made quite a point of the fact that a NAFTA tribunal decision cannot be appealed to the Supreme Court of the United States. But why would a disagreement between, say, Mexico and the United States, be tried in a court of the United States? He also did not say that any government may ignore a judgment against it. NAFTA has no army; it will not invade us and put George Bush in jail if the US refuses to pay a judgment it deems unfair. All that would happen would be that the plaintiff government would have the right to retaliate with trade or other sanctions, just as if there were no NAFTA to prevent that from happening.

The only case in the Bill Moyers show that has been decided by a NAFTA tribunal was that of a U.S. company that had signed an agreement with the Government of Mexico to clean up and manage a sanitary landfill. But the villagers next to the landfill objected - even rioted - so the Mexican Government broke the contract. Whose fault was it? Clearly, the Mexican government, because they should have known how their own villagers would feel. But they didn't, so they misled the corporation. This case seemed to me to be a simple breach of contract, so the American company should be compensated for its investment. But Bill Moyers made it seem that the big, bad American company was harassing the poor people of Mexico.

Bill Moyers was right in one respect. The NAFTA tribunals should be more open. But this would be easily corrected. It is not necessary to shout down NAFTA.

Much ideological literature surrounds NAFTA, globalization, and multinational corporations. It also surrounds literature from the Christian Right, or others who proclaim "causes." The characteristics of ideological literature are: (1) It does not approach its topic with an open mind. Thinking (though not necessarily writing) starts with a preconceived conclusion. (2) It perceives only information that supports its cause, ignoring any other side. (3) The truth of a proposition seems less important than defeating those who take an opposing belief. (4) Often it makes extreme, emotional statements, exaggerating the ill effects of the opposite cause. (5) Sometimes it contains outright lies. Since all these characteristics can be expressed strongly or weakly, any literature can be more or less ideological.

Non-ideological literature, on the other hand, perceives all the information that intelligent observers would agree pertains to a question, states arguments pro and con, and explains why, on balance, it arrives at its conclusion. Although my own books often open with their conclusion (to alert the reader), my thinking did not start that way - it built up as I have gathered facts about international economics and history, over the past fifty years.

Nevertheless, one of the biggest problems for me is to define my ideology (for everyone has an ideology). I must constantly test my conclusions and try to prove myself wrong. Even with that, I can never be sure.

Ideological literature emanating from CEOs of multinational corporations usually neglects the ways in which they have tried to bribe or overthrow foreign governments, how they have falsified their accounts to deceive stockholders and banks, and how they have bargained, cajoled, or threatened governments to influence political decisions. It neglects the ways MNCs have deceived their employees while catering to the interests of their management elites (See CLQ #34 on Enron.) It also neglects the attempts of MNCs to damage the environment, such as by promoting oil wells in the primeval forests of Alaska. Nor does it always tell the truth about the quality of its products or their effects on human health.

The literature condemning MNCs, on the other hand, usually neglects that, on average, they pay higher wages than their domestic counterparts in any country or that they provide safer working conditions and better health care, and education and housing where it would otherwise be unavailable. All the above has been shown by different researchers, including the International Labor Organization.

The anti-MNC literature usually "forgets" that the United States and Europe have signed agreements to make bribery a criminal act, and that American MNCs have supported these agreements (to bring the Europeans in line). This literature also "forgets" that multinational corporations bring capital, technology, and training that would otherwise be unavailable to many countries in which they invest. Especially in less developed countries, jobs with MNCs are a plum, widely sought.

Literature opposing profits - calling them "greed" - usually neglects that many firms operate on the margin of loss; that often bosses are not greedy, or that usually a firm finds that profits are enhanced by good working relations with staff, workers, and community. Mostly, this literature neglects the economic theories that show how profits determine which goods will be produced in response to consumer demand, as well as how the technology to produce them will be selected to consume a minimum of resources. It neglects that every other system - socialism, dictatorship, feudalism, etc. - has failed to create a viable economy.

Ideological literature supporting globalization often neglects the job losses as industries move from country to country, the towns that suffer deeply when the principal employer moves away, and how whole industries become lost, as would be the future for shipbuilding, steel, textiles, and maybe even farming, in the United States.

On the other hand, the literature opposing globalization usually neglects that trade barriers infringe on the liberties of producers to seek the most profitable markets, and, above all, trade barriers slow job formation in poorer countries where jobs are most needed. Indeed, some of the literature argues that globalization harms the poor, even though both history and economics show overwhelmingly that globalization leads the poor out of their penury. (See my book, *Centuries of Economic Endeavor,* for case study after case study).

Ideological lies are told even in the highest circles. A few years ago the Pentagon opened the Office of Strategic Influence, "to provide news items, possibly even false ones, to unwitting foreign journalists to influence public sentiment abroad" *(New York Times,* 2/27/02). To his credit, the President asked that it be closed, rightly fearing for the credibility of the U.S. government.

As readers of CLQ know, my ideology lies in favor of globalization and MNCs which, I believe, will together be the major forces lifting the poor from their poverty the world over. By insisting that the full story - both sides - be told in each controversy, I recognize the problems that my positions engender. In each case, however, the question is: do we overthrow the system, or seek corrections in it?

One final comment: I have often said that in CLQ I set forth only my position and do not try to persuade. I have been told there is a very thin line between the two. Perhaps. But I find that if I try to persuade, I tend to be ideological. If I just set forth my position, I can be objective. The thin line broadens into one between ideology and objectivity.

What do you think?

Thank you, and Peace, Jack

READERS' COMMENTS ON LETTER NO. 37

This kind of direct commentary on general debates is really helpful for your readership. For laymen, it's good to get an economist's viewpoint, especially one that runs counter to the main tenor of debate.

Geoffrey Williams, Bethesda (MD) Friends Meeting

It is comforting to hear that you think Methanex will lose its case, but obviously Methanex itself does not think so or they would not invest in the trouble and expense of making their case. They must believe that they have at least a fighting chance of winning. Why do they believe that?

Roger Conant, Mt. Toby Meeting, Leverett (MA)

ANSWER (I usually answer only when asked): My intent in CLQ #37 was more to show how an ideological presentation can be made than it was to predict what would happen in the Methanex case - though you are right, I think Methanex will lose. Sebastian Mallaby in the *Washington Post* (February 18) thinks the same (Look up his article on www.washingtonpost.com).

I wondered why Moyers mentioned only California. So I looked up MTBE on the web and found that it is used widely in other states, and there are even concentrations in Denver, right near where I live. Why haven't other states forbidden it?

To answer your question: Methanex may believe that MTBE is not sufficiently harmful to be banned and California is merely trying to protect its own producers of alternative products. If the court so decides, Methanex would win. Another possibility is that Methanex knows that defending the case will be costly and it wants the US Government to settle simply to avoid having to pay that cost.

I really don't know the answer. All I can judge is that Bill Moyers presented a very one-sided case, and that is what CLQ #37 was about.

I'm delighted to hear a balanced evaluation of the charges of the anti-globalization people, especially with regard to the Methanex situation. I hope you will send this issue of CLQ to Bill Moyers.

Virginia Flagg, San Diego (CA) Friends Meeting

Tom Coyner kindly forwarded CLQ #37 to me (on Ideological Literature). Beautifully put. I didn't know of you until now, and have hastened to subscribe.

What a refreshing tone you manage. A still, small voice, amid the babel of shrieks and chatter. I tend to shrillness and polemic myself; but should learn from you.

Aidan Foster-Carter, Hon. Senior Research Fellow in Sociology and Modern Korea, Leeds University, England

NOTE from Jack: That's the first time, *ever,* anyone said anything like that to me.

I am not certain whether I am a Classic Liberal Quaker or not. I am on some issues: I like local involvement. But locals must live up to some standards of civility which often need some pressure to achieve anything like equity (the civil rights movement). I have no idea how small communities can effectively influence the use of undue force that is often applied by the national government, especially when it seems so many want what is now being offered as patriotism and security. Which puts me in the ... "I wish big government weren't so big" camp.

Charlie and Jeannine Thomas, Pima (AZ) Friends Meeting

What I've noted about the positions of the "liberal left", as you call them, is that instead of asking 'What is wrong to have caused such poverty?' (for example), their question is 'Who is wrong ...?', and they usually find some answer in WTO, NAFTA, Corporate America, the Republicans — not a charitable answer, not an understanding that (as the Dali Lama states it) 'Almost all men strive for what they understand is the good', but a demonizing answer which doesn't help at all.

John Janda, Orange County (CA) Friends Meeting

Reply to Asa Janney, who questioned whether the Olympics are worth the cost:

As a rabid sports fan and a college student majoring in sports management, this is a subject near to my heart. My reaction is that whatever it takes to help your team win, within the bounds of legal and ethical behavior, is worth the cost as long as you are turning a profit. Obviously this is nothing profound; it is just good business. When your team is winning, people want to spend money to watch the team in person. In the case of the Olympics, that would spill over into other international sports events like the Goodwill Games and Pan-American Games, and also national competitions. These competitions bring the USOC, as well as the national governing bodies for each sport, more revenue. Considering ticket prices at the Olympics, I'm sure they made more than $20 million. In addition to that, they profit from sale of hats, sweatshirts, and other paraphenalia. Business-wise it makes sense. And make no mistake,! as much as the Olympics want us to think they are about "lighting the fire within," they are a business.

Beth Stevenson, Boulder (CO) Meeting of Friends, now living in Tulsa (OK)

Also for Asa Janney:

Good questions. I believe that sports is a substitute for real wars. As such, I support them. Perhaps the real discussion needs to be about what sports is doing to colleges and universities around the country. Why are they paying coaches millions of dollars to "teach" football and basketball?

Free Polazzo, Anneewakee Creek Friends Worship Group, Douglasville, GA

The emphasis [Bill Moyers] seemed to take was that any law which threatened profits, which could be challenged, was an outrage. There was no discussion of the criteria the tribunal would use for its finding other than government action amounted to a substantial taking.

He emphasized that the threat of challenge by the party suffering loss was enough to prevent environmental laws from passing. This would depend on the criteria the tribunal is to use, which was not emphasized. Maybe the laws are not based on good science, and need to be challenged.

Jim Booth, Red Cedar Meeting, Lansing (MI)

I read most of your letters yesterday and today and enjoyed them. I feel you truly advocate an open discussion and it is a pleasure to see these issues discussed with an air of openness, acceptance of others, desire for peace, and feeling of love for humanity. Thank you.

Milton Janetos, Agate Passage Friends, Bainbridge Island (WA)

In response to your final paragraph in CLQ #37: Some people think there is a fine line between setting forth your position and trying to be impartial. The way I see it is a well-reasoned position is very persuasive if only people will open their eyes.

Dennis Bentley, Morganton NC

I attended a legal seminar on NAFTA. It was suggested there (by me) and confirmed (by one of the lecturers) that the Chapter 11 provision may lead (and by now surely has led) to an AMERICAN corporation, desiring to do business IN AMERICA forming a wholly-owned Canadian or Mexican subsidiary organized especially to conduct this business with the intent to benefit under Chapter 11. (And, of course, it can go the other way as well).

The essence of Ch. 11 is (a) the treaty-language was stuck into NAFTA (and other similar trade agreements) by special interests such as oil and chemical businesses, much as VP Cheney allowed the same sorts of groups to "write" US energy policy recently; (b) the Ch. 11 dispute-resolution mechanism has neither "common law" precedents nor "civil law" rules to govern its outcomes, nor any court (or other mechanism) to REVIEW its outcomes; (c) it places governments and perhaps especially local govern-ments "*in terrorem*", fearing any sort of regulation whatever; (d) it does NOT treat all companies the same, because any company can make use of the non-treaty legal system but only foreign companies can use the Ch 11 mechanism, giving the foreigners more legal possibilities than are given to local companies or non-company citizens.

Peter A. Belmont, Brooklyn (NY)

We have dozens of cases now and environmental protection laws and civil court rulings overturned. The problem ~is~ NAFTA chapter 11. If Chap-ter 11 was removed from NAFTA or modified, then NAFTA could be what it was meant to be. As it is NAFTA is dangerous and anti-democratic. Bill Moyers is not raising a false alarm. Chapter 11 and fast track are unjust and undemocratic. And why "secret tribunals". Justice demands open and transparent proceedings.

Greg Austin

I was startled and provoked by your thoughts in #36 about the role insurance might play three hundred years from now.

Let me suggest that insurance as we know it, for most events, will be impossible. Most things will be predictable, and thus you will not be able to buy into a risk pool for anything less than the simple cost of saving up for the event you want to insure against. For example, the year of your death will be known (barring accidents) from birth, and so it will be impossible to purchase insurance against outliving your resources at any price less than then cost of a savings account. The same will be true of floods, storms and earthquakes. Since the economy and demography will have reached steady state, and your abilities to earn a living determinable by analyzing your body and brain, it will be possible to determine exactly what your life-time earning power will be. Since unemployment will be predictable, the only way insure against it will be to save when you can.

Allan Abrahamse, Orange County Friends Meeting, Santa Ana (CA)

THE QUAKER ECONOMIST

March 13, 2002

Letter No. 38

Dear friends:

Should a rich person take a job from a poor person just because he can do it better?

"Thousands of Thai farmers have been performing black magic rituals in front of the US embassy in Bangkok protesting the United States and World Trade Organization (WTO)." They have burned effigies of President Bush and the head of WTO, Mike Moore.

"Jasmine rice is one of the most sought after strains of rice in the world and is grown by over 5 million families in Thailand many of whom are in debt and very poor. In 1999 the average income of farming households was 26,822 baht (US$600), significantly lower than the average household earning of 78,875 baht (about $1800). If the small-scale farmers in Thailand lose the markets for jasmine rice, in particular its main buyer the US, then the viability of their livelihood will be threatened in the future." (*Bangkok Post,* 2/27/02).

Into this poverty-stricken situation stepped Chris Deren, an American entrepreneur who had obtained seeds for rice very similar to jasmine. Helped by the University of Arkansas, and funded by the U.S. Department of Agriculture, he genetically mutated the rice with gamma rays so he could plant crops suitable to the American climate and capable of being mechanically harvested. The crop can be planted in U.S. soil in any season, does not depend on seasonal fluctuations, and ripens in 90 days. Furthermore, Deren claims that "his rice is just as aromatic and delicious as Thai jasmine rice."

But Gate Kong Ngam, a Thai peasant farmer, says, "Jasmine rice belongs to Thai communities, and Thai farmers. Our grandfathers, grandmothers, great grandfathers, and great grandmothers have been growing it for millions of years" (*Bangkok Post,* 2/27/02). If Deren's rice takes over the American market, over 5 million small-farmer families in Thailand will lose their means of livelihood.

Now look to Mexico: With the North American Free Trade Agreement (NAFTA), U.S. farmers can sell corn in Mexico, putting out of business Mexican farmers who plod out their existences on small farms with obsolete (by American standards) equipment.

What should be done about this?

But wait a bit! The same is happening right within the United States. "All along the nation's back roads," the *New York Times* reported (2/16/02), hundreds of towns . . . are teetering in the recession, and some worry that they may never recover. Uranium mining has stopped in Falls City, Tex. In Loving County, Tex., oil exploration has stalled. For farmers in Pima, Ariz., and Bartow, Ga., cotton prices have sunk to 30-year lows. . . Ranchers who raise goats for angora wool are victims of low prices and competition from New Zealand and Argentina. Stretched across the southern tier, from Arizona and New Mexico through Texas and Georgia and into Virginia, these small rural communities form the base of the national supply chain. They produce most of the oil and much of the ore, fiber and food. In past recessions, even if they did not bounce back entirely, at least they survived. But this time around, as the overall economy begins to show some signs of healing, things are ominously different in many of these towns."

Where does the competition come from? From China, Russia, and other former Soviet republics, plus less developed countries in Africa and Latin America. True, the U.S. poor are not on the poverty level of the Thai, but does that make much difference to them?

The consumer is king

No matter what we hear, and what else we would like, the world is tending toward a free market. Some believe it is only "the rich" who want this, but evidence is strong that poorer manufacturers, of steel, textiles, and even farming, would like to crack the markets of the more developed countries, because with their low wages they can produce more cheaply than we can. Many Americans resist this - demanding tariffs on steel and textiles, and boycotting sweatshops. Yet steel, textiles, and sweatshops may be the only jobs available for the poorest of the poor if (for example) we drive them out of farming rice. If we deny them these, they will turn to whatever they can - including prostitution and sex slavery. No, in many ways, we do not live in a pleasant world.

In economics, however, the consumer is king. Economics teaches how the world functions (in the economic sphere), not how it *should* function. Here, the consumer rules. Some feel that multinational corporations rule, or governments rule, or rich people rule. Some feel that workers *should* rule, or stakeholders (employees as well as consumers and stockholders) *should* rule. Maybe so, but these are "should's," not "are's." History shows that over long periods, consumers overcome multinational corporations that urge us to buy Edsels. It is to recognize consumer sovereignty that the world is deregulating.

When consumers rule, we pay more attention to the Mexican urban poor, who want cheap corn for their tortillas. With NAFTA, they can buy that from the United States, and their children become better fed. What about the Mexican farmer? Well, he must either seek off-farm employment or improve productivity to compete with American farmers (cheap labor is his advantage). The same for Thai producers of jasmine rice. If American consumers can buy the same (or better) product more cheaply, they will do so. (Try to stop them!) Then thousands of years of Thai rice-growing may come to an end. Thai farmers must move into manufacturing or service jobs. And finally, so must small-town Americans.

Small-town Americans have long been adapting. A century and a half ago, the U.S. population was over 50% farmer. Now it is less than 2%.

If we were asking this question a century ago, it would be: should automobile producers hold off, in order to save the jobs of horse farmers and buggy makers?

What we must do versus what we want to do

It has been easier to dislodge the King (or Queen) of England from his (or her) power than it is to dislodge the consumer. Nor should we. A world of consumer power is a world from bottom up - a classic liberal world.

But is there nothing we can do to alleviate the pain of those who lose? Of course, there is much. First, we in the more developed world can buy the manufactures of those in the less developed world. Political pressures have led our President to declare duties on steel up to 30%. This is a despicable act, which we should all protest strongly. We also protect textiles much more than we should. Second, we can provide technical assistance and capital to those who must change their lifelines. We can invest in Thailand and hire their erstwhile farmers. We can also invest in small towns in the United States - in the many industries where location is not a significant factor. Third, we can promote training schools, both at home and abroad, where new skills for a new world can be learned. Whatever we do, we must assist the transition, not try to hold it back.

What can I do, I keep asking myself? At age 81, for all the above I have "been there, done that." Now the best I can do is keep teaching in the university as long so I am able, and keep producing CLQ, to urge the world to move in salubrious ways.

What are you doing? If you are disagreeing with me, Fine! That is the way I learn. Please let me know about it.

> Yours in friendship,
> Jack

READERS' RESPONSES TO LETTER NO. 38

Repetition does not make a truth. Saying the consumer is king over and over does not make consumerism the equivalent of an ethical or moral principle. It may reveal the "true religion" of today however, led by a Wall Street Messiah. The dominance of most economic bully pulpit preachers does not make them speakers of truth, and certainly not of human compassion.

I believe that truth is found in a compassionate economics that places value in all workers, that does not exploit just because one can, that applies rules of fairness and equality regardless of where geographically one may be operating. The policy of free trade too often becomes unbridled greed and ignores such principles of justice and equality.

Your opening examples of "adjustments" in agriculture due to free trade are good illustrations of an economy that has lost its way. They illustrate how far removed most of the world has become from the most basic of all human needs, food. They illustrate how distorted an economy can become when it does not properly value that most basic of all needs by compensating very highly what should be the most treasured industry and occupation in the world, farming and the farmer.

No, pure economics is and should not be a religion as you seem to have made it. It will always be missing compassion and humanity as long as it can disconnect the parts from the whole.

Anonymous (exceptionally, by Jack's choice)

Has anyone factored into this equation the true cost of the water that would be needed to grow such a large amount of rice in the United States? If the process does not rely on seasonal fluctuations, Deren may well be assuming he will use a large amount of water from our rapidly depleting aquifers. And then, of course, there are a host of environmental factors resulting from irrigation, again multiplied by the scale of this sort of endeavor. Basing the cost of the rice merely on the short-term dollar investment and return would be a mistake. Before being able to decide which rice to buy, I would want to know what is the true cost we would pay in the long term?

Merlyn Holmes, Unitarian, Boulder (CO)

Is it possible to "look ahead" on this issue, much as one would use that strategy in a chess game? Suppose consumers decide the issue and producing jasmine rice in Thailand is no longer a viable occupation. What "moves" would the former Thai farmers have available to them? Unlike workers in developed countries who are displaced from an industry, they have few options which are *under their control.* You have suggested what we in the developed world can do to alleviate their suffering, but I'm interested, too, in what means of self-determination those former Thai farmers could have.

Ann Dixon, Boulder (CO) Meeting of Friends

How did consumers become king? My conclusion is that it is the very fact that consumers are not organized like workers, etc., that put them on top, assisted by competing providers. Each consumer has to be persuaded individually to buy this brand rather than that brand. Empirical tests are required and undertaken every day: this tastes good, that one has too much salt. Does this sound like a liberal society, with choice and decision power at the base? If consumers are not king, are the institutions of liberal society likely to evolve? Where consumers have not been king, as in Russia through the early 1990s, autocrats have been. As a consequence consumers were treated shabbily in an economic sense and atrociously in a political sense. Their humanity was denied by their relative lack of choice. Consumers value choice, and choice creates the possibility of freedom.

> J.D. von Pischke, a Friend from Reston (VA)

What about the agricultural subsidies that keep prices in the US higher than world market prices and/or protect the export of stuff that could not be exported without them? Are you sure the consumer is king? If he is, he's a very modern king, more a figurehead than a ruler. Absent those subsidies, would the Thai farmer have this problem?

> Tom Cooper, Lafayette (CA)

The only way a multinational corporation becomes big is by fulfilling the wants of others. If it doesn't do that it's not going to survive. Isn't it the height of presumption for us to sit back and say, "Oh, but providing all those Thais with CocaCola is destroying their culture?" It's like the Thais telling us that we shouldn't be patronizing all those Thai restaurants in the USA because it's destroying our wonderful culture of hamburgers and potato chips.

Critics seem to look upon the MNC as some externality that is sucking the well-being out of society. They fail to recognize that the MNC is an integral part of society, simply an aggregate of people fulfilling others' wants. And they overlook the fact that in the typical large business enterprise most of the revenues, say from 30 to 70%, goes to the workers, while the "evil capitalist owners" get from 2 to 10%, sometimes nothing at all.

> Don Marsh, Seattle (WA)

Our mutual friend, David Edinger, lent me a copy of your book, *Seeking Truth Together* this week, and I have just finished a first read-through. I enjoyed your analysis of so many problems which are of perennial concern to Friends — and I appreciate your courage in offering analyses which run counter to conventional Quaker wisdom, backed with solid economic thinking.

Josh Brown, Pastor, West Richmond (IN) Friends Meeting

I have read two of your books, *The Moral Economy* and *Centuries of Economic Endeavor.* It seems to me you make an excellent case for showing that the dispersion of power and development of mutual trust as people negotiate as equals, trusting they will not be taken advantage of, are prerequisites to the free market. If so it would seem that the example America portrays by our actions and our description of the basis of our way of life would the best way of bringing about free trade, while on the other hand bullying others to our way might be the least effective.

Lyle E. Smith, Motor Friends Church, Milo (IA)

I was intrigued (but confused and unpersuaded) by Messrs Belmont and Austin and their points. I would be interested in seeing further discussion of this, especially by Chapter 11 cases where it was decided for the foreign company.

Are Belmont and Austin referring to cases where the environmental law was simply a scheme to protect local industry? In that case it might be very revealing to look at such a case in detail and demonstrate that virtue was triumphant in the overthrow of an "environmental" law.

Geoffrey Williams, Bethesda (MD) Friends Meeting

Thanks for Letter #38 which we find provocative and perplexing in that no answer seems to suggest itself to a problem brought on by (supposedly) good intentions.

Joe Roberts, Noblesville (IN) Friends Meeting

The automotive industry destroyed my grandfather's harness shop. Capitalism is finished. Communism is the answer.

Guy Grand (A grand guy.) "The Magic Christian"

NOTE from Jack: I don't know what this all means, but it comes anonymously from Maurice Boyd, Friends Meeting of Washington (DC)

Thanks for your objective report on NAFTA and the Moyers show (in CLQ #37). It is a breath of fresh air for these days when we are inundated with ideological views in all sectors of the press and government.

Lorna Knowlton, Boulder (CO)

The US could help Thai farmers be more efficient if it wanted to. That's not the purpose of US policy. US policy purpose is to make US as rich as possible. If that's done by any means necessary and a few millions starve in other countries because of it, just don't tell the voters. We elect our politicians to make the country rich and not tell us what they had to do to people in other countries to make it rich, so on Clinton's desk it said "It's the economy, stupid". As Pogo said, "we have met the enemy and he is us."

Doug Fenner, Queensland, Australia

You recommend law and international treaties as correctives to the abuse of power by multinational corporations. I agree, but it seems to me that, as things currently stand, those legalities are worked out by the agents of those very same corporate entities. The by-laws of the international trading organizations and political financing regulations could do much better toward preventing the abuse of office.

Thanks for your thoughts and the opportunity to reply.

Riley Lynch, Seattle (WA)

THE QUAKER ECONOMIST
March 22, 2002

Letter No. 39

Dear friends:

What is economics?

The first Readers' Response, to letter no. 38 helps me understand what has been happening to me over the past quarter century. I have always been part of the family I will call "progressives," because I love them and feel at home with them. Progressives are people who care about the environment, who want to improve conditions of the poor, and who want a more just world. My problem is, that most of the progressives that I know and love have never studied economics.

David Korten makes that clear in his book, *When Corporations Rule the World,* which is known to virtually all my progressive friends. This book begins with a thesis and "proves" it by selective perception: citing evidence in its favor, and ignoring all else. Had Korten studied economic statistics, he would have known better.

In a review comparing my book, *The Moral Economy,* with that of Korten, the late Paul Heyne, economist with the University of Washington, asks: "How can intelligent and informed people with almost identical concerns construct such contradictory recommendations for a world they have in common? Let me suggest the answer. Powelson employs the perspective of economic theory. Korten, on the other hand, tells us in the prologue to his book" that he is proud of not having studied economics. Heyne goes on to say that *The Moral Economy* is "rich in insights, instructive examples, and practical proposals."

As an exception to my rule, I keep the first Readers' Response anonymous because I do not want to seem critical of a real person. By referring to an economics that has lost its way, and a true economics as compassionate, this respondent seems not to understand that economics is an instrument, like a hammer. A hammer can be used to build a beautiful house, or it can bash in someone's head. Hammers and economics have no values or compassion.

Economics describes how the economy functions. It is people who are moral or immoral, compassionate or not compassionate. It would make just as much sense to say that physics is immoral, because it created nuclear weapons. But physics merely describes how the physical world functions. People could make nuclear weapons only within the laws of physics (or, they might not make them; their choice). Economics has laws that are as fundamental as those of physics.

When I was in my twenties, I was part of the New York Young Friends (who would be called "Adult Young Friends" today). We were bound together by our pacifism in a hostile world (WW II was on!). We also sat in restaurants to test their racial policies. Bayard Rustin and Jim Farmer (who later became prominent in the civil rights movement) would sit with some Whites at one table, while other Whites (a comparison test) would sit elsewhere.

Many of us were socialist. Evan Thomas, the brother of Norman Thomas, Socialist candidate for president, met with us frequently. I had met and admired Norman when he visited my high school.

I was also pro-union. Whenever I saw a picket sign, I would talk to the picketers. Once I marched down Boylston Street in Boston in a union parade, singing "Solidarity Forever." I sought out the communist leader of the union (C.G.T.) in Lille, France, to dine in his home and become his friend. Traveling to Europe with the Experiment in International Living for several summers while in graduate school, I tried to learn about other cultures. When the AFSC formed summer high school institutes in world affairs, I was on their faculty. When the AFSC ran an educational program on student ships to Europe in 1948, I was lecturing and conducting discussions.

Those were the years that I felt most at home with progressives.

Then I went out into the world. I took a PhD in Economics and a CPA, worked for the International Monetary Fund and Price Waterhouse, then taught at Harvard, Johns Hopkins, and finally, the University of Colorado. From these universities, I took frequent leaves of absence to help lift the Third World from its poverty. I "advised" presidents, cabinet ministers, and governors of central banks. ("Advised" is in quotes because rarely did they take my advice). I lectured in universities all over the Third World. In every capital city to which I was assigned, I wandered around the slums, talking at length with the poorest of the poor. In 1973, I decided that in "advising" the elites, I was helping corrupt people enhance their power. Though they mouthed platitudes about the poor, they rarely communicated with them. In any given country, I knew more what the poor thought than the president did.

So I quit doing that and returned to my loved ones, the progressives in the United States, bursting to tell them what I had found out. But I discovered that, mainly, they did not care to hear me. They did not respect me as an economist, nor my knowledge of history, nor my experiences in the Third World. At one Gathering of Friends General Conference, Friends listened with rapture to an astronomer who said she believed in the Big Bang, not God. They respected her for her scientific knowledge. But they did not respect economics.

I soon found out that for progressives, economics is different from other fields. They think they *know* the answers to economic questions, and if an economist tells them differently, often they will not listen. (Fortunately, not all of them. In fact, readers of CLQ are a major exception). In fact, I am a fairly mainstream economist, not an extremist. Most economists think pretty much the way I do. Mostly, our differences involve policies to correct ills, such as depressions. In how the economy functions, however, we are re-markably agreed. Do I have to choose between being an economist and being a Quaker?

Writing CLQ provided an answer. In doing so, I discovered many Quakers understand the importance of economics in their everyday lives and are willing to consider economic precepts and historical principles in fashion-ing their decisions. You don't have to be an economist, just a logical thinker who does not miss a single step on the way to a conclusion.

Many understand that sometimes gut reactions that at first seem right and moral turn out to be the exact opposite once the complex economic/histori-cal logic has been fully run. For example, the minimum wage increases unemployment among Black teenagers and women; forgiving Third-World debts keeps corrupt dictators in power; boycotting sweatshops forces women into even worse jobs, etc.).

If you read my article in the April *Friends Journal,* you will find my expla-nation of why I am leaving Quakers. I have given up on modern, political Quakerism. I will continue to write CLQ because many responses from readers show they value the original Quaker philosophy, the classic liberal one. I still think of myself as Quaker, and I keep my membership in my local Meeting. But I will no longer travel under concern to Yearly Meetings and Friends General Conference. I will continue to hang out with progressives, because their hearts are in the right place.

But it is your responses that keep me going. Please keep it up!

Sincerely your friend,
Jack

READERS' RESPONSES TO LETTER NO. 39

I think *The Quaker Economist* is fantastic, and I am glad you have chosen this method to put forth your ideas. Who knows, maybe from time to time, some people will questions their own assumptions as you once did.

    Mel Dodd, Atlanta (GA) Friends Meeting

I feel very much the same way and have been looking around at other churches also. I have stopped talking about political or economic issues to Quakers as I just get them upset. I have been involved in the Wharton Global Consulting Program over the past three years, but have simply stopped telling Quakers about it.

    Mark Cary, Wallingford (PA)

Thanks for the account of your unique background and journey in CLQ #39. I found it rich and illuminating.

    Michael Jack, Friends Meeting of Washington (DC)

I have been reminding Friends here in North Pacific Yearly Meeting and in my home Meeting (South Mountain, in Ashland, Oregon) - and anyone else who will listen - that opposition to globalization is hypocritical from a people who not so long back carried bumper stickers that said "one planet, one people - please." If one really wants to help Central Americans combat economic colonialism, I tell them, buying fair-traded coffee is much more useful than demonstrating against the WTO. Fighting against supply and demand is pretty useless, like fighting gravity and thermodynamics, which are also laws of nature. Like you, I have found this message not particularly welcome, but I do continue to give it. I have taken much heart from your stand, as a Quaker economist, on these issues.

Bill Ashworth, South Mountain Meeting, Ashland (OR)

I've found your last two issues, on the proclivity of unprogrammed liberal Friends toward anti-capitalist politics and economics, fascinating. What I found especially interesting was your memory of a time, perhaps half a century ago, when there was more political diversity among Friends. I don't question that, but I think that it may have been an unusual interlude. Largely, the history of American Quakerism has been characterized by political uniformity.

Thomas Hamm, New Castle (IN) Monthly Meeting, Professor of History, Earlham College, Richmond (IN)

I resonate with your core premise, that we as Friends struggle to be inclusive, almost as if we have the truth before discerning it by listening to the voice of God in meeting. We are not alone in that among the faithful, I suppose. But I think Friends, fearful of our internal conflict, have forgotten how to listen to the rich diversity of opinion.

Paul Alexander, Mountain View (Denver CO) Friends Meeting

Economists have spent enormous amounts of time looking at the way people collaborate, the way people respond to incentives, etc., and have assembled a major body of data and theory. Since both economists and Quakers spend enormous amounts of time thinking about voluntary arrangements, collaboration and non-violent persuasion, Quakers would be well advised to learn more about the work of economists.

Geoffrey Williams, Bethesda (MD) Friends Meeting

I was touched by your frustration with progressives. I too used to be a "progressive" but became most disillusioned decades ago. What I learned was that good intentions do not necessarily lead to good outcomes — as a matter of fact, they often lead to terribly evil outcomes. Example: Progressive admiration for the various Stalinist dictators - Stalin himself, then Mao, then Castro. . I still remember attending lectures by progressive delegations just returned first from the USSR, later from various "People's Democracies", still later from Red China, then Cuba, finally Nicaragua, even Albania, and all of them reporting enthusiastically on the Brave New World they had encountered in those countries, and how contrary reports were just lies propagated by US disinformation.

Arthur Bierman, Jewish, Boulder (CO)

I use the hammer analogy myself, but it's simplistic. In physics, for example, others than physicists provide money for research. The donors' priorities do not include, explicitly, the discovery of the principles of the universe, but they influence the direction of physics research. A hammer-but the sponsors would prefer it to be convertible into a sword.

Jim Caughran, Toronto (Ontario) Meeting

Your CLQ Letter #39 made me think of this passage from Landsburg's *Fair Play.* "Economics breeds not just tolerance but compassion. The economist's method is to observe behavior closely, the better to understand other people's goals and other people's difficulties. That kind of understanding is the basis of all compassion."

Asa Janney, Herdon (VA) Friends Meeting

I appreciated the frustration articulated in CLQ #39. I also despair of a high level discussion about many issues and policy situations with my fellow Quakers. And unfortunately it corrupts my attitude toward our entire denomination. However, their thought is similar to my non-Quaker radical friends who rail against corporations, free trade and empathize with every dissident group in conflict with governments anywhere.

> Jim Booth, Red Cedar Meeting, Lansing (MI)

I'm still rooting for you. In your own way you are speaking truth to power. I read every issue you send out and bless you for your logical presentation.

Keep up the good work.

> Rich Ailes, Middletown (PA) Meeting

I know where you're coming from, and I share your reaction. I remember one time after I had spent several Sundays in after-meeting "seminars" with the Honolulu Friends, somebody pointed an accusing finger at me and said, "You're wrong. Nobody has a right to cut down trees just because they own the forest." I tried to explain that people didn't cut down trees "because they owned the forest," but because people needed houses. I tried to point out that, no matter how we wanted to solve the problems of clear-cutting and environmental preservation, we had to begin with this fact. But I was written off as a worshiper of the uncontrolled market.

> Dan Suits, Quaker Economist, Michigan State University

"Economics has laws that are as fundamental as those of physics." Exactly. I am sure you have read Von Mises introduction (or is it the 1st chapter?) to *Human Action* where he provides the reasoning for this truth based on an analysis of human nature and behavior. A part of his opus often overlooked.

> Ken Allison, Episcopalian, Paradise Valley (AZ)

I disagree that the laws of economics can be compared so directly with the laws of physics. Economics is a human construct and depends upon human behavior. I think the law of gravity prevailed before humans walked the earth and will continue to prevail after we are extinct.

Vici Oshiro, Minneapolis (MN) Friends Meeting

I think Ms. Dixon in her comment after CLQ #39 touches on an important point. The Thai farmers whose product comes to be supplanted in the market by a similar product grown in another country cannot easily adjust themselves to the market because they cannot pick themselves up and come to the US or some other country to farm. There is no free international market in people, and there is not likely to be one for the foreseeable future and beyond. As long as people cannot move internationally to where the work or profits are, won't free international trade in capital result in inequity and unemployment? But which First World country is going to be the first to open its borders entirely, i.e. no restrictions on anyone coming in and taking any job?

Frank Perch, Philadelphia (PA) Meeting

Jack, I admire and respect your yearning and more for the company of progressives such as those you describe from the 1940s and those involved in a collective search for Truth at Boulder Friends. These types of folks are indeed exciting and lively, and some good may come out of what they do. My quest for association has been more toward the good but creative quiet life and those who enjoy it by simply trying to do the right thing from day to day, and being quite serious about it. I tend to associate progressives with greed, in the sense of trying to force others to pay for their agenda, using the tools of the State. (NPR is a minor example.) The ones I'm trying to hold in the Light often pronounce "conservative" and "Republican" in a clearly pejorative manner, denoting something right down there with the slime. I find their sense of rectitude and moral superiority discouragingly cavalier. (This is stereotyping, but no more so than your description of folks with their hearts in the right places, etc.) The good but creative quiet types are more likely to do it on their own and in a different way. Hatred (possibly too strong a term to use here) of existing institutions and practices and of the rich or the poor are not part of their frame of reference or the basis for their activism.

J.D. von Pischke, a Friend from Reston, VA

I am amused (or bemused, maybe) by how Friends would react if I for example (or any one MD) were to offer up pet/imagined remedies for arthritis (or any other human physical ills) — and how respectfully (and naively) they do react when MD's and other non- economists, non-historian, non-MSW folk pontificate in Meeting, in social hours, and even in print on their pet/imagined remedies for poverty, social ills (e.g., homelessness), WTO, etc. There ought'a be a law . . . but then it wouldn't be a democracy, or a Quaker Meeting, would it? I couldn't agree more with your disaffection for 'modern political Quakerism' —and its foundation of intellectual immodesty.

John Janda, Orange County (CA) Meeting

I can understand how you must feel rather "beaten about the head and shoulders" to judge from some of the responses I heard when I was present at some of your workshops. I am very sorry about that. As you know Jim and I always counted ourselves among your supporters. That doesn't mean that I have always agreed with you about everything (for example: I have some cruelty to animals issues with things that have occurred under the aegis of NAFTA) but I think we could discuss things like that and still feel quite happy with one another. I am deeply sorry that this seems not to be the case with many "liberal" Friends. I put liberal in quotes because it seems to me illiberal to infuse rancor into what should have been open, honest, and to the best of one's abilities, informed discussion.

Pat Corbett, Tucson (AZ) Friends Meeting

I agree with what you say about "progressives" who either cannot or are unwilling to see economics as an essential part of any society. Economics is the science of the natural laws that bind our lives together - the necessary material half needed to maintain the balance between abstract and reality. I don't understand why so many liberally-minded thinkers tend to leave out what seem to me to be obvious economic considerations in their hopes for a better world. Your letter reassures me that there are people out there who are willing to call attention to this. Thank You.

Anonymous (at reader's request)

I take your point about Quakerism. I still believe it's now just a poorly funded liberal PAC, not a religion any more than any other political movement. (Of course, Quakerism probably has more than its share of "true believers".)

Tom Cooper, Jr., Boston (MA)

The current Quaker outlook is a remnant of an older upper class ethos, based on inherited wealth, in which "We" are folks of privilege, cultivation, and benevolent concern, who "Do Good" to "Them," the oppressed, etc. Indeed, it is specifically the outlook of the children of those who no longer need to "work for a living," and feel themselves beyond the gritty, soiling arenas of vulgar commerce (note the affinities with antecedent British aristocratic attitudes). Our "socialism" is thus strictly of the Fabian variety, I think.

Chuck Fager, Director, Quaker House, Fayetteville (NC)

Friends' Attitudes Toward Business in the USA

by Mark S. Cary
515 Scott Lane, Wallingford, PA USA
Comments can be sent to markcary@att.net
Second Month 2002

The Attitudes

Unprogrammed liberal Friends today seem publicly almost uniformly negative about most business activity. I have been to talks at the Pendle Hill
Conference Center (Wallingford, PA USA) where speakers casually state
that capitalism is the cause of all the injustice and inequality in our world,
where being employed by a large corporation is treated as a badge of shame.

For example, Paul Rasor, who directs the Social Issues program at Pendle
Hill considers the "deep-seated ethic of competition that underlies our economic system" to be "a form a cultural violence, it is also a form of physical violence as well." Paul write that this violence "has been accorded the
status of a religion, demanding from its devotees an absolute obedience to
death." Certainly, with language like this, the average business person might
wonder about their moral legitimacy.

These negative views of business are not limited to Friends. Laura Nash
and Scotty McLennan (*Church on Sunday, Work on Monday*) have found
that many liberal clergy share these negative views. Knowing little about
how business works, many clerics take a view that includes simple protests
and academic position papers full of "oughts."

Attitudes of the average "Quaker in the Street" are not as negative as some
of the more public Friends. We have two recent sources of data here, both
of which I conducted as a volunteer using my survey research background.
The first was a survey members and attenders at three Meetings in
Philadelphia Yearly Meeting (PYM) which was done to learn more about

outreach and diversity issues. The second was a survey of people on the Pendle Hill mailing list who live outside the Northeast and Middle Atlantic states. This survey was about Friends' attitudes toward money.

Both studies show these Friends are mostly upper income people with high levels of education, and thus good earning potential. In the PYM study, 53% percentage have a graduate degree, with 79% percent having a graduate degree in the Pendle Hill sample. Few, however, are in business. Previous survey work suggests that most Friends are in education or social services. Those in business rarely have management responsibilities. Few Friends appear to be small business persons or entrepreneurs.

Friends are much more politically liberal than the general population. As shown in the table below, 88% of the Quakers on the Pendle Hill list and 65% of the PYM Quakers self-identified themselves as liberal or extremely liberal, compared to only 15% of the general US population. Thus, these Friends are 4 to 6 times more likely to be liberal or extremely liberal than the US population. Few Quakers are leaning conservative or conservative politically in these samples. Compared to the US population, Quakers are definitely on the "far left" of the political spectrum.

Their attitudes toward business appear to be leftist, but with considerable range. We only have data on these attitudes for the Pendle Hill sample, but given their overall similarity in liberalness, we might expect PYM to be roughly similar.

In the table below, we have divided the responses into "agree" meaning "agree" or "strongly agree", "Neither agree nor disagree", and "Disagree" meaning "Disagree or Strongly disagree."

Almost all these Friends agree that there is too great an income disparity in America today, and most agree that they themselves have enough money. Likewise, there is substantial agreement that spiritual and emotional poverty is more important than material poverty and that income does, in the end, come from business economic activity.A number of issues split the respondents into thirds. About a third think socialism is a better economic system than capitalism; about a third disagree. About a third say they would agree to some taxation scheme to level incomes across all Americans so that everyone would have about the same income—a third disagree. Such a program would require a much higher marginal tax rate than we have today. A third agree that the WTO should require world-wide wage standards.

	US Population 1998 GSS Survey %	PYM Quakers (Three Meetings) %	Non-Eastern Pendle Hill Quakers %
Extremely liberal	2	15	23
Liberal	13	50	65
Leaning liberal	13	12	8
Moderate	37	15	0
Leaning Conservative	16	5	3
Conservative	15	4	0
Extremely Conservative	3	0	0

There is little support for free international trade as a solution to world poverty.

In more conservative circles, the entrepreneur who develops new methods of production or new products is seen as a creator of wealth, a person who lifts all boats even if some gain disproportionately. Most Friends disagree. Quaker entrepreneurs are not likely to be held in high esteem.

Other Friends are more positive. In a talk given at the 1994 Consultation of Friends in Business at Earlham, John Punshon wrote that:

> In recent years, convinced Friends like myself have come to be a fairly large majority in the Society, and we wanted to join a religious society that did good because we were already doing good

ourselves. But we do not work, as the old philanthropists did, with their own money, but with taxpayers money. We are a sustained class and not a sustaining class. The link between the production of wealth which the community can use for socially productive purposes, and the good ideas about what those purposes are, has been severed.

Far too often then I find Friends speaking in critical or condescending ways about business, and it annoys me, because such attitudes show no awareness of how Quaker history has developed, let alone the importance of the vocation to economic life. Suppose there is a cherry pie. It is easy enough to share it out,

Attitude	Agree %	Neither %	Disagree %
There is too great a disparity between the highest and lowest income levels in this country	97	0	3
I have enough money; I do not need more	76	9	15
Spiritual and emotional poverty is a greater problem in the world today than material poverty	57	26	17
Almost all income for government or non-profit organizations comes, in the end, from commercial and busines economic activity	52	35	13
Overall, socialism is a better ecomomic system than capitalism	36	32	33
The WTO should require world-wide wage standards so that all workers are paid equally for comparable work	35	40	25
Capitalism is the main cause of problems in the world today	34	33	34
The government should use taxation and other means to equalize income so that every person has about the same income	31	35	34
International free trade is the best way to raise the world out of poverty	17	33	51
We need people with the gift of generating wealth, for we are all raised from poverty by them	14	54	33
Pursuing a for profit career is contrary to many Friends testimonies	11	36	52
Rich people are rich mostly because they are greedy and grasping	9	24	68
Rich people are morally inferior to poor people	2	20	78

but who is going to pick the cherries and go in the kitchen and actually make the pie? The answer is the business community and Friends in business. I think that it is sad that the prevailing opinion in the Society of Friends seems to be more concerned with eating the pie than cooking it.

Richard Wood, then President of Earlham, and a philosophy professor, makes a similar point. He contrasts the utilitarian approach to ethics to the Kantian. Being concerned with the greatest good to the greatest number, the utilitarians pay attention to the size of the pie, even if it is not always distributed evenly. The Kantians can tend to focus exclusively on fairness and distributive justice. Wood believes that "Much Quaker hostility to business in recent decades seems to me to lie in an uncritical adoption of largely Kantian views. As Plato has Glaucon argue in *The Republic,* a society might be fair but otherwise hardly worth human habitation."

Many Friends who live in "clean" professions like teaching, social work, and the like, are living off a tax base drawn mostly from business activity. In Punshon's terms, we are a "sustained class" and not a "sustaining class." Even the Friends School teacher who complained about capitalism admitted in her talk that their Friends School could not exist without the money from these same capitalists. While the work we do may well be useful, we are more like the little fish that symbiotically clean the teeth of the big fish than the big fish themselves. We want to divide the pie, leaving the work of making it to others.

There are also social class and status distinctions that affect business. Thorstein Veblen wrote of the leisure classes and their distain for useful work. As we become more academic, we are holding ourselves to be doing "high status" work rather than business work—teaching, research, art, literature, pure research and theory. But, someone has to run the local grocery store, manage the garbage collection, and be a fireman or policeman. I think some of our resistance to business is a matter of prestige—we are now wealthy enough to indulge ourselves in the pursuit of "higher" things.

Discussion

I personally believe that excluding the pro-business and more politically conservative views from today's liberal Friends' communities is a mistake.

In doing so we become less diverse, our political and religious dialogue becomes more one-sided, and Friends become increasingly out of touch with the wider diversity of views in our society.

As a Quaker who is in business, I feel increasingly isolated within my faith community. Where do we turn for help?

There are some Quakers in business. The British Quakers and Business Group has a web site at www.quakerbusiness.org that contains literature and other resources. They have also published *Good Business: Ethics at Work* which are advices and queries on personal standards of conduct at work. Here in the USA, we do not have a national Friends Business organization—and it appears that few would be interested. However, Philadelphia Yearly Meeting does have a group that meets from time to time.

However, other religious persons have thought deeply about these issues. Laura Nash and Scotty McLennan's *Church on Sunday, Work on Monday* is the most detailed discussion of the split between the church and person of religion in business. Their books attempts to explain the view of each side to the other, and ends each chapter with questions to consider. Michael Novak, a Catholic, has also written a book called *Business as a Calling*, which summarizes many of the pro-business views.

Given Friends history of success in business and the many businesses that Friends founded, what happened to Friends in business? I'm not sure that this has been researched, but I suspect that there has been a gradual drift of more conservative and free enterprise oriented Friends out of the Society and into religious denominations that are more supportive. We have no quantitative data on whether this trend is continuing.

The Author

Mark S. Cary operates a survey research and data analysis business. He was worked in the past for Research International USA (a company within the WPP group, head-quartered in London), The Walt Disney Company (the Chilton research division of the ABC Broadcasting Company), Friends World Committee for Consultation, and was on the psychology faculty at

Indiana University in Bloomington, Indiana. He has also been adjunct faculty to the Wharton Global Consulting Program. His web site is www.caryresearch.com.

References

Nash, Laura, & McLennan, Scotty. (2001). *Church on Sunday, Work on Monday: The Challenge of Fusing Christian Values with Business Life*. San Francisco, CA: Jossey-Bass.

Novak, Michael. (1996). *Business as a calling: Work and the Examined Life*. New York: The Free Press.

Punshon, John (1994). "An Historical View of Friends and Business," in *Friends Consultation on Friends in Business*. Richmond, IN: Earlham School of Religion and Quaker Hill Conference Center.

Quakers and Business Group. (2000). *Good Business: Ethics at Work—Advices and queries on personal standards of conduct at work*. London: Quakers and Business Group.

Rasor, Paul. (2001). "Materialism, violence, and culture: The context of our faith." Pendle Hill Monday night lecture. Wallingford, PA.

Wood, Richard J (1994). "Virtues, Ethics, and Friends in Business," in *Friends Consultation on Friends in Business*. Richmond, IN: Earlham School of Religion and Quaker Hill Conference Center.

READERS' RESPONSES TO LETTER NO. 40

As I was reading Mark Cary's article, I found myself wanting to stand up and sing for joy. Granted, I'm in college, so as yet not actually in business. However, I've noticed the quiet clearing of throats when I mention among Friends that I am majoring in (gasp!) Management. I started college with a typically negative view of business, but also knowing that I wanted to pursue a business degree. I'm not saying I know all the solutions, but as I've taken my economics and business classes I've started to understand two important things: 1) A good number of Quakers seem to be out of touch with some basic realities of economics; and 2) Most seem to be in the happy position of being able to complain about "the system" without having to think up workable alternatives.

Beth Stevenson, Boulder (CO) Meeting of Friends, now residing in Tulsa (OK)

Hear! Hear!

Chuck Fager, Director, Quaker House, Fayetteville (NC)

As a small businessperson I have always felt what is mentioned in the article. The scorn and then the minds closing as I say things that run counter to "popular belief." I run into resistance to my reality about work in the business world from folks who have never worked (or very long) in that environment. I have the advantage of work which brings me into many businesses as a person who gets let in to many "secrets" about the businesses who's accounting, distribution and manufacturing systems I am replacing.

At FGC Gathering, AFSC meetings and FWCC conferences, it seems that everyone needs an enemy, even Quakers. So we have picked business people and corporations. I guess we are just like everyone else, except that we can maybe listen harder to the minority, even if they are not part of an "affirmative action group" or part of an "oppressed class". That is my hope.

Free Polazzo, Anneewakee Creek Worship Group, Douglasvillle (GA)

I especially appreciate #40 as I've been a small scale general building contractor for the past twenty years. Engaging in that activity has helped me make the transition from a lukewarm, left-leaning radical sympathizer and middle class misfit with tentative academic ambitions to a convinced conservative and to a proud and conventionally productive member of the American middle class.

Tom Webster, Santa Barbara (CA) Friends Meeting

I though your article provocative, well stated, and unfortunate in the sense that it is descriptive of the real Quaker world in at least some, and perhaps most, situations. Newtown Meeting, happily, seems to be an exception. We have, by my estimate, about 1/3 educators/social workers, 1/3 professional artists, and 1/3 business people.

Norval Reece, Newtown (PA) Friends Meeting

The suggestion regarding some kind of Friends in Business organization seems to be a constructive idea. What about starting as a listserv? How many would constitute a critical mass at FGC?

Vici Oshiro, Minneapolis (MN) Friends Meeting

THE QUAKER ECONOMIST
April 3, 2002

Letter No. 41

Dear friends:

Palestine and Israel

Ariel Sharon has just declared that Israel is at war after the suicide bombing of March 31, just as George Bush declared the United States at war after September 11. Neither needed the approval of the legislature.

Here are my opinions (note opinions only). Together, Bush and Sharon are diminishing both their credibility and the Israeli state. The Palestinians have finally discovered a weapon successful against the powerful Israeli military: suicide bombing. They have an unlimited supply in their arsenal and continue to train more. Suicide bombers will destabilize Israel by making it less attractive to foreign investment and tourism, on which the economy depends, and by frightening Israelis into staying home instead of patronizing restaurants and malls. All except for the diehards, including political tourists.

Sharon acts out of ideology. Bush may be doing what he thinks is right, but he is also acting out of desire for power and reputation. Sharon thinks this war is like World War II, where we defeated Germany, reconstructed it, and went home. It is in fact more like the Vietnam War, with its unending guerrillas. Bush wants to go down in history as a great warrior on a par with Washington, Lincoln, and Roosevelt. He does not know that he would impoverish Israel in his wake.

The Palestinian position

We lived here for centuries as independent peoples. When Selim I defeated the Mamluks in 1517, we fell under the power of the Ottoman Turks. In 1858 the Ottoman Land Law established private property, under which agricultural settlements were formed by French, Russians, and Germans, many of them Jewish who – as a Zionist movement - hoped for a Jewish national state. This movement was given impetus by the British under the Balfour Declaration of 1917.

The Turks, who had allied themselves with the Germans, were defeated in World War I. The victorious powers promised the Arabs that the land would become theirs, but Britain and France made secret, conflicting arrangements to divide the former Ottoman (Turkish) Empire into their own spheres of influence. In 1922 the League of Nations declared us to be a British mandate. We have never had our own national state.

After World War II the Jewish people, suffering from Naziism, migrated massively to Palestine. At first the British tried to stop them, but the movement obtained such force that the British gave up and went away. The Jews landed, and Israel declared itself a national state in 1948. They say they bought all their property from the Palestinians in voluntary sales, but how can a sale be voluntary when massive numbers of armed immigrants frighten the people away? We have never had our own land laws, so if the Jews "bought" property, they did so under British or Israeli laws, not ours. They have taken our entire seacoast (except the Gaza strip), so a Palestinian state would (except for Gaza) become landlocked. Those who fled were placed in refugee camps, where they and their descendents remain today, seething in anger and wanting their property back.

Israelis are now settling the West Bank, in territories previously conceded to us. We believe they want to settle the area from the present line to the Jordan River. With so many Israelis, how can Palestine be given back to us? Could the U.S. give California and Texas back to Mexico now?

This land is ours. While some of us are willing to make peace with Israel, others feel they are a usurping power and should be driven to the sea.

The Israeli position

God gave us this land. He directed Moses to lead the Israelis out of Egypt in Biblical times. We lived here for centuries until we were driven out by the Romans. Our temple was destroyed in 70 CE (only the West Wall remains), and the Jewish Diaspora (scattering) began. Since then Jews have been discriminated against everywhere we have settled – in northern Europe (the Ashkenazi Jews) and Spain and northern Africa (the Sephardic Jews). Sephardic Jews were tortured by the Christian Inquisition. We now deserve to have our own national state.

We have allowed the Arabs to remain in Israel if they wished. They have all the rights of Israeli citizens, even to sitting in Parliament, except that (for security reasons) they cannot join the army. But many Palestinians demand the "right of return" – that is, all refugees should have the right to come back. If they all did, then half of Israel would be populated by Arabs, and we would not be a secure state. We would like to live in peace with the Arabs, but they will not. The Oslo Peace Process (1993-2000) was intended to create a Palestinian state as part of a proposal by President Clinton in 2000. But Yasir Arafat was unwilling to agree, and the dispute continues.

Jewish settlements on the West Bank are essential for our defense.

The Arab position (continued)

The Oslo peace process began to break down in October 2000 when Ariel Sharon, not yet prime minister, led an Israeli delegation on to the Temple Mount, which is sacred territory to the Palestinians. He did it solely to aggravate us, because in his heart of hearts he wanted to undermine the peace process. This so angered the Palestinians that suicide bombings began to pick up. Now we will never make peace.

The opinion of a pacifist (me)

Bush wavers. He is strongly influenced by the Jewish vote, but he does not really know how the Jews in the United States feel about Sharon. At first, he backed Sharon because he found the suicide bombings to be similar to the attack on the World Trade Towers. Then, as the situation became out of control, he tried unsuccessfully to hold Sharon back. The United States is rapidly losing influence in the Middle East.

Bush and Sharon both blame Arafat for destroying the Oslo peace process. In fact, Arafat has no power. Although he has arrested a few token terrorists, if he were to do so massively he would be immediately swept away. He cannot do what Bush and Sharon both demand that he do. As Uri Avnery of the Israeli Peace Movement said (International Herald Tribune, April 2, 2002):

> When a whole people is seething with rage, it becomes a dangerous enemy, because the rage does not obey orders. When it exists in the hearts of millions of people, it cannot be cut off by pushing

a button. When this rage overflows, it creates suicide Bombers fueled by the power of anger, against whom there is no defense. A person who has given up on life is free to do whatever his disturbed mind dictates.

How should a pacifist feel about this? I have always refused military action, but my proposal is for police action (which Quaker pacifists have long allowed). The Israelis and Palestinians have had over half a century to settle their quarrel, and they have been unable to do so. The United States should request the United Nations to declare a Palestinian state and to set the boundaries, probably close to the present ones (not the original ones declared by the United Nations in 1949). The U.S. and NATO forces, as police, should defend that boundary.

Israelis settled in Palestine would be given the choice to remain and become Palestinian citizens, or return to Israel.

No state should be associated with a religion. There should be no Jewish state, no Christian state, no Muslim state, no Buddhist state, etc. Religious states were ended in Europe in the sixteenth century. Why? Because the Europeans were gradually becoming more interested in economic prosperity than in religion. Trade led to compromises whose resulting rules overcame the dominance of religion. The Arabs were also traders, but their trade was not strong enough to overcome religious rule.

We should revive a 1940's plan to pump water from the Mediterranean, desalinate it, and dump it into the West Bank, which is lower in altitude to the sea. The entire area would flourish with new agriculture. Then Israel and Palestine would be forced to cooperate.

We should establish American-run schools in Muslim lands, particularly Pakistan, to replace the *madrasas* where thousands of impoverished children are sent because only there can they get enough to eat. But they are indoctrinated as terrorists.

We should recognize (which we have not so far) that the Arab-Israeli dispute lies at the heart of the worldwide struggle against terrorism. We should ask the nations of the world to agree with us that any terrorist act (military action against civilians) is unacceptable anywhere, whether in, or originating in, Palestine, Israel, Northern Ireland, Bosnia, Africa, or elsewhere.

Anyone committing a terrorist act should be kidnapped and tried before the international court in the Hague.

We should make it clear that the United States, and indeed the entire world, suffers from a continuation of the war in the Middle East, and that the world must take action to stop it.

Neither the chronology (below) nor the present CLQ should be considered a complete history. For more information, please consult your history books, the encyclopedia, or the web.

Sincerely your friend,

Jack

CHRONOLOGY OF ARAB-ISRAELI DISPUTE

November 1947: UN General Assembly votes to partition the British Mandate of Palestine into two independent states.

May 1948: British depart. Israel declares itself a state. 5 Arab armies invade Palestine.

Feb. 1949: Armistice. The state of Israel acquires the borders, now called the Green Line, which defined it until June 1967. The West Bank and East Jerusalem were taken by Jordan, Gaza by Egypt.

Jan. 1964: PLO was established to liberate their homeland.

June 5, 1967: Six-day war. The West Bank, East Jerusalem, and Gaza were occupied by Israel.

June 16, 1967: Israel offers to withdraw from almost all conquered territory in exchange for a peace settlement.

Sept. 1, 1967: Israeli offer rejected by Palestinians at the Khartoum Conference. "No peace, no negotiations, no recognition."

Oct. 1973: Yom Kippur war. Israel almost defeated.

May 1977: Likud wins majority in Knesset. Begin elected as Prime Minister. He begins a policy of establishing settlements.

March 1979: Israeli-Egyptian peace treaty. Israel evacuates all of Egyptian territory.

June 1982: Israel invades Lebanon.

Dec. 1987: Intifada begins.

Aug. 1988: Hamas established. Calls for elimination of Israel.

July 1991: Rabin elected. Calls for peace with Palestinians.

Jan. 1993: Oslo talks begin in secret.

1995: Hamas begins terror campaign, including suicide bombing. Israel continues with Oslo.

Nov. 1995: Rabin assassinated. Peres elected Prime Minister.

1996: Peres defeated by Netanyahu.

Dec. 1996: Amnesty International condemns Palestinian Authority for human rights abuses.

Feb. 1997: Netanyahu and Arafat start working together.

May 1997: Human rights groups accuse Israel of torturing Palestinian prisoners.

May 1999: Barak defeats Netenyahu. Resumes Oslo.

Jan. 2000: Barak decides upon Final State negotiations with Arafat.

July 2000: Barak approves a plan to share administrative control of Jerusalem's Palestinian neighborhoods.

July 2000: Camp David negotiations. No resolution.

October 2000: Ariel Sharon leads a delegation to the Temple Mount, upon which the Dome of the Rock and al-Aqsa mosque stand.

September 28, 2000: Intifada II.

Dec. 2000: Clinton offers bridging proposal.

Jan. 2001: Taba (Egypt) negotiations.

Feb. 2001: Sharon elected.

nesses who's accounting, distribution and manufacturing systems I am replacing.

READERS' RESPONSES TO LETTER NO. 41

In recent years the Quakers I have known have sided, often stridently, with the Palestinians. They have warped history to make that seem plausible. I have grown more and more concerned because I see no Quakers who are seeking to understand and bring together both sides, Quakers who recognize the enormous pain on the part of both peoples, Quakers who are looking for ways that we can be instrumental in facilitating understanding and support to both as they struggle to find a balance. I am deeply uncomfortable with our taking one side against another. I sense a degree of anti-Semitism in such a one sided approach. I have been a Quaker since the day of my birth. But I believe we have changed. We have taken up positions. We have decided what shall be politically correct for all Quakers. The old method of sorting and respecting seems to have disappeared, as does the mission to have no enemies, but listen to all and seek to bring a light to the conflict.

Nancy Summers, Warrington Friends Meeting, Wellsville (PA)

Thanks for sending me letter # 41 — just what I am interested in. I am anxious to do more reading in *The Quaker Economist*; I need that kind of stimulating discussion.

Howard Baumgartel, Oread Friends Meeting, Lawrence (KS)

Suppose a large group of little old ladies in Palestine were to march up to the Israeli tanks and just stand there? The group would have to be large enough so that the soldiers could not easily arrest them all. There is the memorable vision of the people of the Philippines swarming around Marcos's tanks when he tried to enforce his claim that he had won the presidential election instead of Corazon Aquino. The soldiers were given flowers and food, and they could not fire on their own people.

Virginia Flagg, San Diego (CA) Friends Meeting

Throughout the history of Israel there has been a very disturbing unwillingness on the part of the Arab states in the region to accept its existence. In *The Wealth and Poverty of Nations,* Landes tells a story of some liberal Israelis visiting an Arab country and talking about how if Jews and Arabs cooperate, they would be able to create great things, "make the desert bloom", etc. etc. The Arabs responded that the best path to prosperity would be to defeat Israel. Add to that the invasion right after the UN declaration, the unwillingness to normalize relations, and there seems to be an unwillingness to cooperate.

Geoffrey Williams, Bethesda (MD) Friends Meeting

I'm deciding whether I've got to leave my meeting over the bias of its members in the Middle East conflict - since I have a Jewish daughter with relatives in Jerusalem, Netanya, Haifa, and a few other places there. There seems to be no room for me in religion dominated by Political Correctness. I was much interested to learn from you that it has not always been this way.

Bob Richmond, West Knoxille (TN) Meeting

I really appreciate the work that went into issue 41 (and the results, too). I am about to post it on the Middle East Dialogue Group list that exists here in Atlanta. (started before 9/11!).

Free Polazzo, Anneewakee Creek Friends Worship Group, Douglasvillle (GA)

CLQ #41 is badly needed. The Peace Testimony really does not permit us to ignore Palestine: For any of us paying taxes, we paid for a share (albeit small) of each of the tanks we see destroying towns.

Will Candler, Annapolis (MD) Friends Meeting

Many Arab states ban Jews as citizens and Saudi Arabia bans them from even entering. There were more Jewish refugees from Arab states (over 800,000) than Arab refugees from Israel (400,000-500,00). Israel absorbed and assimiliated its refugees, the Arab world (apart from Jordan) prefers the Palestinians as stateless sticks to beat Israel with. Many Palestinians are descendants of migrants attracted to Palestine by the economic revival the incoming Jewish settlers generated from the 1880s onwards (the 19th century population of Palestine, including Jordan, was only about 400,000 while Jerusalem was already a majority Jewish city in the mid 19th century). Palestinian notables — who sold land to Jews at high prices — started using terror as a weapon back in the 1920s because the increased wages and opportunities, plus the new Arab migrants, weakened their hold over the Arab peasantry. Anti-Zionism remains a tool of oppressive Arab elites.

Michael J. Warby, Melbourne, Australia

Violence is (of course) not in the best interest of either side. Israel is likely to create more martyrs than it prevents by invading with tanks and gunship helicopters. Palestine is exerting far too much of its resources for retribution against Israel, rather than caring for the needs of its population. However, two things are clear: violence will only breed more violence, and the world is rapidly growing tired of the same old "we'll quit when they quit" stories from both sides.

Beth Stevenson, Boulder (CO) Meeting of Friends, now living in Tulsa (OK)

"We should recognize (which we have not so far) that the Arab-Israeli dispute lies at the heart of the worldwide struggle against terrorism"

Perhaps so, but just as easily perhaps not. South America is full of ideological and drug-related terrorism having nothing to do with Israel. Ireland had nothing to do with Israel. Plenty of evidence exists that Al-Qaida cares little for Israel compared to their hatred of a certain lifestyle and set of values. Shall we talk about Indonesia, Somalia, Ethiopia (or most sub-Sahran African states), the Balkans, the Phillipines? The Arab-Israeli dispute may be the mother-of-all terrorist initiators but to accept your claim requires a certain intuitive leap.

Milt Janetos, Agate Passage Friends Meeting, Bainbridge Island (WA)

I thought the Israelis could defend themselves and should, but now I don't thinks it's possible. Only the U.S.A. can provide the solution—by admitting all Israelis eligible under the I.N.S. rules, which may need to be expanded. The hard core Meir Kahane element will not leave but probably will hole up in the hills, or the desert, for endless guerrilla action. We would tell them we would have nothing further to do with them. I know this creates all kinds of problems and there are 1000 reasons why people say it can't be done. More prayer, real soon, needs to be done.

Maurice Boyd, Friends Meeting of Washington (DC)

You open CLQ 41 with a statement that George Bush didn't need the approval of the legislature for his Afghan war (which he is trying to expand to virtually anywhere he alone sees fit). This may unfortunately be true in practice in the last 50 years but is constitutionally absolutely not true (see Article I Section 8 of the U.S. Constitution). Only Congress can declare war in the United States...except they have abdicated that responsibility ever since WW-II.

Rich Andrews, Boulder (CO) Meeting of Friends

The PLO was founded in 1964 when West Bank and Gaza were Arab. Its aim: to destroy Israel for nationalist reasons. Hamas was founded in 1988. Its aim : To destroy Israel for Islamist reasons. First suicide bombing in 1994, one year after beginning of Oslo Peace Process. The Oslo negotiations failed because of Arafat's insistence upon Unlimited Right of Return of Refugees - a formula for Israel's suicide. How does one negotiate with a "partner" who wants either your immediate or your delayed death? I welcome comments at arbier@ aol.com.

Arthur Bierman, Boulder(CO)

The Arabs decided that their fellow Arabs should be left to fester in horrible refugee camps. They did give them money, but this money has produced almost nothing in the way of an economy. It's probably in Swiss banks. Jordan has a majority Palestinian population, but the Palestinian refugees have not been invited to assimilate into the population. It is this situation which has created the despair of the Palestinians. They are hopeless – they indeed have no future in the hell holes in which they live. However, this is not Israel's fault: it is the fault of their fellow Arabs, who are using them as a political weapon in their eternal hope of destroying Israel.

Judy Warner, Lutheran, with a Jewish father

I have to commend you on your encyclopedic knowledge of the Palestinian- Israeli conflict.

Dennis Bentley, Morganton (NC), No Friends Meeting in town.

NOTE from Jack. It helps to look it up in the encyclopedia.

THE QUAKER ECONOMIST
April 11, 2002

Letter No. 42

Dear friends:

The Living Wage

"Despite the harm to low-wage workers, including those who clean city buildings, drive city contract buses, and help build the city's bright new structures, cities regularly stretch their tax dollars on the backs of these low wage workers." So writes Steve Herndon, a member of the Boulder Living Wage campaign, in the *Daily Camera* of Boulder, Colorado (my home town). The Living Wage Campaign aims to require cities and universities to pay their employees a "living wage" and to buy their supplies only from producers who pay similarly.

The living wage campaign started in Baltimore in 1995 and has spread to over sixty metropolitan areas. Students have taken up the campaign in universities, including Harvard in the spring of 2001. When I gave a series of talks at Swarthmore College last September, I met with the student living wage committee. They had studied the minimum it takes to live in the Swarthmore area, about $12.50 an hour they said, and were campaigning to persuade the college to pay that amount to all its menial employees.

What causes wages to be what they are? (Please pardon the tiny lesson in economics that follows – only two small paragraphs).

Employers pay workers the value of their product (technically, their marginal product, meaning the value one worker adds to the total product). If the worker does not produce a value equal to his or her wage, he or she will not be hired. If one produces more, one's wage must be increased, because if not, the worker will be lured away by someone else.

But how do you determine the "product" of a janitor in a university, or a school bus driver for a municipality? That is determined by comparison with workers in industry (in this letter, "industry" includes agriculture and services). Normally, the municipality/university does not pay more than it has to, just like industry. If wages in the municipality/university fall below those in industry, workers migrate to industry. Nor does the university/municipality see any need to pay more than industry. Thus the wages of university/municipality workers are determined by the productivity of similar workers in industry.

Unionized workers may earn more than non-unionized, but they cannot stray far from the productivity test. Harvard's settlement with the living wage campaign was not to raise wages to the level demanded by the students, but to agree to pay its non-unionized workers the same as unionized workers of equal skill.

I would like to see all workers earn the comfortable wage of at least $12.50 an hour. For this to be sustainable, however, the economy must produce goods and services worth at least $12.50 an hour times the number of worker/hours, plus what is paid in taxes, profits, and other costs. If the economy does not do that, then higher wages only bring inflation – too much money chasing too few goods.

If we truly want all workers to earn more, we must find ways to increase the productivity of industrial workers. For municipality/university workers to earn more, industrial workers must produce more. If the living wage is put into effect but the productivity of industry does not increase, the consequences are adverse. First, labor will become two-tiered: higher earners in municipalities and universities than in industry for the same work. More workers than are needed will line up for jobs in municipalities/universities, and industrial workers will be dissatisfied. Second, inflation will cause the "living wage" to be eroded. It will buy less and less. Third, someone has to pay the living wage. For municipalities, that will be taxpayers. Since we are a democracy, they may very well refuse, and the city will be left with a deficit, to be paid by our children and grandchildren.

When I asked the Swarthmore students if they would be willing to pay higher tuitions to cover the living wage, they answered "No." The higher wage should be paid from the college's endowment. But the income from this endowment reduces their tuition. (As in most colleges, Swarthmore students do not pay their full cost). If the endowment is diminished, their tuition would increase, or else their library would buy fewer books and their laboratories less equipment. Swarthmore would not be Swarthmore, and new applicants might go to Haverford (unless Haverford did the same).

There are even more adverse effects. Studies of an increased minimum wage have shown that it usually causes employers to shift from workers to machines (where possible). This leaves unemployed workers. Guess who they will be? Mostly minority groups and women, against whom employers are prejudiced. The minimum wage was increased almost yearly from 1961 to 1981. During that time unemployment for African American teenagers increased fourfold, to 40.7% (see my book, *Seeking Truth Together,* page 25). Thus higher than market wages discriminate against women, African Americans, and teenagers.

What do we mean by a living wage, I asked the Swarthmore students? When I was their age, I told them, menial workers earned about one tenth what they do now (adjusted for inflation). How did they live? Their reply, reasonably, was that today's culture is different. Standards of housing, health, and other necessities are higher, and we must keep up with the times.

Yet it seemed that those demanding living wages for others were also demanding that still others pay for them (taxpayers, library users, their children, etc.) Is this the trend of the times? – that we are so kindhearted that we wish others would have the standard of living that we do, but we always want still others to pay for that? Do we demand that the poor live like the middle class, without having the skills or education to produce the standard of living of the middle class?

This is the dilemma that I leave you, readers. Please let me know what you think.

Sincerely your friend,
Jack Powelson

A QUESTION BY JACK

Some responses to The Living Wage have referred to the high salaries of CEOs and say that if these could somehow be redistributed to the menial workers, living wages could be paid, and no one would suffer. I too wish this could happen. But how?

If a high-earning baseball player does not receive an excessive salary, he will leave for another team.

It is the same with CEOs. Many of us who understand baseball do not understand the worth of a good CEO to a corporation. David Balkin, a professor of management, puts it this way: CEOs "need to have leadership, a vision, and bring diverse people together on a large scale. [They must] also possess political skills and inter-act well with the Wall Street investment community. Public speaking and the ability to lobby government regulatory boards are also important" (quoted in my book, *The Moral Economy,* p. 27).

Some think of large corporations as troves of treasure, greedily garnering profits and paying their favored management vast sums. In a few cases (Enron?) this may be so, but mostly it is not. Many corporations are on the verge of bankruptcy. If they go belly-up, their workers and stockholders lose, sometimes their life savings (as in Enron). Often, only an extraordinary CEO keeps them afloat. But he demands extraordinary emoluments to keep him from leaving for another company.

I shudder every time I see a huge mansion – too many these days, belonging to multibillionaires. But what can you do about it? Please, someone, answer this question for me.

[My solution is to ignore it. They are small fry in the big picture. Let us instead concentrate on increasing the productivity of the poor.]

READERS' RESPONSES TO LETTER NO. 42

Peter Belmont of Brooklyn (NY) has suggested a universal stipend paid by the government, along with minimal lodging and cheap food, to keep people alive. Beyond that, we would have a free market economy and no need for a minimum wage.

Unfortunately, Peter's letter is much too long for me to publish, and I do not see a key paragraph for my usual excerpt. REMINDER TO OTHER READERS: PLEASE KEEP YOUR LETTERS SHORT. My correspondence is approaching my capacity of 24 hours a day. Until that capacity is reached, I will answer longer letters but cannot publish all of them. Thank you.

My city, Lansing MI, has an income tax of 1% on residents and 1/2% on non-residents that work in the city. In the 40 years or so, virtually all commerce has relocated outside of the city limits and all of the high income housing developments. Our downtown is limited to a community college, a law school (nation's 2nd largest) and state, city, and county governments. It takes huge tax breaks to retain the historic auto plants and they are just assembly units with the parts being manufactured in area plants also located outside the city.

The "living wage" will be death to most urban economies.

A much better device is the Earned Income Tax Credit. This tax credit matches earning of low wage workers based on the number of dependents. It is national so it does not discriminate against certain communities.

Jim Booth, Red Cedar Meeting, Lansing (MI)

The logic of your comments here reminded me of a radio-talk-show caller who recently complained about her taxes and then opined that corporations should pay a greater share of the nation's tax burden (thereby reducing her own obligation, presumably). She clearly had no idea as to who ultimately pays corporate taxes. Advocates of the "living wage" are afflicted by the same sort of short-sightedness: they advocate for one group in society at the expense of everyone else—especially those who can least afford it. You make the point nicely, Jack.

Ken Allison, Episcopalian, Paradise Valley, AZ

As I have said before I don't believe I have a firm grasp of economics. However it appears to me that students and "liberals" are idealistic but naive. The "Living Wage" folks were communists/socialists 30-100 years ago but now that those dreams have crashed they're trying to dress the same notions in new clothes, and thus it ever will be.

Maurice Boyd, Friends Meeting of Washington

I appreciated your analysis of the economically flawed arguments of the living wage movement. I have made a similar case regarding the minimum wage (see William Ashworth, *The Economy of Nature* [Houghton Mifflin, 1995], pp. 284-286). However, I suspect neither one of us has much chance of being listened to, because the real point of concern for living-wage advocates is not economic but moral - it has less to do with what people earn at the bottom than it does with the excess that is being scarfed up by people at the top. Distributional issues are real, and the problem is worsening. According to the latest figures from *Forbes*, America's 400 richest individuals are worth a combined total of $1.2 trillion, or an average of $3 billion each. If we let those 400 keep $150,000 each and then parceled the rest out among the remaining 200 million of us, we would end up with nearly $5,000 apiece. This is a problem for which I have yet to see a satisfactory solution, aside from the old suggestion made by Charles Ives (yes, THAT Charles Ives) to create a maximum allowable income. Does *The Quaker Economist* have any thoughts on this matter?

Bill Ashworth (South Mountain Friends Meeting, Ashland, Oregon)

NOTE by Jack: Yes, see above.

Friends, I am a business executive. We can only pay what the worker earns in economic terms as you have said. The next challenge is to increase the value of the contribution that the worker makes so that we can afford to pay them more. This is the fun challenge. It is the great win-win.

Lee B. Thomas, Jr. Louisville (KY) Friends Meeting

An alternative that might be worth considering to achieve the same goal would be reducing the standard of living to the wages that will support it for everyone. Not likely to be a popular edict if handed out from above, but the voluntary simplicity movement might be more effective in the long run than the living wage + increased production approach, especially when you compare the long-term environmental impacts of either approach.

Merlyn Homes, Unitarian, Boulder (CO)

Unlike the students you discussed "living wage" with, I'm willing to pay more so that those at the bottom could live better. This is, in other words, a redistribution of income. Some years ago Cesar Chavez began a grape boycott to force growers to recognize a union so that wages would be higher for agricultural workers. It didn't work. We are accustomed to buying inexpensive food while we exploit those who produce it.

Virginia Flagg, San Diego (CA) Friends Meeting

OK Jack, explain how CEO salaries are set, how come American CEO's earn so much more than European CEO's. Tell me why CEO salaries maintain during down cycles when companies are laying off workers and losing money? Why aren't they subject to market forces??

Charlie Thomas, attending Cascabel Worship Group, Arizona

NOTE by Jack: The reader has the last word. Usually (not always) I do not reply, so as not to keep the dialogue going interminably. Especially is this so when someone hits me with a one-liner that requires extensive, complex economics to answer. The short answer here would be that the productivity of European businesses is, on average, much lower than the American. The long answer would be to explain why, and you have to look for that in a more sophisticated economics journal than this one.

The problem with all these economic discussions is that people see that they do not apply to CEO's and other high managers who get paid fabulous sums that do not appear at all related to the value of their work. The market is skewed because the board members who employ them tend to be in the same position themselves and so their self-interest skews their perception of the real value. And people perceive the luxuriousness of the management quarters (in many cases) compared to the workers. I know, as you do, that these expenses are a drop in the bucket (but just try and tell people that). Cutting them would not make a real difference to a large company, but it would make an enormous difference to public perceptions.

Bruce Hawkins, Northampton (MA) Friends Meeting

I enjoyed the discussion of "living wage". Apparently it has perverse consequences, like rent control. In a more perfect world, people working a lot
more than 40 hours a week would be able to afford rent and medical care,
including prescription drugs. I think real estate prices are on a separate
track (especially out here), owing to land scarcity. Drug prices puzzle me,
since prices are lower in Canada and Europe.

Trudy Reagan, Palo Alto, (CA)

ANSWER by Jack (because the question was asked, sort of): Drug poducers
have very heavy fixed costs, including the costs of research in seeking drugs
for particular ailments, and the drugs do not pan out. Somebody has to pay
theses costs, and they stick them on consumers who can pay more. If Americans are richer than Canadians, drug prices will tend to be higher in the US
than in Canada. Also, if the Canadian government (with its health care program) puts a cap on drug prices (I don't know whether they do or not), then
they would shift those costs to US consumers. If every government put a
cap on drug prices, pharmaceutical companies would go out of business.

Thanks for this piece. I think it sets up one side of the argument. Good for
discussion. I'm not sure that the labor market works as rationally or as
equitably as your model. The push for a living wage here in Lawrence fo-
cuses only on firms moving into town with substantial tax benefits and
public financing of one kind an another. I'll forward your message to one
of the key people in the living wage movement here, incidentally funded by
AFSC or some Quaker source.

Howard Baumgartel, Oread Friends Meeting, Lawrence (KS)

THE QUAKER ECONOMIST
April 24, 2002

Letter No. 43

Dear friends:

The Commanding Heights

When Lenin introduced the New Economic Policy in the Soviet Union in 1921, he declared that the "commanding heights" (large-scale industry, foreign trade, banking, and transport) would be managed by the state. Later on, the USSR brought all business and agricultural enterprises into state ownership. The commanding heights therefore refers to the ability to pull strings (regulations) that tell the economy to act this way or that.

On three Wednesday evenings (April 3, 10, and 17, 2002) Public Broadcasting presented *Commanding Heights*, an overview of the world economy during the twentieth century. The gist was that early in the century the governments of many countries decided that market principles were not working fast enough to alleviate poverty and to distribute income and wealth well enough. Therefore (in country after country) the government pulled the strings of the economy as if it were running a puppet show. By the end of the century, it became clear to most that manipulating the economy was not working. Economies were devastated and increasing numbers driven into poverty. The Soviet Union and other socialist states, plus India, Chile, Argentina, Bolivia, and Mexico were prime examples. I could add several more where I have had professional experience. The main reason was that governments either did not know enough about the billions of transactions they were trying to control or they became mad for power. Corruption is rampant. Now deregulation is sweeping the world, and free markets are being re-created everywhere.

Whenever the government assumes control of the commanding heights, it pits the power of the politicians against the power of the market. The market is the outcome of decisions made by billions of individuals, each acting in his or her own interest. Every transaction (such as buying and selling) in a free market – without coercion – implies that both parties feel their welfare is improved. Most economists say that this mutual improvement – multiplied billions of times – constitutes the most advantageous society possible. Adam Smith argued (1776) that one cannot act in one's own interest in an uncoerced market without satisfying the interest of someone else. Therefore a free market economy is led by an "invisible hand," which he thought was the hand of God, to produce those goods and services that most satisfy the people, at the lowest cost and saving of resources possible.

Those who would seize the commanding heights declared that this argument was fallacious. Monopolies spoil the opportunities of others. (Smith made the same criticism). While bargaining in the market improves the conditions of both sides, nevertheless the bargainers do not start from positions of equal power. Often they are poor, powerless. Nor does the market prevent depressions, which cause many to be unemployed, some even starving.

Part One of PBS's *Commanding Heights* dealt with depressions. Before the 1930s economists widely believed that a depression was a temporary imbalance caused by wrong guesses: consumers demanding different goods from those producers had guessed. Once the imbalance was corrected, the economy would straighten out again. Or, they believed that overproduction had produced a glut, and once the excess goods were drawn down full employment would return. As the Great Depression dragged on, an English economist, John Maynard Keynes, proposed that a depression was not necessarily self-correcting. If savers were so discouraged that they would not lend for capital investment, the depression might go on forever. From this, some economists (known as Keynesians) concluded that government expenditures could jump-start an economy. Franklin Roosevelt "bought" this idea with the New Deal.

The first part of *Commanding Heights* deals with attempts to control the macro-economy by manipulating total government expenditures (borrowing as necessary) and adjusting the interest rate. While watching this, I felt my life being re-run: I was in college from 1937 to 1941, studying economics, when Keynes's book (published in 1936) swept the field. I became a thorough Keynesian and remained so through graduate school. Friedrich Hayek, the Austrian economist who thought Keynes was leading us down "the road to serfdom" (his 1944 book) was a "reactionary devil."

But *Commanding Heights* shows that deficit spending did not always alleviate depression – not even usually. Furthermore, while Keynesians proposed that the government borrow during depressions and pay back during prosperity, in fact they would not pay back. To no ostensible purpose, government debt continued to mount. Hayek's popularity gained relative to that of Keynes.

Macro-economics – the study of national income, over-all employment, and fiscal and monetary policy – was born with Keynes. It so fascinated me that I wrote my first book on that subject (*Economic Accounting,* McGraw-Hill 1955). But when stagflation (simultaneous inflation and stagnation) – impossible under Keynesian theory – hit us in the 1970s, I joined many other economists in changing my mind.

After World War II, the temptation to speed up the economic development of poor countries once more led governments to seize the commanding heights. But now they depended more on traditional economics, or *micro-economics* (the study of which particular goods and services are produced, and how resources are used). By dictating the amounts of consumption and investment, and setting their prices by fiat, economic planning violated the rules of the market, all over the world. We thought that forcing investment would speed development. I became an economic planner, advising governments on how to do it.

Once again I was wrong. The second part of *Commanding Heights* shows the failure of micro-planning. Instead of responding to the needs of "the people," planners fed their own egos. They passed laws designed to give themselves power to grant licenses and privileges, then they demanded bribes to grant them. Setting up a business became so onerous that many would operate on the "black" or "informal" market, where they constantly broke the law. Had they not done so, many economies would have gone bust (like Argentina today).

These were the conditions in virtually all countries in Latin America, Asia, and Africa. Interest groups (such as labor unions and businesses) would vie for the favor of the government. Among the responses were requirements that a business could not fire a worker without paying up to several years of salary. So businesses found ways not to hire. Many used machines instead of labor. One government enterprise in Mexico shut down but still had to pay its workers. It would bus them in to the factory, where they would sit idly all day, and then bus them home again.

During my career as economic advisor, I gradually came to understand that I was a lacky for the wealthy elite. They rarely communicated with the poor, and their purported interest in the poor was hypocritical. On one occasion, the planning team that I headed up in an African country decided to transfer resources from road-building to small-scale agriculture. The minister who oversaw road-building was furious because he had already let out contracts for five years in excess of what we had proposed. He got his way. On another occasion, high civil servants wanted to keep interest rates low so that they might borrow cheaply from a development bank that they owned, to build a tourist hotel – in a country where agricultural extension services were virtually nil and education grossly underfunded.

Micro-economic planning could not last forever, because governments could not finance all they had planned, and they had planned vast projects the market could not sustain. (One saying among economists was, "Don't plan vast projects with half-vast ideas." Part Two of *Commanding Heights* tells about its failures in country after country. How the Soviet Union and Argentina collapsed, and how China, Mexico, India, and others are selling off their bloated state enterprises and deregulating their economies. Even the United States is deregulating, slowly. Finally, at the turn of the twenty-first century governments are coming to understand what economists knew in the nineteenth – that the free market provides the greatest employment, the highest wages for workers, and the most egalitarian distributions of income *given the resources of the country.*

If you criticize the free market – and I encourage you to do so – please do not criticize it in a vacuum. Always tell what your alternative is.

The third part of *Commanding Heights* takes us up to the present, including the protests against the World Trade Organization, the International Monetary Fund, and the World Bank. The protesters have a message: we have not yet arrived at a fair and equal economic world.

But globalization has brought millions of jobs and higher incomes for the poor all over the world, even though most countries have not yet broken the bonds of poverty. (The poor *are* getting richer, contrary to much belief; I'll do another CLQ on this in the future). *Commanding Heights* shows how representatives of the Third World have overwhelmingly favored globalization, but they complain (correctly) that the rich countries do not practice what we preach. We and the Europeans still maintain tariffs against Third World products, such as textiles. Toward the end of *Commanding Heights,* the President of Tanzania is shown declaring that his country would gain much more by selling its textiles to the United States than it does by receiving foreign aid.

Commanding Heights maintains (and I agree): if you are going in the right direction, don't turn around just because you haven't arrived. Globalization and free trade have come a long way toward economic justice, but we still have a long way to go.

If you want a copy of the complete tapes and/or book for *Commanding Heights,* phone WGBH in Boston at 1-800-255-9425.

> Sincerely your friend,
> Jack Powelson

READERS' RESPONSES TO LETTER NO. 43

Jerry Frost, retiring head of the Quaker library at Swarthmore and history lecturer, reminded us at a Pendle Hill lecture that Quakers during the 1800s saw free markets as the path to peace. According to Frost, British Friends backed peace groups with free trade agendas but made sure they were led by Church of England types so they wouldn't be negatively branded as tools of Quakerism. It was a lecture on the peace testimony, not economics, but it seems to fit your argument.

> Signe Wilkinson, Chestnut Hill (PA) Friends Meeting

Your comment that we should ignore the mansions of the multi-billionaires is on target both practically and morally. I see that some of your correspondents have forgotten, or do not care about, the Commandment against coveting. I think that breaking this Commandment has caused more harm than any other. If it had been kept, we would not have had any of the evil communist movements of the last century that brought the death of millions and the misery of hundreds of millions. And we would have a happier, more productive society today.

> Judy Warner, Lutheran, Rohrersville (MD)

P.S. I enjoyed the typo that identified someone as being from a "Fiends Meeting." It gave me a few minutes of amusement imagining what a Fiends Meeting would be like.

This piece is excellent - and it is encouraging that your education and change of perspective continued throughout your life. Alas, too many people I know still have the same ideas and worldview that they had in their 20s - never adjusted, never updated and never truly tested for reality.

Michael Schefer, Jewish (non-attending), Philadelphia PA, children in Germantown Friends School

---

While viewing The Commanding Heights I was struck by the contrast between "that of God in everyone," and "that of control over everyone." CLQ 44 introduces "greed." The 20th century champions of greed were the left-wingers. They wanted and got, to varying degrees, something for nothing — redistribution rather than creation. Their systems were unsustainable and collapsed with tremendous economic and human costs. Being coercive and monolithic, they contained no inherent self-correcting mechanisms. In modern capitalist economies most people get something for (almost) nothing, too, but at much less or almost no cost to others because capitalism is largely voluntary and diverse. The East Asian failures, Brazil and Argentina also have great costs, and by not controlling everyone the capacity for self-correction is greater, faster and more humane. Why? Could it have anything to do with "that of God in everyone," a more elevated view of the individual? In any case, we still have some distance to go.

J.D. Von Pischke, a Friend from Virginia (editorial board member)

Hi my name is Brandon I am fourteen years old and live in Los Olivos California. I am very interested in politics. I am a big follower of the Republican Party. I heard about you from my neighbor Tom. Los Olivos is in Central California and in Santa Barbara County. I am in the eighth grade. Please tell me what you have done in your life and a little bit more about you. Sincerely your friend,

Brandon Griffith, Los Olivos, California

REPLY: Thank you, Brandon, for your interest in me. If you will send me your snailmail address, I will send you, with my compliments, a copy of my Quakerback book, *Seeking Truth Together,* which tells about me and what I have done. If you need more information, visit my web page at http://spot.colorado.edu/~powelsoj, where you will find my Vita. If you have any more questions, write again. Jack

---

The summary of the "commanding heights" seemed to imply that there is nothing more to do in both advanced and developing countries than to let free markets do their thing. This is not correct, as even in theory free markets cannot do many things. First, capable, honest institutions are needed to oversee the markets to set the rules and make sure they are followed—these activities are on the financial pages of our newspapers every day, Enron, Microsoft, Merrill Lynch, etc. Second, we must have monetary institutions and policies that no free market will provide. Third, we must have legislative and fiscal institutions to decide and spend funds on public and merit goods and transfer payments, influence income distribution by determining who bears the tax burden, and decide how much of a deficit or surplus is needed; free markets cannot do any of these things. Fourth, we must have institutions to control the effects of private markets on the public and global commons—air, water, oceans, wildlife, etc. Fifth, we must decide who can immigrate to our country. All these activities are accepted by both political parties in the U.S. and elsewhere, and our newspapers are full every day of controversy on carrying out these activities. Even the most doctrinaire free market Friend can participate in the Friends Committee on National Legislation with a clear conscience.

Bill Rhoads, Germantown Meeting, Philadelphia [PA]

NOTE from Jack: I agree with most of that. My major lifetime opus, which took a quarter century to write (*Centuries of Economic Endeavor,* University of Michigan 1994), is about how and why these institutions were formed in the Western World and Japan, and how and why they developed much less and more slowly in the rest of the world.

I have recently heard quite a bit about the merits of limiting a CEO's pay. I remain unconvinced. My reasons:

1) We live in a market economy. That includes labor markets, where people sell their knowledge, skills, and abilities on the open market to the "highest bidder." Isn't this what capitalism is all about?

2) American culture encourages people to achieve the highest rank possible. By limiting the pay of a CEO, we would be punishing the CEO for being successful.

3) We aren't Japan or Europe. Our economies and ways of life are different. It's quite possible that the reason American CEO's are paid more is because we value their work more (in an economic sense) than Europe or Japan.

Beth Stevenson, Friends Meeting of Boulder (CO), now in college in Tulsa (OK)

---

1. Why can't we have a vibrant free market and restrain the massive inequality of income by a truly progressive income tax as does Sweden, I believe, so that no one can retain huge earnings? Would that dry up the urge to earn more money? If being the CEO meant earning a top salary much less than what one earns now, would that mean competent people for the job wouldn't seek it?

2. Who will restrain the free market from actions that help the corporation but harm the general welfare, such as polluting the environment, selling unsafe products, or running an unsafe factory? Doesn't the government have to do that by enforcing regulations?

3. Does the free market work best for all services, such a medical care? If the government provides some services such as water and roads, why not health care?

Arthur Rifkin Manhasset (NY) Friends Meeting

THE QUAKER ECONOMIST
May 3, 2002

Letter No. 44

Dear friends:

Profits

Are profits the life blood of the economy, or do they reflect greed? My answer: Both of these.

Profits are the return on capital (interest and dividends), just as wages and salaries are the return on labor. Land, labor, and capital (the factors of production) all combine to produce what we consume. Real capital consists in the physical sources of production, such as factory buildings and machines. Machines enable workers to produce more than they could without them. Buildings keep both workers and machines dry, warm, and undamaged. The entire gross domestic product of any country can be divided into the amounts arising out of land (rent), labor (wages), and capital (profits). Can you think of any good whose value is not ultimately divided among these three? (I can't).

NOTES: (1) Economists call the returns to land "rent," but that is a technical term, different from the ordinary concept of rent; (2) Financial capital (stocks, bonds, etc.) evidences the ownership of real capital.

Greed applies to wages, rent, and profit. The worker may be greedy by demanding extremely high pay, such as a baseball star or a CEO . A farmer may be greedy by demanding price floors that force others (including the poor) to pay higher prices for sugar. (Most farm subsidies are paid to the rich, not the poor). A capitalist (owner of capital) may be greedy by demanding a monopoly or by violating the environment to ensure higher profits.

The greedy ones make the news with their transgressions, so we usually ignore the many, many people who do not demand more than their due. While greed is characteristic of all types of people, not just capitalists, many of "all types" are not greedy. Hence I believe greed is a characteristic of some *individuals,* not of a "system" or of organizations such as multinational corporations. We should not condemn MNCs for their greed. If anything, it is people within them who are greedy.

If you think capitalists are greedy, please reflect on yourself. How much will you depend, in your retirement, on profits of corporations? What would you pay for education were it not for profits on university endowments? Would you pay more for insurance (fire, life, health, auto) if the insurance company did not earn profits on its investments? If you saved up for a house, then the services provided by that house (warmth, protection from the elements, etc.) are the profit from your investment. Are you greedy if you keep that profit to yourself, instead of opening your house to the homeless?

Our society values creativity and change. In the economic sphere this is part of competition, which tends to reduce costs. Our society rewards innovation with higher profits than those earned in the ordinary course of business. If you write a book, you get royalties, but only if your book sells well (my books sell reasonably, but nothing like Harry Potter). If you patent an invention, you receive a higher than normal return, but only if your invention sells well. (The inventor of skateboards must have made a killing). Our society generally thinks this is fair. But any bonanza is usually temporary; after some years the investment sinks back to a "reasonable" return.

We also think it is fair that those whose inventions do not pan out should earn no profits, indeed should lose their investments. Thus, risk is rewarded if it succeeds, and the risk-taker takes the lumps if it does not. Pharmaceutical companies make up for losses on experiments that don't pan out by charging higher prices for those that do. Whenever you buy a prescription, you are also paying for many unsuccessful attempts.

Externalities

Some companies make profits based on capital that is not their own. Pure air, for example, is the common property of many. A company that fouls the air without paying for it receives a stolen profit, stolen from the people who suffer. The same for water and other goods provided by nature. These are known as external costs (someone other than the producer pays them). Logging companies using federally-built roads take advantage of external costs. Environmentalists should lobby to internalize the externalities by requiring firms to pay costs of pollution. Loggers should pay for the logging roads. If everyone paid all costs (and passed them on in the price to the consumer), environmental degradation would sink to restorable levels.

Stockholders insist on profits

Stockholders press their management to make the greatest profits possible, because doing so increases the market values of their holdings. Is this moral? According to our system, yes, because profits are earned through (1) inventions, (2) producing goods that people want, and (3) operating efficiently, to reduce costs and conserve resources. Especially in the latter respect, environmentalists should favor the pressure on corporations to earn high profits.

Look at it another way. Income reflects resources created, since goods that are sold are resources. Expenses reflect resources consumed, such as labor, depreciation of machinery used in production, and raw materials. The excess of income over expenses, which is profit, therefore reflects the excess of resources created over resources consumed. This balance should cheer environmentalists.

Of course, the wrong resources may be created, if we feel we should drive VW bugs rather than SUVs. But that is consumer choice. That problem lies with the *people,* not the system. Likewise, *of course* producers dump waste in public waters or belch exhaust into public air. So we pass laws (or file lawsuits) to prevent them from abusing externalities. Our system is one of checks and balances. If corporations violate the environment, it does no good to blame them for trying to maximize profits, for that is what they are supposed to do. There's no point in saying: "Please be good little boys, and don't do that." We must have laws with teeth, to hold them in line.

It is sometimes thought that high profits are taken at the expense of workers. Well, *surprise:* the firms that earn the highest profits are the very ones that pay the highest wages. In 1942, Joseph Schumpeter, one of the world's greatest economists (under whom I had the privilege of studying) observed that this had been happening at least since 1899. *The Economist* (5/30/98) noted that "numerous studies, looking as far back as the 1920s, show that industries where profits and average productivity are higher tend to pay all workers more."

Other researchers, including the International Labor Organization, have reported that multinational corporations, on average, pay higher wages and offer more social services (health care, pensions, education, housing, etc.) than their workers could earn with other employers. Through worker training, they bring needed skills to less developed countries, which could be obtained in no other way.

Nevertheless, the greed for profits leads many corporations to violate the environment and to demand monopolies, protection from foreign competition, and subsidies. It leads some to insist on laws (such as taxes) in their favor, and a few to try to overthrow "hostile" governments. These practices *must,* over time, be outlawed either legally or culturally. If culturally, corporations will not engage in them because "it isn't right" or because their neighbors do not. Slavery, whipping workers, child labor, and unsafe conditions have all been abolished, both culturally and legally, in the more developed countries but not in all the less developed. Since "the system" that includes profits is far from perfect, we must continue to correct it. Since it is the life blood of our economy, we must also preserve it.

If instead, you would propose dismantling "the system" because it promotes profits (and greed), please tell me what system you would suggest instead. Surely not one that concentrates power *more* than it is concentrated under our present system? If you propose to correct the system for its faults, you are on my team.

Is greed inculcated by the system, or is it learned in families, church,and schools? I think both, but change will come mainly from families, churches, and schools, and only later from passing laws.

To keep this letter to a reasonable size, I have not taken up (1) capital gains, (2) socially desirable investment, (3) non-profits, and (4) short-term versus long-term profits. I have also summarized a very complex issue, which deserves more extended treatment: external costs, especially environmental costs. Possibly others. These will be the topics of future letters. Any comments, questions, or additional topics? Thank you.

> Sincerely your friend,
> Jack

READERS' RESPONSES TO LETTER NO. 44

Not all markets are equal in terms of making information available, allowing different actors comparable choices, etc. Just as there are circumstances where workers can use pressure to negotiate higher wages unfairly (and so diminish profits), sometimes managers can use pressure to unfairly negotiate higher profits, and so diminish wages. A strong market, with transparency, other options for actors, etc, limits this as much as any human institution can, but a weak market may not be able to.

Geoffrey Williams, Bethesda (MD) Friends Meeting

Unfortunately the greedy and the media coverage have created a crisis for legitimate profit makers. I am trying to get Bellarmine University, where I am Executive in Residence, to call a conference of the top local business executives to address the question: "What can we as local business executives do to help restore confidence in the system?"

Lee B. Thomas, Jr., Louisville (KY) Friends Meeting, Business Executive

---

I thought CLQ #44, on profits, was spot-on: but I wish you had spent a little time on the technical difference between normal and monopoly profits. I think it would be useful if those whose tendency is to excoriate all profits could understand the functional distinction between those profits which arise from the normal operation of the system (and are necessary to make it work right) and those which arise from distortions of the system (and tend to interfere with its operation). Your piece pointed out that some profits are indeed excessive, but it might have been good to remind your readers that the differences are economically as well as morally significant, and that it is at least theoretically possible to tell which is which.

Bill Ashworth, South Mountain Meeting, Ashland (OR)

Suppose a company never paid dividends, how much would you pay for its stock? You might buy the stock on the assumption that there was a bigger fool, who would pay even more for the company once its profits had grown (even though these would never be paid out), but surely we would not want to say that the allocation of capital in the US is basically built on the bigger fool theory? Yes I know about the double taxation of dividends, but if the logical end-point is that dividends should never be paid, where does that leave the allocation of capital?

Will Candler, Annapolis (MD) Friends Meeting

NOTE by Jack: You hit the nail on the head with double taxation of dividends. Some companies, such as Microsoft, do not pay dividends, preferring instead to retain earnings for future investment. In that case, the value of the company increases, so the value of the stock grows, and stockholders who sell their holdings earn capital gains instead of dividends.

I'd like to express my curiosity about whether classical liberalism accommodates worker ownership of enterprises. I'd also like to know if you think that environmental and social costs can truly be comprehensively internalised in the prices of goods and services (by road-pricing, land and resource privatisation, liability assignments, etc.).

Paul Connor,

Brief response: Modern technology has made some of this possible, (for example, electronic devices to count cars as they speed along), but not for everything. Jack

---

THE QUAKER ECONOMIST
May 14, 2002

Letter No. 45

Dear friends:

Economics distorted

Dear Friends:

In CLQ #44, I said that profits are earned through (1) innovations, (2) producing goods people want, and (3) operating efficiently. But Will Candler of Annapolis MD reminds me that profits also arise out of (4) pay-back (including tax breaks) for political support and (5) financial engineering. Will is right, but there are even more: (6) monopolies, (7) subsidies, and (8) rent and price controls. However, only the three that I mentioned are genuine profits; the rest being economics distortions.

The economic system becomes distorted when gimmicks are used to alter not only profits but the income from land and labor as well. Besides those mentioned above, gimmicks include the minimum wage, the "living wage," agricultural subsidies, tariffs, and other barriers to trade. These gimmicks all have in common that they reduce total production to less than would be physically possible with any given expenditure of resources, and they redistribute income from the politically invisible to those with greater political clout.

How? Well, the minimum wage and living wage cause employers to hire fewer workers and use machines instead, at greater total cost than workers alone at market wage. Those still at work benefit, while the invisible are those who are dismissed or who cannot be hired because their skills are worth less than the minimum or "living" wage. Farm subsidies cause farmers to grow the wrong crops, those that would not otherwise be marketable. Tariffs and other trade barriers lead us to produce goods that can be made abroad with less expenditure of resources.

I have told you before how I spent 25 years reading history books to discover how the world came to be divided into rich and poor. One of my conclusions, which I set forth in *Centuries of Economic Endeavor* (University of Michigan, 1994), is that those nations that became rich are the very ones that traded most and that formed the freest markets, with fewest economic distortions.

Their wealth did not come from imperialism. The greatest imperialists of twenty centuries were Rome, Russia, Spain, Portugal, Ottoman Turkey, Mongolia, the Incas, the Aztecs, and the Islamic countries. None of these became wealthy. On the other hand, a highly-praised book by Angus Maddison (*The World Economy: A Millennial Perspective*), just published last year, estimates that the development of Britain and France began before 1000 CE, much earlier than their imperialist days. Their wealth correlates more closely with inventiveness, innovation, and trade. No, the rich nations did not get rich by stealing from the poor.

As I explained in CLQ #44, profit is both the life blood of the economy and one of many ways in which greed is made manifest. The other founts of greed include excessive wages (as in baseball players, speaking engagement fees charged by former high government officials, and CEOs), and in government intervention to transfer resources, in nonmarket ways, from some persons to others. The latter include farm subsidies, which cause the politically invisible poor to pay rich farmers excessively for their food. They also include all those activities, such as social security and health care, which could more efficiently be undertaken by private companies.

Social security and health care? Those very basics of human existence, that everyone should have? Yes, everyone should have them, but they need not be provided by government. Unlike my libertarian friends, I am even ready to say that we should tax the rich to subsidize social security and health care for the poor. But pay it in cash, require that it be spent for its purpose, and let the recipients choose the providers. Consider the money value of the hours and days spent by Congress deciding how much of these, and what kinds, *everyone* should have (one size fits all), and one easily sees what an inefficient use of time that is!

What, *subsidize* the poor? Did I not say that subsidies cause distortions? Yes, that too. Subsidies cause people to produce what would not otherwise be bought. In this case, retirement benefits and health care. True, a distortion, but I did not say all distortions are bad. Only most of them.

Now, let me turn to my omissions in CLQ #44: (1) capital gains, (2) socially-desirable investment, (3) short-term capital flows, and (4) nonprofits.

(1) Are capital gains among the profits that are the life blood of the economy? The main difference is that profit is part of the real value of goods sold. Except for distortions, cost plus profit equals real value. But capital gains *might* be a nominal increase only. Suppose I sell you a house for $100,000, then all prices go up 50%, so you sell the house for $150,000, you have a capital gain, but it is the same house, with the same value relative to other goods. No real value has been created.

However, capital gain reflects an increase in real value when dividends are reinvested. For example, the reinvested earnings might buy new machinery. The monetary counterpart to this is an increase in the value of the stock held by the stockholder, therefore a capital gain.

The free market directs profit, whether in dividends or capital gains, to go where it is needed most. But in the Soviet Union and many less developed countries, profit was invested largely in political boondoggles, such as war, white elephant projects, payoffs to maintain and increase the ruler's power base, etc. This explains much of why the USSR collapsed and why most of Asia, Africa, and Latin America is today underdeveloped.

It also explains why Hong Kong, Singapore, South Korea, and Taiwan raised the levels of their poorest to European standards in fifty years. It even explains why, after a quarter century of both consulting in the Third World and reading history, I converted from an economic planner into a classic liberal.

(2) Should Friends invest in socially-desirable investment (no liquor, no guns, no war support)? Of course, if you wish. You can do that in a free market. The less free the market, the less possible it is for you to invest in line with your morality. It may be that you happen to agree with the morality of market interventions, but what about those times when you don't? Only a free market lets you act morally at all times.

(3) What about short-term money, that flits from country to country in search of the highest income, often destabilizing economies in their flights? This is sometimes known as "hot money." Nobel Laureate James Tobin, who died earlier this year, suggested a small tax on foreign exchange transactions (the "Tobin tax") to hinder such movements.

While most economists think of hot money as negative, I look at it a different way. Its adverse consequences chastise volatile governments for creating the conditions that cause money to come to and go suddenly. The Tobin tax is another way by which government tries to offset a problem that government creates. (Actually, Jim and I were in graduate school together. He was a good friend whose astuteness I often envied.)

(4) What about nonprofit organizations? Well, here it depends on the organization. They do require capital, provided by charitable persons. Some nonprofits are good, some not. I can't make any generalization. I do remember a sign in a store window once: "This is a nonprofit company. It wasn't intended to be, but that is the way it turned out."

Any comments?

> Sincerely your friend,
> Jack

READER'S RESPONSES TO LETTER NO. 45

Call me cynical, but what about serfdom, wage slavery, and slavery??? Could France and Britain have become so wealthy without the exploitation of human beings that occurred during this time period? I don't know how you or anyone can assert that these nations and others "did not get rich by stealing from the poor." Stealing human beings and enslaving them, forcing human beings to be tied to the land for existence and exploiting the labor of human beings without just compensation is certainly stealing in my book. But then, maybe it is just the "free market" price of doing business then as it is now.

Jennie Crystle, Manitou Springs (CO)

I enjoyed your most recent edition of CLQ. As you may well know, however, there is a powerful counterargument to several of the comments that you made regarding the creation of wealth by Western nations, particularly Great Britain. Eric Williams, in his 1994 book *Capitalism and Slavery*, argued that a significant fraction of the wealth used by Great Britain to launch its Industrial Revolution derived from the labor performed by black slaves on the sugar and tobacco islands of the West Indies during the early

322

The Quaker Economist
/

and mid-eighteenth century. Williams stated his thesis in fairly extreme terms, maintaining that, in effect, slavery launched British industry. Even though most historians have not adopted this extreme viewpoint, and many have taken issue with various of the details in his book, I do think that Williams' work has convinced many that at least some of the new wealth created in Great Britain during the late eighteenth century was indeed stolen from enslaved Africans.

Chris Johnson, Manitou Springs (CO)

But Jack, if you "require that [government subsidy for social security and health care] be spent for its purpose," aren't you preempting my right to prioritize my own life – to choose high living before 65 over comfortable (or any) life after 65? By the way, I'm 66 and enjoying it, but there may be others who would not choose as I did. So maybe I don't have to spend the subsidy at all, but then I shouldn't be taxed for it, should I? Also, why retirement and health care? Aren't food, clothing, and shelter even more important? –

Bob Sheffield,

COMMENT: You are absolutely right in all of this, and I share your sentiments. But I am thinking of "free riders," or those who specifically do not pay for goods that society, out of its compassion, will provide for them anyway. Our society will no longer allow people to die in the street because they do not have health insurance (I hope).

Nice to hear favorable words about profits and free markets in a religious or moral context; so many persons seem to think they are always in conflict. How do you describe the effect of a criminal statute, such as penalties for distribution or possession? Or a regulatory statute, such as FDA testing, licensing and prescription requirements? Are these distortions or subsidies of the drug market? or morally based? Or both? Justified? Same questions for environmental issues. My view is that government has a role to play in setting the rules, but I dispair of finding a method to minimize those rules and to keep the politicians from constantly declaring the need for more and more detailed rules. Thacherism raised some hope for a middle way between ossification and revolution, but it seems to be losing force.

Richard Decou, Moorestown (NJ) Friends Meeting

Perhaps if we take your statement that the rich nations did not get rich by stealing from the poor... we still must deal with the fact that they did go on to eventually do that: take over the resources from other (poor) places without commensurate compensation. What then is the role of ethics? Much of the effort to "tinker" with free economy, whether competent and effective or misguided and tragic, is born of real needs for equity and justice, to improve the status quo that has resulted if a strictly free economy runs on its own. Whereas the market does maximize profits, it has no compassion. People with compassion have the power to impose ethics on their actions. If we don't allow ethics to postulate that certain wages are exploitive of dire need, if we say that if someone who has not been able to produce something worth trading can just starve, if we say that people must accept the free market consequences without interference, then where is the role of ethics, or of charity?

Steve Willey, Sandpoint Friends Meeting

COMMENT: Ethics and charity can be expressed by sending such people money and/or offering to help them produce something worth trading, if that is what they want (but don't do it if they don't want it). In a compassionate society, no one should starve. Jack

---

I would like one of your future letters to treat irredeemably low-productivity professions like nursing, care giving, social work, artists, musicians, writers, teachers and child care workers, police and firemen and so on. I notice that a capitalist society doesn't necessarily
deliver all the things we may desperately need. A little distortion in this direction would be fine with me!

Trudy Reagan, artist, Palo Alto (CA) Meeting

I am an advocate of socially responsible investing. I have usually beaten the bench marks slightly. But I have a different twist on it. I am looking for well managed companies. Companies that try to protect the environment, have a loyalty to their employees, and learn from diversity tend to be well run. I also like a decentralized management structure. I do analyze their financials. I do not make a bad investment just because it looks like a well run company. I tend to be a long term investor. That saves transaction costs. It is remarkable how often in a free economy that you can do well doing good.

Lee B. Thomas, Jr., Friends Meeting of Louisville (KY)

I would like to express my appreciation to you for having produced one of the few intelligent and interesting web sites that I have encountered to date.

William Hibbs, Philadelphia (PA) Friends Meeting

Economic theory is truly distorted!! It is distorted in assumption. I urge friends to visit various parts of Dieoff at yahoo for intelligent discussion of the reasons that economics fails the test of science. There is a large literature in ecology that discusses the failure of economics.

Economics fails to address the issues of thermodynamics. This may seem strange reason to question it, but all other sciences subsume the more basic sciences. Biology does not reject the laws of chemistry, does it reject the laws of physics. Economic theory totally ignores the fact that it is contained within the earth's ecosystems. It does this because it has to explain why exploitation of natural resources, slave labor, are Good for the earth. Economics is the constant reinterpretation of human history in the service of those who favor accumulation of wealth; the hubris is incredible. It does not address the ecological/ biological reality in which it is subsumed!! The incredible rate of other species extinctions is a serious indictment of the whole field of study, but economists as a whole totally ignore these 'losses.' Only human centered wealth is valued!

For those of you looking for religious references please read about Jubilee, biblical teachings of Jesus. Forgiveness of debt, redistribution of wealth, was a concept Jesus clearly supported.

Charlie Thomas, Cascabel Worship Group, Tucson (AZ)

TWO COMMENTS: (1) That's not the economics I studied, and (2) Charlie, do you redistribute only your own wealth and forgive only debts to you, or would you require that others do the same? Jack

THE QUAKER ECONOMIST
May 30, 2002

Letter No. 46

Dear Friends:

Victimhood and The Mystery of Capital

I've been getting flak from my assertion in CLQ #45 that exploitation was not the principal cause of the economic development of the West. So I want to clarify. I agree that some slave owners profited from their human capital, but slavery was not the *principal* cause, or even a major cause, of the economic development of the West. One reason is that no kind of capital is ever the major cause of economic development. The major cause is innovation, invention, and promotion of new ideas.

How do I know? Well, I don't really, but this seems to me the most likely. How would an economic historian address that question? He or she would list all the possible causes of economic prosperity, including slavery, colonialism, other exploitation, innovation, invention (and many more). Carefully examine how each coincides historically, or does not coincide, with economic prosperity.

When one does that (I repeat from CLQ #45), one finds that the greatest imperialists of twenty centuries were Rome, Russia, Spain, Portugal, Ottoman Turkey, Mongolia, the Incas, the Aztecs, and the Islamic countries. None of these experienced an industrial revolution. Britain and France were also imperialists and slave holders, but to a much lesser degree. Rather, their wealth correlates more closely with inventiveness, innovation, and trade.

Not only is this shown historically, but a recent book by William Baumol, noted economist at Princeton, explains how modern firms build innovation into their systems. In *The Free Market Innovation Machine,* Baumol argues that "the ability to produce a continuous stream of successful innovations . . makes capitalism the best economic system yet for generating growth." This happens because "innovative activity, which in other types of economy is fortuitous and optional, becomes mandatory, a matter of life and death for the firm" *(The Economist,* 5/18/02).

Slavery and colonialism were heinous crimes. I detest them as much as anyone. But they did not make their perpetrators wealthy. Wealth came to Britain and France long before they engaged massively in slavery (as I said in CLQ #45), and it did not come to other countries that took slaves massively. (I say "massively" because, before a certain period, "everybody" was enslaving. In particular the Africans and Native Americans took slaves.)

A series of articles in *The American Economic Review* in the 1970's debated the profitability of slavery in the United States. While they did not reach total agreement, the authors recognized that slavery was expensive to society as a whole (not just to the individual slaveholder). The cost of maintaining slaves, their low productivity, and the cost of recapturing them when they escaped was too great. Some have argued that the North won the civil war largely because of the greater productivity of free labor.

Furthermore, slavery ended without a war in every European country, and in all the countries of the Western Hemisphere except the United States and possibly Haiti. From this I presume that our slavery ended not because of the civil war or because owners saw the Light, but because it specifically was NOT profitable in a mechanizing age.

Still more: as I lectured in universities in Asia, Africa, and Latin America, and as I conducted seminars (over ten years) for Marxist students in Latin America, I was struck by the paralysis of victimhood. Students and many others felt that the more developed world was responsible for their underdevelopment. "We are poor because you are rich," President Nyerere of Tanzania once said.

Much beloved by the Left in the Western world, Julius Nyerere was in fact a tyrant. He forced farmers into his socialist (*Ujamaa*) villages. When they escaped and ran back home, he sent in the army to burn their houses so they would not do it again. He shut down a voluntary cooperative because it did not suit his socialist mold. The *Ujamaa* villages were a disaster, setting back Tanzanian development probably by a quarter century. We Americans do not encourage the development of the South when we adulate such actions and assume their guilt as our own. (The story is told in full in Powelson and Stock, *The Peasant Betrayed.*)

The Mystery of Capital

How, then, will the less developed countries advance?

In Asia, Africa, and Latin America the poor own more wealth than the rich. This startling fact was discovered through painstaking research conducted in many countries by a Peruvian, Hernando de Soto, for his latest book, *The Mystery of Capital: Why Capitalism Works in the West and Nowhere Else.* Of course, one reason they own more wealth is that there *are* more poor than rich. De Soto counts all the property that the poor effectively possess, through occupation in city slums and on farms. Mostly, they cannot be dispossessed of this property (although the elites often try to drive them out of the slums).

The inability of the poor to convert their assets into capital is a major cause of poverty. In the West, you can mortgage your house to finance a business. The poor of the less developed world cannot use billions of dollars worth of farmland and buildings to form businesses because they cannot prove ownership. Mostly, no property registry exists. If they cannot prove ownership, they cannot sell, buy, mortgage, or legally inherit property.

By contrast, the West has developed a common set of laws of ownership and financial instruments. These include not only property registries but also promissory notes, rules of performance in contracts, intellectual property rights, bank accounts, stockholdings, forward contracts, and the right to sue in court. Once in Kenya, I gave a check to an African friend who wanted to open a bank account in an African bank. To do so, he needed references from a "reliable" person; most Africans could not find such a person.

Knowing that if we borrow we must pay back, or if we lend we will most likely be repaid, or if we violate a contract we might be sued, we can draw on the capital of others to finance our innovations. We can draw on a little bit, or a lot, depending on our financial condition and our needs. On the other hand, we can invest our own assets in projects of others (as through stocks and mutual funds). Thus capital is fungible, like grain and money, whereas raw assets, like a house and a spoon, are not. Fungible capital is essential to economic development.

De Soto tracked the rules of the informal (or extralegal) economy throughout the less developed world. He finds that poor people do possess the concept of property rights. ("You know whose property you are on by whose dog barks," he says). But without proof of ownership, the ability to use banks, enforceable contracts, and legal protections, the poor cannot engage in the kinds of business that lead to advanced economic development.

These protections emerged slowly in the West and Japan (though they need not be so slow in less developed countries today). They did so through the dispersion of power, in which the lower classes captured the ability to negotiate and make the laws, and through trade, whose rules were composed mainly by negotiation and common law. Once the king (or shogun) lost the power to control the lower classes, the poor gained the ability to make their own property laws and financial instruments, and have them stick as the law of the land. This has not yet happened in the less developed world. (All this is explained in my book, *Centuries of Economic Endeavor,* but you don't need to read it because its 500 pages are summarized in this paragraph).

All these amount to economic democracy and rule of law and property rights determined by the people and not by the rulers. It is too simple to say that this is all of economic development, but it is a large part. If we in the West assume that our own actions (imperialism and slave holding) have caused the plight of the less developed world, we are not only wrong, but we do them no favor.

> Sincerely your friend,
> Jack Powelson

READERS' RESPONSES TO LETTER NO. 46

Economics is not a neutral and value-free discipline. When someone of good training and values figures out how to serve people instead of saying "butthat's how the system works" the result is transformative.

Trudy Reagan, Palo Alto (CA) Meeting

COMMENT: Most of us tend to attribute to a "system" (not usually described) what really reflects our own morality. For those willing to go along with what we call "the system," the ECONOMIC system responds in one way; to those who buck the conventional wisdom, the ECONOMIC system responds in a different way.

For example, it may be "the system" to discriminate against the poor, against minorities, etc., or it may be "the system" to destroy the environment. However, it is not the ECONOMIC system, as economists describe it, that does these things. It is the personal morality of people. The ECONOMIC system explains the reactions of the ECONOMY when people of different values and different policies act in different ways. The ECONOMIC system is therefore neutral, but people are not.

One of my purposes in writing CLQ is to bring these differences out to Quakers, so that we will take more personal responsibility for our actions instead of blaming them on some undescribed "system."

This is quite up to your usual standards. You are one of the most trenchant thinkers writing today - and you write well, to boot. Debunking the Marxist myths of slavery is a welcome contribution to our understanding of the human economy.

Bravo! Michael Schefer, Philadelphia (PA), children in Germantown Friends

---

I would like to see an issue devoted to moral concepts that have seemed to escape corporation officers of late: fair treatment of employees (lifetime employment is a fantasy, but truth-telling to employees should not be) and responsibility to shareholders rather than to the officers themselves.

Rick Brooks, Green County Friends Meeting, Tulsa (OK)

COMMENT: I have been thinking along the same lines. Keep tuned! I will write on that subject soon. Jack.

I just want to let you know how much I have enjoyed reading what you have written. As they say; "This friend speaks my mind."

Peter D'Angelo, Oakland (CA)

Jack, you are the most lucid economist I've ever known. Keep it up.

Tom Selldorff, Weston (MA)

Thanks for your thought-provoking article, and one that seems especially NOT politically correct. I certainly don't know the historical developments as well as you, but I am inclined to agree simply because they make common sense. The most intriguing part of your article for me was the idea of 'victimhood.' As I understand it, 'neurosis' is commonly understood as the inability to move away from being dependent (in some sense) to accepting personal responsibility. What alarms me is how prevalent a sense of 'victimhood' is in the US, not just other parts of the world. What I wonder, and would like your feedback, is what forces, internal and external, help develop a greater sense of personal responsibility in people? Any ideas?

Bruce Messinger, San Antonio (TX)

COMMENT: Your question is a tough one, because for the most part the ideas must come from the persons concerned, and they must think of them (but historically, they have done so). From the outside, we can open up our trade (steel, textiles) and stop subsidizing agriculture. These subsidies cause people in the less developed world to buy our farm products when theirs would be cheaper to produce (without the subsidies). Our rich farmers gain a bonanza while poor farmers are denied their own national markets. But you know what a problem that is, with selfish people like us!

Another excellent statement. The flak gives us a barometer of how we are doing. More is better, as it engages more folks.

J.D. von Pischke, a Friend from Reston (VA)

British and French prosperity preceded slavery, and our prosperity has continued to grow after slavery was abolished.

Further evidence that we should look for a different cause is the failure of other slave-holding countries to become prosperous. If slavery was the

cause of our prosperity, then surely slavery would have caused prosperity in other countries.

Look, for example, at Rome's failure to exploit the rich coal resources in Europe. Rome had slaves to dig the coal where Britain never did.

Russ Nelson, St. Lawrence Valley (NY) Friends Meeting

COMMENT: Peter the Great visited Holland and England to seek the reason for their prosperity. Failing to notice their free labor, he returned to Russia to build identical factories with slave labor.

THE QUAKER ECONOMIST

June 26, 2002

Letter No. 47

Dear Friends:

To whom are we accountable? (Part One)

From Enron, we have learned that corporations have no brains and no souls. Only the people within them have brains and souls. Without brains, corporations cannot think of their bottom lines. Only people can. If the bottom line of the corporation happens to coincide with the bottom lines of management as individuals, they promote it. If not, they do not. Economists have known this for decades. But many noneconomists have been confused.

Enron's chief "sin" (if a non-brain can sin) was that its management had different bottom lines from the company. But the different bottom lines were not consolidated. When I was a practicing CPA (fifty years ago), we would always consolidate a client's accounts (i.e., consider the corporation and all its subsidiaries as a single entity) if its operations were better understood that way. Normally there were no "off-balance-sheet" transactions (such as Enron's putting expenses in a subsidiary whose accounting it did not disclose). Or if, by valid exception, there were such transactions, we always revealed them in a footnote. Thus individual interests that may have been different from those of the company were always revealed.

Times have changed. First, corporations have become more complex, with different lines of enterprise combined under a single management. If you want to know the profits of an energy company alone, you don't consolidate them with its subsidiary in the hardware business. Etc. Sometimes it is hard to know what to consolidate, and what not. There can be legitimate differences of opinion, not related to corruption. Does all this mean that companies should not merge with "unlikes?"

Not necessarily. Sometimes a conglomerate can be better managed (at less cost) than if it were separate companies. But sometimes not. Often companies are merged, and often the mergers are broken (companies are split off). Who is better positioned to decide, than the management? But managers can err, and sometimes their "mistakes" reflect their different bottom lines from those of the company. Mergers, or splits, that benefit them do not necessarily benefit the company. Enron's management was guilty of this.

Is government regulation the solution? Not necessarily. The government does not always know what is best for (1) the stockholders, (2) the employees, (3) the lending banks, (4) the vendors, or (5) the customers. Whom among the above would government favor, anyway? The most "deserving," or the ones with the most political clout?

My answer is that each of the above groups should have its own organization to defend its interests. Labor unions should study what the company is doing, demanding certain kinds of information, and pressuring the company to defend the interests of labor. So should banking organizations, stockholder organizations, and yes, customer organizations. Of course, ordinary stockholders or customers would not want to do that alone. So they should subscribe to agencies that would protect them. Government treats them as if they all had the same interests, and besides, it too is subject to bribery (known as campaign contributions) by particular interests.

Why have these groups not formed, to protect themselves? Mainly, I believe, because we live in an age in which we depend on the government to solve whatever goes wrong (with pensions, health care, education, anything else), so naturally labor unions, etc., lose their umph. Despite our instant tendency to run to government for action, I believe the twenty-first century (maybe fifty or one hundred years from now) will discover the failures of government and revert to the Toquevillian concept of groups, and the democratic concept of balance of power among them.

Second, our national ethics have declined over fifty years. In my day as a CPA, no accountant would give management advice to a client, much less accept a job with a client without first quitting the CPA firm. Today, these conflicts of interest are commonplace. They are, indeed, what sank Arthur Andersen. The auditing CPA has an interest in the client's success, so it tends to slant the audit (e.g., not consolidate with loss-making subsidiaries) to make the company appear more successful. CPAs no longer recognize their separate accountability to investors, banks, employees, or the general public.

What is the solution to that? Congress is considering laws requiring the forced separation of auditing and consulting firms. Accountants oppose these virulently, because their bottom lines are improved by the connection. Though I certainly favor this outcome, it will be difficult to get such a law passed with sufficient teeth.

There are problems with the law anyway. The government would treat all cases alike, when in fact they differ from each other. Accountants should (and did in my day) give advice on how to improve the accounting system. How can they separate that from advice on how to manage finances? Once again, government please keep out. Instead, let us strengthen the labor unions', bankers' and stockholders' organizations, and customer guilds, to defend their interests through their studies of particular companies. This is happening already. Fidelity Investments, for example, is forming a unit to put pressure on the auditors of companies in its portfolios.

But I said our ethics have declined generally, over fifty years, didn't I? I do believe that in the heyday of information technology, and a rising stock market, we have all tended toward guarding our own bottom lines to the sacrifice of traditional ethics. Fifty years ago Merrill Lynch recommended investments that it honestly believed lay in the interests of clients. Now it is charged with recommending investments in the interests of the brokers, who would sell out, leaving clients holding the bag. In the long run, this behavior would not promote the bottom line of Merrill Lynch, but in the short run it promotes that of the brokers. They can retire on their loot and let the company go dang.

So, what is to be done? Laws to promote honesty and ethical behavior will have no force in the face of the overwhelming temptation of a rise in the business cycle. Instead, we must learn from our mistakes, as Enron and Andersen and others go bust and as all investors, employees, and customers learn how rough and tumble the free market is. But let us not fall into the opposite pit, of demanding that the government regulate and protect us, since that has its hazards as well (see CLQ #43). Let us learn to live in the nineteenth century again, or (I hope) the latter part of the twenty-first) in which the cycle will swing back. Let us rely primarily upon ourselves and the cooperative organizations we can form.

Let the ethos of self-reliance and cooperation at lower levels again permeate our Friends' Meetings, as it did when I first joined Quakers in 1943.

Letter No. 48 ("To whom are we accountable? Part Two") will take up accountability for the environment. It will also carry us beyond the Enron/

Andersen/Merrill Lynch debacle, to explain why I think our over-all economic ethics have declined over fifty years. But it will also explain why I remain optimistic that we are on the mend.

Sincerely your friend,
Jack

READERS' RESPONSES TO LETTER NO. 47

I appreciate your work on these CLQs. They are always insightful, well-written, and non-confrontational. I learn something in every one, including this one.

Carol Conzelman, anthropology graduate student, University of Colorado

---

Very intelligent, and light years ahead of how the mainstream press understands these issues.

Michael Schefer, Jewish (non-attending), Philadelphia PA, children in Germantown Friends School

---

As usual a thought-provoking letter. It is hard for me to see how such a theoretical object as a "Enron customers' group" (etc) could possibly be created, so the solution you pose seems hopelessly idealistic. And I wonder if unions (etc) would have access to the information they need to guard their interests and keep Enron (and the others) on the straight and narrow.

Roger Conant, Mount Toby Friends Meeting, Leverett MA

COMMENT (by Jack). If you had lived in George Fox's time and I had described to you the world economy of today, my guess is that you would call me "hopelessly idealistic." Given time, society changes more than the people of any generation can possibly imagine.

Yes, I entirely agree that citizens organizing can make a lot of corrections. Feedback is necessary in a healthy system, and a well-functioning democracy has that built in. Plutocracies and dictatorships are weak in this department. I hope the new tools in place to fight terrorism aren't used to squelch people organizing in the ways you suggest. Some unions were pretty crippled by the McCarthyites in the fifties.

Trudy Reagan, Palo Alto (CA) Friends Meeting

It has seemed to me that there is a lot of pressure for accountability from some of the state pension funds, notably Calif and NY. Obviously not enough, but with the disaster that Enron constituted for Fla. pension funds, they are all on notice now. This leaves the rest of us as free riders on their work, though.

Dave Schutz, formerly of Berkeley (CA) Meeting

While the number of Americans investing in the public stock markets has increased over the last several decades, I would hazard that the number of us with a stake in our own businesses has decreased. In an age of Walmart and McDonalds, it is harder for an individual or a family to secure their own livelihood by serving others in their community. Some of your earlier writings on the shrinking number of Friends engaged in for-profit business may have as much to do with this trend as anything else. Could it be that work in the publicly-held corporate environment is less in alignment with Friends values than work in small business? While you say corporations do not have souls, I feel that small companies that are natural extensions of their owners and customers just may.

Charles Rathmann, Milwaukee (MN) Monthly Meeting

COMMENT by Jack: The number of enterprises hiring less than 20 employees decreased from 89% of total enterprises in the United States in 1990 to 86% in 1999. (From *Statistical Abstract of the United States, 2001*, table 723.) Is that what you mean? (These figures do not include the self-employed, for which I could not find data).

Transaction costs! Transaction costs! As a shareholder I appoint a Board of Directors, who appoint the management, now I have to form a cooperative group to see they do their job? What is the point of owning shares if you cannot trust the directors and management? I'm much better off to invest with Warren Buffet whose staff look after his interests and where he will use his clout to discipline management. Where were the big players TIAA-CREF, other pension funds, CALPERS, Fidelity in holding Enron, Global Crossing, and the other big disasters? Were they monitoring management as they should have been. There is no way I can know as much about a company as CALPERS. Transaction costs!

Will Candler, Annapolis (MD) Friends Meeting

I was intrigued by your comment that ethics have generally declined over the past fifty years. I believe, as you do, that people should be responsible for themselves, and that the culture of victimhood is deplorable. But I've noticed in my recent studies how there often seems to be a strong structural reason for a social or cultural development (such as the pork taboo in Islam and Judaism). I am thinking of how family life has been diluted since economic production by the family was monetised and outsourced. I'm sure there's more to it, but it seems to be families were half-welded together by necessity in the form of chores, errands and eating the same meal all at once (which I have some hazy memories of myself!). I'd be willing to bet that the perceived decline in ethics has some similar structural foundation.

Paul Connor, Toronto, Canada

The business ethics problem is broader and deeper than just the CPA issue, and I contend that it is in part driven by the overwhelming size and dominance that corporations have been allowed to achieve in recent years. Corporations have become the dominant force in government, not individual citizens. Much more control over excessively large and powerful corporations is in order, to limit dominance in any given market arena and in politics and public policy.

Rich Andrews, Boulder (CO) Meeting of Friends

In practice, the law of unintended consequences has worked overtime. Another, more classical view, of current problems of corporate governance is that current laws and regulations do not give corporate managers the proper incentives to maximize long term stockholder value. For example, stock options have worked to get managers to maximize corporate value in the short run until the managers can cash out their options—and then come the accounting scandals! In this view, national ethics have not declined over the past fifty years, but rather the laws of corporate governance have not been changed enough to keep up with the increasing complexity of the modern corporation. We need to change the tax and other aspects of stock options so that they will serve their intended function of maximizing corporate value over a longer period of time, we need to change the rules for accounting and auditing so that corporate reports will be honest, we need to end the stock brokers' temptations to tout the stocks their firms finances, etc. etc.

Bill Rhoads, Germantown (PA) Meeting

I know that you have a plan for Part Two already, but a Part Three might get into public choice economics. Point out that you can make useful predictions if you treat "civil servants" with the same jaundiced eye as you do "private management", and "not-for-profit public benefit corporations" as corporations that merely happen to have a zero on the bottom of the balance sheet for tax reasons.

Russ Nelson, St. Lawrence Valley (NY) Friends Meeting

What if you are wrong? What if the ECONOMIC system is not neutral? Which it is NOT! Our macro-economics should not dominate all other aspects of life! Government is us we the people. We can support other economic models and not be 'against' Jack Powelson.

Charlie Thomas, Cascabel (AZ) Worship Group

THE QUAKER ECONOMIST
July 8, 2002

Letter No. 48

Dear Friends:

To whom are we accountable? (Part Two)

In the recent splurge of corporation scandals, our first thought is to strengthen the power of government (or the Securities and Exchange Commission) to control them. This is vertical accountability. In *vertical accountability* each person responds to a higher authority. In pure feudalism, serf accounted to lord, lord to king, king sometimes to emperor, and emperor to God.

But I prefer *sidewise accountability* where, with a few exceptions (such as children accountable to parents), there is no social hierarchy.

Why did we not employ sidewise accountability in the corporate scandals? Mainly because we have built up a culture of vertical accountability for over a century, so that government as protector is the first remedy to come to mind. A century ago, this would not have been the case.

So, transplant ourselves to an earlier century. What would our thought processes have been? We might have thought that stockholders, creditors, workers, bankers, and others who suffer from the scandals should be the ones to protect themselves. How? Well, a bankers' association could insist on financial statements audited according to standards that it set. If not, bankers would not lend to the company. A stockholders' association would demand audited statements to its standards, plus the separation of auditing and consulting services. If not, they would sell their stock. Workers through their unions would demand that managers and directors hold their stock during the full time of their appointments, instead of selling it just before a crash. They might also demand independent pension funds, invested in outside companies under the care of fund organizations *of their own choosing*. If not, they would either strike or work elsewhere.

Sidewise accountability implies two groups, each of which holds the other to some consequence if it does not do what the first demands. But no one is forced to do anything. If they do not agree, one party simply walks away.

Accountability to the market is a kind of sidewise accountability. A customer may buy products singly while a producer who fails in price or quality loses business. The customer also has a choice: he or she may prefer one supermarket for bananas and another for peas. This accountability is sidewise because the customer is accountable for payment and the grocer for quality of product, and either can walk away.

The main reason our society does not think of sidewise accountability is historical. Before the sixteenth century, Western society (mostly feudal) held to vertical accountability. From the sixteenth to the nineteenth, as democracy took hold, we gradually shifted to sidewise accountability. King James I thought he was accountable only to God. His son, Charles I, lost his head discovering accountability to Parliament. With the Industrial Revolution, accountability to the market became widespread.

In the latter part of the nineteenth century, we became impatient to correct many social ills: monopolies, excessive pricing by utilities, etc. We had two choices: (1) to strengthen sidewise accountability or (2) to shift back to the vertical by entrusting the control of monopolies and utilities to the government. Mostly, we chose the latter. Social security, health care for the elderly, unemployment insurance, and others followed. All of them might have been handled sidewise, but they were entrusted vertically to government.

Vertical accountability brings several problems. The first is bundling. President Bush has agreed to higher textile and steel tariffs, causing U.S. consumers to pay billions of dollars more for these products, while also undercutting producers in less developed countries. Suppose we oppose this policy but favor Bush's promise of more funds for education. We can't decide on these issues separately because they are bundled. We vote Bush up or down; we don't "buy" his policies singly, as we do products in a grocery store.

Second, with vertical accountability the spending of public funds is also bundled. Often taxes are not spent on the purposes we intend. Every penny I have put into social security since I joined it in 1944 has been blown up over Korea, Vietnam, Bosnia, Kosovo, or Afghanistan (or otherwise spent), and there is zero in the till. Current workers pay my social security, and in another generation there will be too many old people for the young ones to support. If we invested our pension money into funds *of our choosing,* this would not have happened. (NOTE: For any 30-year period in the history of the United States, including years of market crashes, blue chips have yielded on average about 7% per annum).

Third, vertical accountability creates a power center – the government. When the President has power over so many things, he begins to think of himself as God. War is much easier to declare than if most accountability were sidewise.

Finally, the return to vertical accountability has weakened sidewise accountability. We no longer save as much for retirement because social security will take care of us. We do not save for the rainy day because unemployment insurance will handle that. Worst of all, we want more than we are willing to pay for. If it's "free" (government-provided), we want as much as we can get. This is where greed comes in.

Prosperity and the decline in ethics

I believe the shift away from sidewise accountability is part of the reason for the decline in business ethics. Each bit of sidewise accountability had created the ethic that "that way" of doing business (e.g. paying debts) was the proper one. But, accustomed to the Securities and Exchange Commission validating stock issues, we lost "caveat emptor." Not squandering our money because of the "rainy day" and "taking care of ourselves" were among the many other ethics that are diminished. When one by one these ethics were diminished or lost, wealth seeking (always popular) expanded into their places.

I can think of no other reason why the decline in business ethics should have occurred in the latter part of the twentieth century. In the sixteenth century, parents could send their children to Quaker stores, confident that they would not be cheated. When I was a child, and later working as a CPA (in the late 1940s), business ethics were much stronger then now.

The rush toward profits has made us all greedy. Yes, me too. I wanted to sell my house for the greatest value so Robin and I could afford a comfortable retirement. To satisfy all of us, our pension funds have tried for the highest return. Enron employees were happy with the stock boom; now we pity them with the fall. Though Enron, WorldCom and Arthur Andersen managers betrayed trust, they were not the only greedy ones.

Accountability for the environment

The environment belongs to everybody and to nobody. That is its beauty and its problem. When our culture accepts that we can get more than we pay for, we fall into the "tragedy of the commons." Wanting more is the reason for fouling the environment. When accountability is sidewise, our personal budgets constrain us. With vertical accountability and deficit financing, the public budget is not a constraint. We count on the government to preserve the environment, or (if we are big business) to help us profit by destroying it. In reality, we will preserve the environment only when we form institutions of sidewise accountability for its protection.

What would they be? Pollution permits, for a starter. Since some pollution will be nature-corrected, issue tradable permits for that amount and no more. Privatize water and electricity. Count on competition to cause us to produce enough of both and to keep us from consuming too much of either. If we count on legislation, we will be betrayed, because the government protects the polluters as much as (and probably more than) it does the rest of us. There are many ways to re-establish sidewise accountability, and many of you will dispute my suggestions. That's OK. But do let's talk about them.

If sidewise accountability means the poor cannot afford to pay for education, water, or what have you, give them money or vouchers. Don't presume our government knows best about how to spend for them.

Finally, sidewise accountability is *Quakerly.* It respects the individual, honoring that of God in him or her. It does not force others to bend to our will.

If you think these ideas are hopelessly idealistic, read my comment to Roger Conant's message (below).

> Sincerely your friend,
> Jack Powelson

READERS' RESPONSES TO LETTER NO. 48

A little oversimplification, but I like this newsletter. Gets us all thinking in a different mode. Do you have concrete suggestions for the individual on this subject? Is there direct action? don't we have to work through existing governmental structures, e.g. Congress?

Howard Baumgartel, Oread Friends Meeting and retired prof.

ANSWERS by Jack: No, No, and Yes. Changes will come only as we discover that vertical accountability doesn't work. That is happening in most of the world right now. See Letter No. 43 on Commanding Heights.

A lot of concern for institution building in development is based on the realization that institutions shape and guide behavior. Efficient institutions guide behavior into productive channels better than inefficient ones. While it is clear that institutions are created by people, in this other sense institutions are not neutral or without a brain. Rather, they consist of a set of incentives that rewards those whose objectives are consistent with those of the institution and punish those whose are not. This seems ironic: on one hand people create institutions, while on the other institutions shape behavior.

J.D. Von Pischke, a Friend from Reston (VA)

A wonderfully thought-provoking essay! I also believe the world would work better if run with sideways accountability where possible. I was with you till I got to:
" Privatize water and electricity. Count on competition to cause us to produce enough of both and to keep us from consuming too much of either."
Our public water systems has been one strong element in our good public health. We both have visited countries where this is not the case. I heard a better suggestion on NPR: Cities could hire the water management services of private companies, but if they were not serving the public good responsibly, they could fire them. This would introduce competition into what would otherwise be a local monopoly. I think local citizens should have some way of having strong input in this matter.

Trudy Reagan, Palo Alto (CA) Friends Meeting

A tiny caveat to privatising utilities: it has been done in the UK and, in the case of the railways, is a disaster. Privatised companies seem to HAVE to prioritise shareholder interests over safety issues, and are reluctant to spend money to solve a LONG-TERM problem when there is no prospect of an instant return.

K.J. Persson, United Kingdom

It's fascinating to hear about these accounting scandals in the US. I have been in Russia for three weeks, and the local media is thrilled. They see it as the US getting what it deserves after years of saying how corrupt Communism was. Russia is happy that all of our finger-pointing is coming back to us. There was a quote in the English-language paper yesterday that made me laugh, because it was printed about four times in the same paper. I don't remember the exact quote, unfortunately, but it was a Russian official saying how happy he was that the Russian people could now see that Russia was in fact better than the US all along.

Beth Stevenson, Boulder (CO) Meeting of Friends

Sideways accountability can therefore quickly deteriorate into every bit a dominating system as vertical accountability can. Citizens' groups with the most power — where power is not only found in numbers but also in money, and perhaps above all knowledge — will win the fight. That is, unless a number of safeguards are put into place. Who can implement these safeguards unless a (vertical) democratically selected governing body?

Knut Mork Skagen, Trondheim, Norway

Re: the letter about business ethics. My theory is that the quality of ethics has gone down as the number of paid, professional ethicists has gone up.

Signe Wilkinson, Chestnut Hill (PA) Friends Meeting

Your term "sidewise accountability" is very good. In further embellishments, you might add that the sidewise accountants normally have incentives to demand behavior that is in the interests of all (e.g., economizing on inputs).

Steve Williams, Bethesda (MD) Friends Meeting

You mentioned that some people no longer save because they rely on social security, but I wonder. Everything I've ever heard or seen about social security suggests that it will not maintain a baby boomer in the comfortable style to which he or she has become accustomed. And thus I wonder if people really think about it much as a significant force for comfort in retirement.

Roger Williams III, Fort Myers (FL)

If we, the American People, don't get our act together, we are doomed. As I watch the direction this country has been taking over my lifetime, I do worry. Freedom is wonderful however people must be held accountable for their actions under Freedom. Freedom is now defined as 'DO WHATEVER YOU WANT". This must change. I thought I saw this attitude change on 11 September, but it really didn't last long. Are we going to follow the Roman Empire? "The Rise and Fall of the USA".

Semper Fi, J.C. Schiffler, Sergeant, US Marine Corps

Other Books by Jack Powelson

Seeking Truth Together, Quakerback, Boulder, Colorado, Horizon Society Publications, 2000.

The Moral Economy, University of Michigan Press, 1998.

Centuries of Economic Endeavor: Parallel Paths in Japan and Europe and their Contrast with the Third World, University of Michigan Press, 1994.

The Peasant Betrayed: Agriculture and Land Reform in the Third World, with Richard Stock, revised edition by Cato Institute, Washington, D.C., 1990; original edition: Cambridge, Massachusetts, Lincoln Institue of Land Policy, 1987.

The Story of Land: A World History of Land Tenure and Agrarian Reform, Cambridge, Massachusetts, Lincoln Institute of Land Policy, 1988.

Dialogue with Friends, Quakerback, Boulder, Colorado, Horizon Society Publications, 1988.

Facing Social Revolution: The Personal Journey of a Quaker Economist, Quakerback, Boulder, Colorado, Horizon Society Publications, 1987.

Threat to Development: Pitfalls of the New International Economic Order, with William Loehr, Boulder, CO, Westview Press, 1983.

The Economics of Development and Distribution, with William Loehr, New York, Harcourt, Brace, Jovanovich, 1981.

A Select Bibliography on Economic Development, with Annotations, Boulder, CO, Westview Press, 1979.

Income Distribution, Poverty, and Economic Development, Co-editor, with William Loehr, Boulder, Colorado, Westview Press, 1977.

Development Plan, 1974/78, Government of Kenya, Nairobi, Kenya, Government Printing Office, Co-author (government publication, not attributed), 1974.

Employment in Africa, Co-editor (with Philip Ndegwa), Geneva, International Labor Office, 1973.

Institutions of Economic Growth: A Theory of Conflict Management in Developing Countries, Princeton, N.J., Princeton University Press, 1972.

Latin America: Today's Economic and Social Revolution, McGraw-Hill, 1964, with editions in Spanish and Portuguese.

National Income and Flow of Funds Analysis, New York, McGraw-Hill, 1960, with edition in Spanish by Fondo de Cultura Económica, Mexico

Economic Accounting, McGraw-Hill, 1955, with edition in Spanish by Fondo de Cultura Económica, Mexico.

Articles in Quaker Journals by Jack Powelson

"Why Are Some Nations Rich and Others Poor?" in *Friends Bulletin,* March 2002.

"Why I am Leaving Quakers," in *Friends Journal,* April 2002

"Why I'm Coming Back to Quakers," submitted to *Friends Journal.*

"Emweakenment and The Moral Economy," in *Quaker Life,* March 1999 and *Friends Journal,* December 1998.

"World Without Borders," in *Friends Bulletin,* December 1998.

"The Brown Cushion," in *Friends Journal,* May 1993.

"Seeking the Truth," in *Friends Journal,* August 1991.

"Civil Disobedience: When Do I Break the Law?" in *Friends Journal,* May 1989.

"Sanctuary," in *Friends Bulletin,* May 1985.

"The Soviet Union, South Africa, and Us" (with Kenneth B. Powelson), in *Friends Journal,* November 1, 1984.

"How to Achieve Social Justice with Peace and No Champions" in *Right Sharing News*, Friends World Committee for Consultation, Philadelphia PA, vol. XI, no. 1, January/February 1984.

"Military Spending and the Economy," in *Friends Bulletin,* vol. 52, no. 5, January 1984.

Holistic Economics and Social Protest, Pendle Hill Pamphlet, Pendle Hill, Wallingford, PA, 1983.

"El Salvador and Quaker Credibility," in *Friends Journal,* pp. 7-10, August 1-15, 1981.

"Friends' Affluence and the Third World," in *Friends Journal,* pp. 11-13, March 15, 1981.

"Feeling Comfortable," in *Friends Journal,* p. 17, May 15, 1980.

"Manuel and Tom," in *Friends Bulletin,* pp. 88-89, April 1977.

"Values and Membership," in *Friends Bulletin,* pp. 71-72, March 1977.

"When Would I Kill?," in *Friends Bulletin,* pp. 21-22, Oct. 1976.

"The Decline of Commitment," in *Friends Bulletin,* pp.105-106, May 1976.

"China, Freedom, and Friends," in *Friends Bulletin,* March, 1976, pp. 88-89.

"Friends and Crises of Conscience," in *Friends Journal,* pp. 107-108. February 15, 1976.

"The Inverse Arrogance of Friends," in *Friends Bulletin,* September, 1975, with continuation in October, 1975.

"They Saw and Were Broadened," in *Friends Journal,* June 15, 1966.

"A Boatload of Students," in *Friends Intelligencer,* 1948.

For a complete bibliography, including articles in scholarly journals, visit http://spot.colorado.edu/~powelsoj